*The impact of early
separation or loss on
family development*

Maternal-infant bonding

MARSHALL H. KLAUS, M.D.

Professor of Pediatrics
Case Western Reserve University School of Medicine
Rainbow Babies and Children's Hospital
Cleveland, Ohio

JOHN H. KENNELL, M.D.

Professor of Pediatrics
Case Western Reserve University School of Medicine
Rainbow Babies and Children's Hospital
Cleveland, Ohio

WITH 49 ILLUSTRATIONS

THE C. V. MOSBY COMPANY
SAINT LOUIS 1976

Printed in the United States of America

Distributed in Great Britain by Henry Kimpton, London

Library of Congress Cataloging in Publication Data

Klaus, Marshall H
  Maternal-infant bonding.

  Bibliography: p.
  Includes index.
  1. Infants (Newborn)—Family relationships.
2. Mother and child.   3. Infants (Newborn)—
Diseases—Psychological aspects. 4. Death—
Psychological aspects. 5. Deformities—Psychological
aspects. I. Kennell, John H.,
1922-   joint author. II. Title. [DNLM:
1. Maternal deprivation. WS105 K625m]
RJ251.K56   618.9′201   76-5397
ISBN 0-8016-2630-7

VH/VH/VH 9 8 7 6 5 4

Contributors

BERTRAND CRAMER, M.D.

Chief of University Child Guidance Center,
Geneva, Switzerland

NANCY A. IRVIN, M.S.S.A.

Research Social Worker, Department of Pediatrics,
University Hospitals of Cleveland, Cleveland, Ohio

MARY ANNE TRAUSE, Ph.D.

Instructor of Psychology, Department of Pediatrics,
Case Western Reserve University School of Medicine,
Cleveland, Ohio

Critical commentators

KATHRYN BARNARD, Ph.D.

Professor of Nursing, University of Washington,
Seattle, Washington

T. BERRY BRAZELTON, M.D.

Associate Professor of Pediatrics, Harvard University,
Cambridge, Massachusetts

ERNA FURMAN

Cleveland Center for Research in Child Development;
Assistant Clinical Professor in Child Therapy,
Department of Psychiatry, Case Western Reserve University
School of Medicine, Cleveland, Ohio

Morris Green, M.D.

Professor and Chairman, Department of Pediatrics,
University of Indiana School of Medicine,
Indianapolis, Indiana

Natacha Josefowitz, M.S.W.

Whittemore School, University of New Hampshire,
Durham, New Hampshire

Betsy Lozoff, M.D.

Departments of Pediatrics, Medicine, and Anthropology,
Case Western Reserve University,
Cleveland, Ohio

Jay S. Rosenblatt, M.D., Ph.D.

Director, Institute of Animal Behavior, Rutgers University,
Newark, New Jersey

Albert J. Solnit, M.D.

Professor of Pediatrics and Psychiatry, Yale University School
of Medicine, New Haven, Connecticut

To our parents;
to our wives

PEGGY and LOIS;

and to our children

DAVID, SUSAN, and JACK
SUSAN, DAVID, ALISA, LAURA, and SARAH

Foreword

This very timely book deals with the issue of "how to make human beings human," starting in the earliest days of life. Its focus is on the genesis of the earliest relationship that a baby develops with his parents— and the factors that may enhance or inhibit this process. It is timely because, in historical perspective, we have reached a point at which our past practices are being reexamined and new directions charted. At such times of ferment it is well to have guidance from experts who are skillful clinicians and scientists aware of the frontiers in the science and art of the care of the family of the normal and sick newborn baby. We can be grateful that, with their professional skill, the authors blend a keen sensitivity to the needs of parents, openness in the reexamination of issues, theoretical orientation that permits them to examine and think critically about the complicated issue of attachment between parent and newborn, and modesty in placing their scientific studies as well as those of others in perspective.

But why are we in a state of rapid modification of practices surrounding the care of the newborn infant and his family? We need to look to the history of medicine since the turn of the century. At that time the advances in the natural sciences made possible the modern era of scientific medicine and particularly clinical investigation. Medical education in its modern form emerged, as did the modern hospital system.

That the results of these developments had a major effect on saving the lives of mothers and infants during the subsequent decades is clear. The growing knowledge of microbiology, immunology, nutrition, and metabolism resulted in improved public health practices, with a lowering of the infant mortality rate (deaths under 1 year of age per 1000 babies born) from 140 in 1900 to approximately seventeen in 1975.

The efforts to apply the new knowledge resulted in an institutionalization and professionalization of obstetrical and infant care that removed mother and baby from intimate contact with each other and with the family. The increasing knowledge and technology in the care of the premature and sick infant has in recent years resulted in the development of intensive care nurseries and the new subspecialty of neonatology or perinatology.

All progress carries with it certain risks, however. The increasing isolation of babies from mothers and of babies and mothers from the family at a time of a major family event has resulted in disquiet on the part of both parents and professionals, with a consequent critical re-examination of these practices. Continued scientific advances make it more feasible to think of modifying long-standing practices. Thus the newer knowledge of epidemiology and infectious disease control and the availability of many antibacterial agents have made it feasible to explore the introduction of family members into the maternity and newborn settings of the hospital. Simultaneously, the growing disciplines of infant observation and child development have focused attention on the importance of studying the interactional and deprivational aspects of this earliest period.

We are fortunate that the authors were among the pioneers in re-opening the nurseries—especially for the premature and sick infant—to parents and their families. We are fortunate, too, that over the past decade they have undertaken to study systematically the effects of this process and that these studies continue. Thus their studies and those of others they review strongly favor this more flexible and liberal policy as being beneficial to babies and families. These studies lead them to present a theoretical framework consonant with their developmental orientation. They posit the existence of a "sensitive period in the first minutes and hours of life, during which it is necessary for optimal later development that the mother and father have close contact with their neonate." They go on to suggest that the newborn must signal back, thus setting in motion an initial interaction that may lead to a profound and long-lasting attachment.

We are fortunate, too, that the authors have shared with us their sophisticated, yet practical, review of the scientific literature that only long-term immersion in a problem can make possible. There is no over-simplification of relevance in the presentation of animal studies and cross-cultural experiences for our society. Yet there is much to stimulate thought about the issues that are considered.

Finally, we are fortunate that the authors are clinicians deeply immersed in clinical practice as well as investigation. This comes through on every page; from their insights and from the literature they draw many inferences that they pass along to us. Other clinicians may have some differences—as clinicians generally do—but none can say that the suggestions are not drawn from struggling with the many complex problems of a rich clinical experience.

Thus they have presented to us a blend of the science and art of the care of the newborn and his family and an important theoretical framework for the study of the earliest relationship between the newborn and his parents.

Fortunately, the state of our science and art supports care that seems to be more humane. The authors, through their pioneering clinical and research efforts and through the uniqueness of this volume, have done a great service to families and the child-caring professions. Since this will serve as a handbook for family care of the normal and sick newborn baby and since so many advances are occurring so rapidly, we can hope that the authors will accept the challenge to revise and update this volume frequently.

JULIUS B. RICHMOND, M.D.

Professor of Child Psychology
and Human Development,
Harvard Medical School;
Psychiatrist-in-Chief,
Children's Hospital Medical
Center; Director, Judge Baker
Guidance Center, Boston,
Massachusetts

Preface

For each of us, learning is a personal adventure; therefore we have deviated from the traditional style and have used several techniques in this book.

One innovation is the use of the patient interview. Some readers may disagree with the inclusion of this material, but we believe a representative interview with authoritative comments is a thought-provoking device worthy of trial. A reading of the text will not be complete without a reading of the interview. It should be emphasized that the comments we have made about each of the three interviews cannot apply to every patient. Since we did not have long-term, in-depth interviews with the parents, there are sometimes many possible interpretations of the parents' comments. They do, however, tell us something about the feelings, thoughts, concerns, and hopes of parents during these difficult days. They have been chosen because they demonstrate or emphasize certain reactions or issues that other parents have repeatedly discussed. Some readers may choose to read the interview first and attempt to interpret the parent discussions before they note our comments. For those wishing a quick review of the subject, we have added a series of recommendations at the end of each chapter.

To demonstrate the many areas of controversy, we have asked expert consultants to comment on each chapter except the first. Some have made notes scattered throughout a chapter. Others have written a single comment, which we have inserted near the case presentation. We strongly urge the reader to consider these short, pithy, thoughtful contributions, since they extend, expand, or differ from our concepts.

This book has been organized in a special pattern that has evolved, in part, as we have developed our understanding of the subject. To understand maternal and paternal behavior in the human, we have found it valuable to learn from the detailed and precise observations of a wide range of animal species, since the requirements of caring for the young may have led to the evolution of similar behavioral patterns in humans and other animals. Because this is so crucial for our understanding, we have presented this information in a separate chapter (Chapter 2). Many studies have been summarized so that the reader may carefully note differences and similarities of parental behavior in a number of species faced with a common task. Chapter 3 describes the studies that provide the theoretical and empirical framework for discussing the care of the human mother and applies this to clinical situations involving care of the normal human mother. Chapter 4 describes studies related to the families of premature and sick infants and makes specific recommendations for their care. For several years we have been interested in Dr. Bertrand Cramer's interpretation of the reactions of parents to their premature infants, and we have included his discussion at the end of Chapter 4. He listens to these parents with the ears of a psychoanalyst having experience in both the United States and Europe. Chapter 5 takes on the painfully sad and difficult problem of a baby born with a malformation, a frequent occurrence in a high-risk nursery. In most pediatric units the greatest number of deaths occur on the newborn service, particularly in the high-risk nursery. The range of parental reactions to the death of a newborn is described in Chapter 6, accompanied by recommended procedures for the physician who has cared for the infant who has died. The latter three chapters (Chapters 3 to 6) first present basic research data, followed by a case study with our comments. Next there are clinical recommendations and a list of practical hints. We hope that the critical comments interspersed in the text will provoke discussion so that the reader will be aware of the many complex and debatable issues that remain unsettled. We conclude with a glimpse into the future.

As we look back, it was the mothers of premature infants who first kindled our interest by showing us that there were difficult problems of attachment after a separation. Our early curiosity was supported and encouraged by thoughtful nurses (especially Jane Cable) who shared their experiences and were willing to take what seemed at the time a hazardous step of allowing parents to enter the monastic doors of the nursery. We gained a richer and deeper understanding of what was going on in the minds of parents of premature infants through long discussions with colleagues in the behavioral sciences (Cliff Barnett, Mary Bergen, Douglas Bond, Anna Freud, Rose Grobstein, Herb Leiderman, Litzie Rolnick, Benjamin Spock).

We were helped immeasurably with our own investigations by the critical suggestions and provocative questions from other investigators concerned with maternal and paternal behavior. Our special thanks go to T. Berry Brazelton, Harry Gordon, Raven Lang, Julius Richmond, Jay S. Rosenblatt, and the late William Wallace.

We have been especially fortunate to work side by side with a series of bright, inquisitive, refreshing medical students who worked long hours and asked searching questions. Each of the medical students made unique contributions. We thank Gail Bongiovanni, David Chesler, Wendy

Freed, David Gordon, Guillermo Gutierrez, Deborah Jean Hales, Rick Jerauld, Chris Kreger, John Lampe, Betsy Parke Macintyre, Willie Mc-Alpine, Nancy Plumb, Howard Slyter, Meredith Steffa, Harriett Holan Wolfe, Steve Zuelke, and the many patient and conscientious research associates who made our studies possible, most recently Billie Navojosky and Diana Voos.

Throughout our studies we have been fortunate to have the benefit of the experience and counsel of Joseph Fagan, Robert Fantz, and Simón Miranda, in the Perceptual Development Laboratory of the Department of Psychology. Special thanks should be given to our department Chairman, Dr. Leroy Matthews, who has been most thoughtful about arranging time to prepare this work.

We would like to acknowledge the expert secretarial assistance and devoted efforts of Janet Negrelli, Jackie Stimpert, and Elizabeth Wilber. Editorial work on the book was started by our former associate Robin White, and then as efforts to complete the book intensified in the final months, skillful help was provided by Alisa Klaus, Laurie Krent, and Susan Schafer.

Our close friend, colleague, and counselor Dr. Avroy Fanaroff has supported and assisted us while we have conducted most of our studies. Since 1973 we have had a highly productive association with our colleague, advisor, and critic Mary Anne Trause. Susan Davis, Dennis Drotar, Nancy A. Irvin, Betsy Lozoff, and Norma Ringler have provided special skills and knowledge for some of our studies. In Guatemala our investigations could never have been carried out were it not for the suggestions and leadership of Drs. Leonardo Mata, Roberto Sosa, and Juan Urrutia, the extremely conscientious and devoted work of research field workers Patricia Baten, Marta Isabel Garcia, Rubidia Méndez, and Olga Maricela Ochoa, and especially the collaboration and expertise of Prof. Gustavo Castaneda and the personnel at Roosevelt and Social Security Hospitals.

Our work would not have been possible without the generous support of the Grant Foundation, the Educational Foundation of America, Maternal and Child Health Grant MC-R-390337, NIH 72-C-202, and the Research Corporation.

MARSHALL H. KLAUS
JOHN H. KENNELL

Contents

Chapter 1

Maternal-infant bonding

MARSHALL H. KLAUS and JOHN H. KENNELL

Most of the richness and beauty of life is derived from the close relationship that each individual has with a small number of other human beings—mother, father, brother, sister, husband, wife, son, daughter, and a small cadre of close friends. With each person in this small group, the individual has a uniquely close attachment or bond. Much of the joy and sorrow of life revolves around attachments or affectional relationships—making them, breaking them, preparing for them, and adjusting to their loss caused by death. This book deals with one of these very special attachments, the bond a mother or father forms with his or her newborn infant.

Over the past forty years, investigators from a variety of disciplines have painstakingly elaborated the process by which the human infant becomes attached to his mother (Bowlby, 1958; Spitz, 1965). They have described the disastrous effects on the infant of long-term maternal separation in terms of his motor, mental, and affective development. Barnett and associates (1970) noted, "While there has been theoretical recognition that separation involves the mother and infant, little attention has been paid to its effect on the mother." This book describes the development of attachment in the opposite direction, from parent to infant: how it grows, develops, and matures and what distorts, disturbs, promotes, or enhances it. This attachment is crucial to the survival and development of the infant. One aspect of its nature is well stated in a Russian proverb, "You can't pay anyone to do what a mother will do for free." Perhaps the mother's attachment to her child is the strongest bond in the human. This relationship has two unique characteristics. First, before birth the infant gestates within the mother's body, and, second, after birth she ensures his survival while he is utterly dependent on her. The power of this attachment is so great that it enables the mother or father to make the unusual sacrifices necessary for the care of their infant day after day, night after night—changing dirty diapers, attending to his cry, protecting him from danger, and giving feedings in the middle of the night despite a desperate need to sleep. It is the nature of this attachment that we will explore. This original mother-infant bond is the wellspring for all the infant's subsequent attachments and is the formative relationship in the course of which the child develops a sense of himself. Throughout his lifetime the strength and character of this attachment will influence the quality of all future bonds to other individuals.

An "attachment" can be defined as a unique relationship between two people that is specific and endures through time. Although it is difficult to define this enduring relationship operationally, we have taken as indicators of this attachment, behaviors such as fondling, kissing, cuddling, and prolonged gazing—behaviors that serve both to maintain contact and to exhibit affection toward a particular individual. Although this definition is useful in experimental observations, it is important to distinguish between attachment and attachment behaviors. Close attachment can persist during long separations of time and distance, even though there may at times be no visible sign of its existence. Nonetheless, a call for help after even forty years may bring a mother to her child and evoke attachment behaviors equal in strength to those in the first year.

In discussing attachment, it is necessary to note that crucial life events surrounding the development of both attachment and detachment have been removed from the home and brought into the hospital over the past sixty years. The hospital now determines the procedures involved in birth and death. The experiences surrounding these two events in the life of an individual have been stripped of the long-established traditions and support systems built up over centuries to help families through these highly meaningful transitions.

An important impetus to studying the mother-infant bond occurred ten to fifteen years ago when the staffs of intensive care nurseries observed that after heroic measures had been used to save prematures, these infants would sometimes return to emergency rooms battered and almost destroyed by their parents, even though the infants had been sent home intact and thriving. Careful studies show an increase in the incidence of battering as well as failure to thrive without organic cause among premature infants and those hospitalized for other reasons during the newborn period when they are compared with infants not separated from their mothers. Failure to thrive without organic disease is a syndrome in which the infant does not grow, gain weight, or develop behaviorally at a normal rate during the first few months at home. Such infants show rapid gains in all aspects of development when given only routine hospital care. Table 1-1 presents observations that have been made throughout the world on the incidence of infant battering and failure to thrive without organic disease and its relationship to earlier separation at or near birth. It was necessary to reanalyze the data from a number of studies (Table 1-1) to highlight this significant association between early separation and the subsequent development

Table 1-1. Effect of separation on battering and failure to thrive without organic cause

	Authors	Number in study	Number affected	Percentage separated
Failure to thrive	Ambuel and Harris, 1963	100	27 prematures	27
	Shaheen, Alexander, Truskowsky, and Barbero, 1968	44	16 prematures	36
	Evans, Reinhart, and Succop, 1972	40	9 prematures	22.5
Battering	Elmer and Gregg, 1967	20	6 prematures	30
	Skinner and Castle, 1969	78	10 prematures	13
	Klein and Stern, 1971	51	12 low birth weight infants	23.5
	Oliver, Cox, Taylor, and Baldwin, 1974	38	8 prematures	21

of these disastrous conditions. The occurrence of these and other mothering disorders have provided a continuing stimulus compelling us to attempt to unravel the mysteries of maternal attachment.

Had we read closely the first text of neonatology by Budin (1907), we could have foreseen and perhaps avoided the tragic problems arising from early separation of mother and infant. In his book *The Nursling* he wrote, "Unfortunately . . . a certain number of mothers abandon the babies whose needs they have not had to meet, and in whom they have lost all interest. The life of the little one has been saved, it is true, but at the cost of the mother." He recommended that mothers should be encouraged to breastfeed their premature infants in addition to their full-term infants to increase the mother's milk production. He designed and promoted the glass-walled incubator, which allowed the mother to look at her infant easily, and he permitted mothers to visit and care for their infants. As a result of introducing these changes, mothers remained attentive to their infants' needs, even though the infants were in hospitals for a prolonged period.

Martin Cooney, a young pupil of Budin, went to the Berlin Exposition of 1896, where his *Kinderbrutanstalt* ("child hatchery"), which specialized in caring for premature infants, was successful commercially. Since premature infants were not expected to live, German physicians gave them to Cooney. He exhibited the infants at fairs in England (Covent Garden) and came to the United States in 1902 for the Pan American Exposition in Buffalo and went on to Omaha, Nebraska, in 1904. From there he traveled throughout the United States. Cooney settled on Coney Island, successfully caring for more than 5000 premature infants during the next four decades. He exhibited the infants in almost all the major fairs and expositions from 1902 until the New York World's Fair of 1940.

It is interesting to note that as late as 1932, Cooney took infants from the Michael Reese Hospital to be exhibited at the Chicago World's Fair. The receipts they brought in were second only to those of Sally Rand, the fan dancer (Liebling, 1939).

Ironically, Budin's desire to publicize this method resulted in the exclusion of the mother from the nursery. Cooney followed all of the precepts of his teacher, Professor Budin, with this one major exception. Women were not permitted to help take care of their infants at Cooney's exhibits, although they were given free passes. Significantly but perhaps not surprisingly, he observed that he could not make a living if he only collected the funds from the mothers. It is also revealing that on some occasions he experienced great difficulty in persuading mothers to take their babies back once they had grown to 5 pounds. In spite of the commercial aspects of Cooney's technique, when premature nurseries were established in the United States, they adopted many of his methods of newborn care. Fig. 1-1, *A,* illustrates the outside of one

A

Fig. 1-1. **A,** Outside of Cooney's exhibit in San Francisco (1915). **B,** Interior of Cooney's exhibit. **C,** Nurses holding six exhibition babies. Cooney's daughter Hildegard is the center nurse.

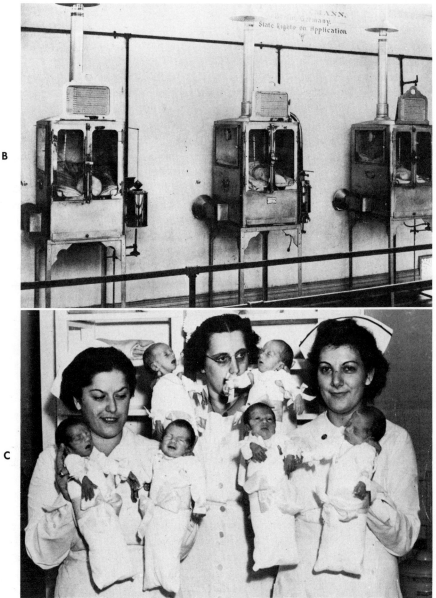

Fig. 1-1, cont'd. For legend see opposite page.

of his exhibits in San Francisco; Fig. 1-1, *B,* shows the interior of one of his exhibits; and Fig. 1-1, *C,* shows the nurses, including Cooney's daughter, holding several premature infants.

In the early 1900s the high rate of morbidity and mortality of hospitalized patients with communicable diseases led to the development of strict isolation techniques for diseased patients and separate wards with protective isolation measures for those patients free of infection. Visitors were strongly discouraged because of the belief that they were the source of infection. The quality of the milk available at the beginning of the century is an example of one of the prevailing problems of the time. In 1903, at the fifteenth annual meeting of the American Pediatric Society, one of the speakers reported that market milk was still sold over the grocery counter from dippered, unrefrigerated, 5-gallon cans (Faber and McIntosh, 1966). Cultures of this milk showed massive contamination. The victory over summer diarrhea was not achieved until general improvements in milk production and distribution were enforced by law, the most important of which was routine pasteurization of milk, including certification. In children's hospitals concern about protecting patients from contagious disorders led to what today appear to be bizarre policies of isolation and separation. In the early 1940s a child was completely separated from his parents during hospitalization. The visiting hours in the major children's hospitals were no longer than 30 to 60 minutes a week. The fear of spread of infection also accounts for the physical barriers often observed between individual beds in the older children's hospitals and the actual spacing between the obstetrical and pediatric divisions in the large general hospitals. Not only was diarrhea epidemic but respiratory infections were a scourge of children's hospitals and maternity and infant units.

As a result of problems of infection, maternity hospitals gathered full-term babies in large nurseries in a fortresslike arrangement in the spirit of the practice established by Cooney. Germs were the enemy; therefore parents and families were excluded. The Sarah Morris Hospital in Chicago developed the first hospital center for premature care in 1923. Following the precepts of Budin, the director encouraged the production of breast milk at home; however, mothers' assistance in caring for the premature infants was not stressed.

Premature units created after the Sarah Morris Hospital followed a standard set of regulations, which have remained in effect until the early 1960s. Standard textbooks on the care of the newborn from 1945 to 1960 continued to reflect the traditions and fears of the early 1900s, recommending only the most essential handling of the infants and a policy of strict isolation (exclusion of visitors).

During the period after World War II, two innovative approaches to premature care appeared. In a study of home-nursed premature infants in Newcastle-on-Tyne, England, Miller (1948) found that the mortality rate was only slightly greater than that of a control group of infants who were nursed in a hospital. A shortage of skilled personnel and equipment was the impetus for an arrangement created by Kahn in Baragwanath Hospital in Johannesburg, South Africa. Here mothers were able to participate in supervised care and feeding of their infants, and they remained in the hospital during their infant's entire hospital stay. Fig. 1-2 shows some of their caretaking activities. Mothers of small premature infants in this unit nursed them on cots in a heated room. With their procedures the rate of infection did not increase, and survival rates were excellent.

Over the last ten years more and more mothers have been allowed to enter premature nurseries. Yet, in a survey of hospital practices in 1970 by Barnett and co-workers (1972), in only 30% of the hospitals were mothers permitted to enter nurseries and in only 40% of these hospitals were mothers permitted to touch their babies in the first days of life. If one adopts the standards of what constitutes deprivation and the levels of deprivation suggested by Barnett and co-workers (1970), it

Fig. 1-2. Mothers in Baragwanath, South Africa. (Courtesy Dr. J. E. Bell, Palo Alto, Calif.)

Table 1-2. Levels of interactional deprivation and component variables[*]

Levels of deprivation	Duration of interaction	Sensory modalities of interaction	Caretaking nature of interaction
I. No deprivation	Full time	All senses	Complete
II. Partial deprivation	Part time	All senses	Partial
III. Moderate deprivation	Part time	All senses	None
IV. Severe deprivation	Part time	Visual only	None
V. Complete deprivation	None	None	None

*From Barnett, C. R., Leiderman, P. H., Grobstein, R., and Klaus, M. H.: Neonatal separation: the maternal side of interactional deprivation, Pediatrics **45**:197-205, 1970.

is apparent that most normal births in the United States are associated with several days of deprivation for the mother (Tables 1-2 and 1-3). A woman who delivers a premature infant suffers complete separation from her infant for at least the first day, since typically, even after the first day she only sees her infant through a glass window. Only mothers who deliver their normal full-term infants at home and live with their infants from birth experience no deprivation.

The need for writing this book arose from this background and, more personally, from our tenure managing nurseries for normal and sick infants. Our interest in this subject has been stimulated by a number of specific cases. For example, Mrs. D. had been married for nine years and for the past five years had planned to have a baby. The infant, weighing 4 pounds 2 ounces, was born in a medical center after a gestation of 35 weeks. Within a few minutes of birth he was gasping and blue and therefore had to be resuscitated. At this early point the mother wondered if the infant would survive. Three hours later he was transferred to an intensive care unit under the direction of one of us, and within the next 36 hours he was placed on a respirator. Two days later the infant was showing considerable improvement, and the respirator was disconnected. At the end of three days the infant was in an incubator and started to take feedings through an intragastric plastic tube. At the end of two weeks he was taking feedings well by nipple, and the staff decided that the infant would soon be ready for discharge. After several days the head nurse came to one of us explaining that the mother was unable to get a few drops of milk into the infant, even though he could be fed easily by the nurses. Some suggestions were given to the mother that were unsuccessful. Three days later one of us observed the infant and noted that the mother was in a very uncomfortable position and continually jerked the nipple in and out of the baby's mouth. At one point she placed the baby on her knees, picked

Table 1-3. Deprivation levels over time, related to birth situations*

Birth situation	Deprivation levels, days and weeks postpartum					
	Day 0	Day 1	Day 3	Day 7	Week 8	Week 9
Home, full term	I, no deprivation	I, no deprivation	I, no deprivation	I, no deprivation	I, no deprivation	I, no deprivation
Hospital, full term, rooming-in	III, moderate deprivation	I, no deprivation	I, no deprivation	I, no deprivation	I, no deprivation	I, no deprivation
Hospital, full term, regular care	III, moderate deprivation	II, partial deprivation	II, partial deprivation	I, no deprivation	I, no deprivation	I, no deprivation
Premature, mother allowed into nursery	V, complete deprivation	IV, severe deprivation	III, moderate deprivation	II, partial deprivation	II, partial deprivation (discharge nursery)	I, no deprivation (home)
Premature, regular care (separated)	V, complete deprivation	IV, severe deprivation	IV, severe deprivation	IV, severe deprivation	II, partial deprivation (discharge nursery)	I, no deprivation (home)
Unwed mother, refuses contact	V, complete deprivation	V, complete deprivation	V, complete deprivation	V, complete deprivation	V, complete deprivation	V, complete deprivation

*From Barnett C. R., Leiderman, P. H., Grobstein, R., and Klaus, M. H.: Neonatal separation: the maternal side of interactional deprivation, Pediatrics **45:**197-205, 1970.

up his head in her hands, looked at his face and said, "Are you mine? Are you really mine? Are you alive? Are you really alive?" Through many similar observations of other patients, we were repeatedly stimulated to take a closer look at this phenomenon. In retrospect this woman believed that her infant would not survive and started to mourn his loss within the first 12 hours after birth. During the first two weeks while the infant was improving, the mother did not expect him to live.

It is easy to see how her interaction with this baby might have easily produced the syndrome of failure to thrive or even child abuse. In fact, she suggested to the hospital personnel that the baby remain in the hospital for a prolonged period, since it took another four weeks for her to develop the necessary caretaking skills. Six months after the infant's birth the mother reflected that those had been the worst six months of her life. One month after the baby finally went home, it was necessary for her to leave him for two to three days so that she could rest.

Another observation raised questions in our minds: A mother who had successfully and skillfully managed two full-term babies was uncertain and anxious as she started to care for a newborn premature infant. She required considerable extra support and instruction to feed the infant and change his diapers and had endless questions during the first three months after he went home.

During the past twelve years we have been excited by the exchange of ideas concerning these issues with individuals from a wide variety of disciplines. This book is our synthesis of this fascinating and complex field. Having the fortunate and unfortunate opportunity to observe daily both normal full-term infants and sick infants in the intensive care nursery and the mothers of healthy full-term infants as well as those separated from tiny infants, we are forced to ask the question: What is the normal process by which a father and mother become attached to a young infant? From our fumbling, early efforts to understand and unravel the mysteries of this process, we have developed our present understanding.

We must confess that although often our behavioral observations stimulated certain productive studies, they often misled us in our understanding of a specific phenomenon. For example, when we first permitted mothers to enter the premature nursery to touch their infants in the incubator, we noticed that they would poke at their infants as women poke a cake to test whether it is done, touching the tips of their fingers to their infants' extremities. We wondered about the origins of this behavior. Our thoughts and ideas about this behavior have evolved as we have gone back and forth from the intensive care to the normal full-term nursery. As will be seen in Chapter 3, poking at premature infants by mothers is possibly an aberration of the normal maternal behavior when the infant appears fragile and an incubator is interposed. When the infant and mother are in a situation more appropriate for their becoming acquainted this behavior is observed only during the first minutes of contact.

The recent accumulation of information in a closely related field has greatly augmented our work. Detailed studies of the amazing behavioral capacities of the normal neonate have shown that the infant sees, hears, and moves in rhythm to his mother's voice in the first minutes and hours of life, resulting in a beautiful linking of the reactions of the two and a synchronized "dance" between the mother and infant (Condon and Sander, 1974). The infant's appearance coupled with his broad array of sensory and motor abilities evokes responses from the mother and provides several channels of communication that are essential in the process of attachment and the initiation of the series of reciprocal interactions just described.

As an example of the infant's role in attachment behavior, Fig. 1-3 shows a mother suckling her infant a few minutes after birth: the in-

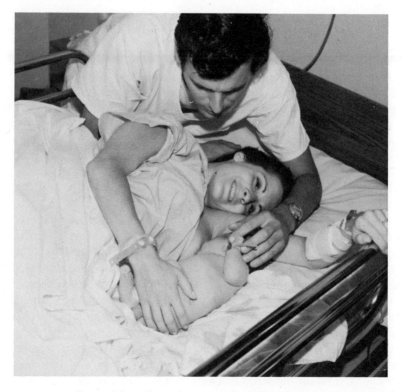

Fig. 1-3. A mother suckling her infant a few minutes after birth as the father looks on.

fant is licking the area around the nipple (Lang, 1972). MacFarlane (1975) has shown that six days later this infant will have the ability to distinguish reliably by scent his own mother's breast pad from the breast pads of other women. On the mother's side, she is intensely interested in looking at her newborn baby's open eyes. The infant is awake and alert and visually follows his mother for over an arc of 180 degrees during this special period immediately after birth (Brazelton et al., 1966). The infant's licking of the mother's nipple induces marked prolactin secretion and oxytocin release, which cause the uterus to contract thereby reducing postpartum bleeding. This early interaction also possibly permits the transfer of the mother's staphylococcus and other bacteria to the infant so that it is colonized with the mother's rather than with the hospital's bacteria. Recent discoveries in endocrinology, ethology, infant development, immunology, and bacteriology have greatly increased knowledge of the reciprocal linkages at many levels between the parent and infant. Throughout this text we will repeatedly consider the interrelationship between the pair and stimulating characteristics of each member. We have learned by our own errors that it is misleading to look only at one member of the dyad in this complex interaction.

It is difficult to understand the factors that determine the interactional and mothering behavior of an adult human who has lived for twenty to thirty years. A mother and father's behavior toward their infant is derived from a complex combination of their own genetic endowments, the infant's responses to them, a long history of interpersonal relations with their own families and with each other, past experiences with this or previous pregnancies, the absorption of the practices and values of their cultures, and probably most importantly, the way in which each was raised by his or her own parents. The mothering or fathering behavior of each woman and man, the ability of each to tolerate stresses, and the needs each has for special attention differ greatly and depend on a mixture of these factors.

Fig. 1-4 is a schematic diagram of the major influences on paternal and maternal behavior and the resulting disturbances that we hypothesize may arise from them. At the time the infant is born, some of these determinants (framed with a solid line) are ingrained and unchangeable, such as the mothering the father and mother received when they were infants, the practices of their culture, their endowments, and their relationships with their own families and with each other. Other determinants (framed with a dotted line) can be altered, such as the attitudes, statements, and practices of the physician in the hospital; whether or not there is separation from the infant in the first days of life; and the nature of the infant himself, his temperament, and whether he is healthy, sick, or malformed. Fig. 1-4 also shows a series of mothering disorders

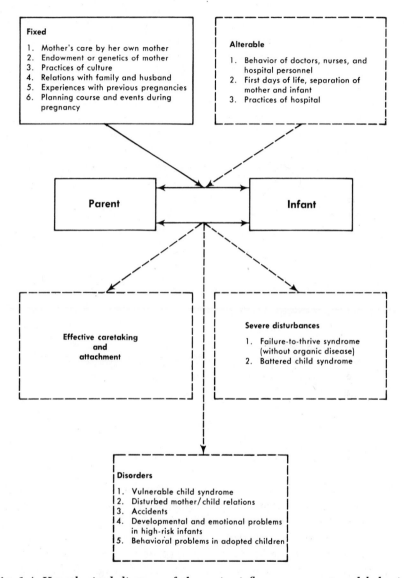

Fig. 1-4. Hypothesized diagram of the major influences on maternal behavior and the resulting disturbances. Solid lines represent unchangeable determinants; dotted lines represent alterable determinants.

ranging from mild anxiety, such as persistent concerns about a baby after a minor problem that has been completely resolved in the nursery, to the most severe manifestation—the battered child syndrome. It is our hypothesis that this entire range of problems may result largely from separation and other unusual circumstances which occur in the early newborn period as a consequence of present hospital care policies. Parent-infant separation and hospital practices during the first hours and days of life are the most easily manipulated variables in this scheme. Recent studies have partly clarified some of the steps in mother-infant attachment during this early period.

Our own studies over the past twelve years have led us to formulate principles governing the mother's attachment to her infant. For several rules we have strong evidence, and for others the evidence is sketchy and fragmentary. At present we believe these seven principles are crucial components in the process of attachment.

1. There is a sensitive period in the first minutes and hours of life during which it is necessary that the mother and father have close contact with their neonate for later development to be optimal.

2. There appear to be species-specific responses to the infant in the human mother and father that are exhibited when they are first given their infant.

3. The process of the attachment is structured so that the father and mother will become attached optimally to only one infant at a time. Bowlby (1958) earlier stated this principle of the attachment process in the other direction and termed it *monotropy*.

4. During the process of the mother's attachment to her infant, it is necessary that the infant respond to the mother by some signal such as body or eye movements. We have sometimes described this, "You can't love a dishrag."

5. People who witness the birth process become strongly attached to the infant.

6. For some adults it is difficult simultaneously to go through the processes of attachment and detachment, that is, to develop an attachment to one person while mourning the loss or threatened loss of the same or another person.

7. Some early events have long-lasting effects. Anxieties about the well-being of a baby with a temporary disorder in the first day may result in long-lasting concerns that may cast long shadows and adversely shape the development of the child (Kennell and Rolnick, 1960).

During the past ten years, as knowledge in the field of infant development and mother-infant attachment has rapidly increased, the field of neonatal intensive care and high-risk obstetrical care has also changed remarkably. The obstetrician caring for the high-risk mother often requests close monitoring of a large proportion of mothers with special devices to measure fetal heart rate and uterine contractions during labor. The neonatologist wants the infant warm, dry, and under close attention. At the same time there is a strong lay movement advocating less interference with normal births and more involvement of and control by the parents. As a consequence, the home birth movement is now growing. Ideally, we would like to use the best of present day knowledge of high-risk obstetrics, neonatology, infant development, and mother-infant attachment and at the same time have family and parent participation in homelike births in the hospital. This book will give our suggestions for the care of mothers and fathers if the baby is premature, full term, malformed, or dies.

We will not attempt to describe all of the many studies that define the factors affecting the development of the infant, that is, the complex requirements for accessory stimulation. This is a book about the needs of fathers and mothers and of their effects on the infant.

Chapter 2

Maternal behavior in mammals

Mary Anne Trause, Marshall H. Klaus, and John H. Kennell

> It is only through a real understanding of the ways in
> which chimpanzees and man show similarities in behavior
> that we can reflect with meaning on the way in which men and
> chimpanzees differ. And only then can we really begin to
> appreciate, in a biological and spiritual manner, the
> full extent of man's uniqueness.
>
> Jane van Lawick-Goodall

Just as the neonatologist who is interested in the respiratory changes occurring at birth has used the models of the fetal lamb and monkey, scientists attempting to understand maternal behavior in humans find it valuable to study maternal behavior in a wide range of other animal species. This is done not to explain human behavior but rather to view human beings within the context of evolutionary development. The requirements of air breathing resulted in similar morphological structures in both human and nonhuman primates; the requirements of caring for the young have led to the evolution of similar patterns of maternal behavior in humans and other animals. The study of human parental attachment has been partly aided by observation of animal mothers.

Kaufman (1970) has described the evolutionary importance of certain reproductive changes in mammals (internal fertilization, the development of the amniote egg, and the development of the placenta) and states the following:

> Of at least equal significance, mammals also evolved a *behavioral* program of reproductive economy, namely, a higher order of *parental care* of the young after birth, without the consequence of which it is impossible to visualize the development of man. Care of the very young was already evolved in fish, reptiles, and especially birds, but what made possible the tremendous advance in mammals was the system of feeding the infant, through special glands, a substance, milk, which contains everything needed for growth and development. The improved feeding arrangement keeps the young physically close

16

to the mother and thus safer from harm. . . . Finally, and very importantly, the close physical relationship and the shared personal experience provided to the infant and mother by the feeding from her body constitute a degree of contact and intimacy which creates a new kind of bond, with durable characteristics.*

In lower primates the infant clings to the mother; in higher primates such as the gorilla and human being, the infant is unable to cling, and the mother must carry him. In these more advanced species, therefore, the mother plays a more important role in maintaining contact with the infant, and his survival hinges on the mother's attachment to him to a greater extent.

COMMENT: Patterns of maternal behavior among mammals appear to be adapted mainly to the altricial (i.e., immature) or precocial (i.e., more mature) status of the newborn. Species with altricial young are usually nest builders or live in burrows or caves, whereas species with precocial young are generally surface-living, migratory animals that live in herds or social groups. In the former group there is an extended period of intense maternal care, then a tapering off as weaning begins, and the young soon leave the mother. In the latter group there is a shorter period of intense maternal care but a more extended weaning period, during which the young are integrated into the social group alongside the mother, and they may never really leave their original social group.

Primates share features of both patterns, since the young are altricial in certain ways but in other ways they are precocial.

J. S. ROSENBLATT

In pursuing the relevant data on the formation of that affectional bond between an animal mother and her offspring, we have relied on ethological field studies as well as experimental laboratory studies. Ethological studies are usually made on animals in their natural habitat and involve painstaking descriptions of behavior in the ecological and social setting where it has evolved and naturally occurs. After these descriptions have been made, attempts to explain the functions of particular behavior patterns, the antecedent conditions, and the underlying mechanisms require field or laboratory experiments. Since experimental interventions are made only after the animals have been carefully observed in their natural environment, a model of behavior emerges that is based on normal rather than pathological conditions.

Even those who caution strongly against an overemphasis on ethology for the understanding of human behavior agree with the usefulness of

---

*From Kaufman, C.: In Anthony, E. J., and Benedek, T., editors: Parenthood: its psychology and psychopathology, Boston, 1970, Little, Brown & Co.

an evolutionary perspective for highlighting significant features of human behavioral development (Bernal and Richards, 1972).

SPECIES-SPECIFIC BEHAVIOR

Detailed observations of parturition in a large number of species have illuminated the evolution of species-specific patterns of parturitive behavior and its relation to maternal care that follows, both of which serve the needs of the newborn young. Parturition is similar in the domestic cat all over the world: Toward the end of her pregnancy the female is less agile than usual, and her activity greatly decreases. For a birth site she selects a warm, dark place, preferably with a soft surface. The degree of seclusion varies, and in home pets it depends on the closeness of her relationship with her human owners. Although pet cats have been known to bear their young in the bed of a sleeping person, more often they find a secluded spot, such as the back of a closet or the space under a stairway.

During parturition the female cat usually licks herself, the neonates, and the floor of the birth site. Invariably, she licks the posterior part of her body, especially the vaginal area, and this often leads her to lick or nose the kitten immediately after birth. Typically she squats during labor to aid in expulsion of the fetuses.

After the birth of the last kitten and eating of the last placenta, the female generally lies down, encircling her kittens, and rests with them for about 12 hours. This encircling is the earliest direct adaptation she makes to her young after birth. She "presents" by lying down around her kittens with her ventral surface arched toward them and with her front and rear legs extended to enclose them. While lying with the kittens, she licks them, stimulating them to nurse. This may begin as early as a half hour after birth and typically before the end of the 12-hour resting period. For the first few days the mother stays with her litter at the birth site, leaving them only once every couple of hours to feed. If the kittens wander away from the home site, they usually begin to vocalize and the mother responds by retrieving them, becoming more skillful with practice.

The mother initiates nursing during the first twenty days after parturition. For the next ten to fifteen days either mother or kitten may initiate feeding, but after the thirty-fifth day the kitten is more likely to seek out the mother for feeding (Schneirla et al., 1963).

Another mammal for which the sequence of mothering behavior at the time of birth has been meticulously described is the rhesus monkey. During the last 5 days of pregnancy the female manually explores her genitals, then looks at, smells, and licks her hands. She removes the mucous plug from her vaginal opening with her hands just prior to the birth. When the fetus's face appears, she squats and pulls it forward, helping to deliver the trunk and legs. Although the infant rhesus sometimes vocalizes during parturition, the mother does not. As soon as its hands are free, the infant clutches the mother's fur, and the mother in turn holds her infant to her chest and alternately cleans herself and the infant, licking it thoroughly from head to toe. When the delivery of the placenta begins, she temporarily ignores her infant while she eats the placenta. Grooming and retrieving of the infant increase during the first month, as does restraining it from leaving her. During this period the mother spends much time holding the infant close or cradling it loosely in her arms (Brandt and Mitchell, 1971).

COMMENT: The role of parturition in the formation of the mother-young bond is the subject of some controversy among animal researchers. Female rats that are not permitted to give birth normally but are delivered by cesarean section readily respond to pups when they recover from the surgery after several hours. This has led some investigators to suggest that parturition does not play a *crucial* role in the establishment of the mother-young bond or in the onset of maternal behavior. A recent study by Bridges,[*] however, has demonstrated how significant the events of parturition are for the mother. He showed that females whose pups were removed immediately after each was cleaned after birth did not show any increased responsiveness to pups twenty-five days later, but females that were allowed to keep their pups until the end of parturition, that is, for about 30 minutes, were very responsive to pups twenty-five days later. My own belief is that this problem has not been studied sufficiently.

J. S. ROSENBLATT

Brandt and Mitchell (1971) report a fascinating observation of a captive chimpanzee mother whose newborn did not seem to be breathing. She held its body and head and covered its mouth and nose with her mouth as if administering mouth-to-mouth resuscitation. One minute later the infant cried out and the mother put it to her chest.

Although two species may be closely related taxonomically, they have not necessarily evolved exactly the same responses to similar environmental demands. For example, although the North Indian langur mother is closely related to the rhesus mother, and her behavior around the time of delivery is similar in many ways, she will allow as many as eight other females to handle her infant after the first few hours, whereas the rhesus mother jealously holds her newborn close and avoids the approach of other animals.

[*]Bridges, R. S.: Long-term effects of pregnancy and parturition upon maternal responsiveness in the rat, Physiol. Behav. 14:245-249, 1975.

Table 2-1. Species-specific mothering behaviors in various animal species

Animal	Preparation for birth	Birth site	Birth	Protection of young	Nursing	Stimulation of young	Other observations
Domestic cat	Genital licking	Warm, dark place	Licks self, young, and floor of birth site; eats placenta	Retrieves vocalizing young	Initiates by presenting; begins ½ to 12 hours postpartum	Licking (Roth and Rosenblatt, 1968)	
Laboratory rat	Builds nest; anogenital licking	Birth nest (Rosenblatt and Lehrman, 1963)	Eats placenta	Nest; retrieves	Mother drapes herself over litter	Licking (Rosenblatt, 1969)	At first somewhat afraid of young (Rosenblatt, 1970)
Goats	Separate from herd	Secluded	Self-licking; licks newborn all over	Butts away all intruders; moves toward vocalizing kids	Adjusts position	Licking	Attempts to steal other young before birth (Ewer, 1968; Hersher et al., 1963a)
Sheep	Separate from herd	Domestic: indoor shelter Big horn: inaccessible mountain area	Licks anal area; licks newborn all over	Moves toward bleating lamb (Hersher et al., 1963a)	Adjusts position	Licking	

Primates					
North Indian langur				Keeps to herself for first hours	Licking, grooming, manipulating, stroking	Allows other females to hold in first day (Dolhinow, 1972)
Rhesus monkey	Floor of cage or metal bar	Explores genitals; removes mucus manually	Squats; pulls fetus forward; eats placenta; licks young	Holds young close, cradles, avoids others for a long time; retrieves and restrains	Grooming (Brandt and Mitchell, 1971)	
Chimpanzee		Moves away from herd	Carries placenta by umbilical cord	Stays away from group for several days; 5 months before allows others to touch (Kaufman, 1970)		Other behaviors similar to rhesus monkey

Elks and moose, two closely related species, also exhibit different patterns of maternal behaviors. The moose cow selects a totally secluded thicket near food and water in which to give birth and remains alone with her calf during the first weeks. They spend the first few days within a dozen square feet but later move around together. The elk cow, on the other hand, seeks a marginal retreat to deliver her young, which allows her to remain in visual, auditory, and olfactory contact with her herd. After the initial nursing the mother gently pushes her newborn down and leaves it in hiding while she grazes nearby with her herd. She remains with her calf at night and at first returns every 20 minutes during the day to nurse. Within a few days, however, the intervals between nursings increase to several hours.

Two related species that show widely differing postparturition behavior are pigtail and bonnet macaques. Normally bonnet adults tend to stay close to each other, whereas pigtail adults make few contacts with other animals in their group. Likewise, after parturition the bonnet mother rejoins her peers, whereas the pigtail mother remains isolated with her infant (Rosenblum and Kaufman, 1967). These examples dramatically illustrate the caution necessary in drawing conclusions about the behaviors of even closely related species.

Table 2-1 summarizes observations of maternal care in a number of mammalian species. It shows that different species have evolved comparable caretaking behaviors to meet similar needs. All mammals prepare for the birth of their young, establish a birth site, and during parturition lick their bodies. After birth they display a profound interest in the protection of their young, ensuring their warmth, maintaining control over visitors, warding off intruders, keeping an eye on the young, and in some species retrieving those which stray. In addition, most mammalian mothers clean and arouse their infants by licking and grooming them.

The universal needs of young mammals are met in a variety of specific ways by different species. Each species has specific patterns of organized behavior that it has evolved in relation to its environment to ensure its survival. Individualized, enduring bonds develop between mother and infant in species such as primates, in which the young are particularly helpless, and in species such as ungulates, in which the young are part of a moving group and can easily be lost.

SEPARATION

In view of the foregoing it is significant that a human newborn is immediately separated from his mother if he is born prematurely or becomes sick after normal term birth. Does this early separation affect subsequent maternal-infant attachment? In our search for clues as to whether the effects of early separation on maternal behavior in the human would be a fruitful area to study, we have looked at the effects of separations in a wide variety of animal species. Especially relevant to our inquiry is the point at which separation occurs, the length of separation, the mother's behavior on reunion with her infant, and species-specific differences in the effects of separation. It is necessary to emphasize that our principal interest is the effect of separation on the mother's attachment behavior rather than the effect on the infant. What aspects of separation interfere with the emergence of maternal behavior?

In attempting to answer this question, Rosenblatt and Lehrman (1963) studied the effects of mother-infant separation on maternal behavior in laboratory rats. An important characteristic of the maternal female is that she will act maternally to pups other than her own young: Under certain conditions alien pups elicit her maternal care. This permitted experimentation in reeliciting maternal behavior by introducing new pups ("test pups") for short periods to observe the reactions of mothers separated from pups for various lengths of time.

Table 2-2 presents the findings of Rosenblatt and Lehrman (1963) and reveals that, in the laboratory rat, separation of mother and infant is debilitating, especially if it occurs immediately after birth. When separation occurred immediately after birth and lasted for at least four days, all pups (which had been fed by their own mothers) introduced to the deprived mother died within five days. When the separation lasted for only two days, half the pups died within the first five days. In each case separation sharply decreased maternal responses to the test pups; new pups allowed to live permanently with the deprived mother reelicited nursing, nest-building, and retrieving behaviors for a short time, but eventually maternal behavior fell to a low level. If mothers were allowed as few as three days after birth in which to establish maternal behavior patterns before they were separated from their pups, they were much more likely to respond appropriately to new pups even after four days without them.

Mother-infant separation affects maternal behavior in goats even more significantly (Table 2-3), since the maternal bond in this species is formed much earlier and is more individualized than in the rat. Because a mother goat will vigorously butt away alien kids, experimenters cannot easily introduce an alien infant for test purposes.

Collias (1956) and Klopfer (1971) have found that dams will not accept their own young after the infants have been removed at birth for more than 1 hour (Table 2-3). Hersher and colleagues (1963a) demonstrated that if goats were allowed as little as 5 minutes of contact with their kids immediately after parturition, virtually all young were reaccepted even after 3 hours of separation. There were, however, **persisting** effects of the separation on nursing patterns still evident two to three months later.

Table 2-2. Effects of separation on maternal behavior in rats*

Beginning of separation	Length of separation	Tested (with a 5- to 10-day old pup that was not her own)	Effects
At birth	Permanent	Weekly for 4 weeks after birth	Rare nursing; retrieving (retrieving slightly more than in virgin females); nest building drastically decreased
After female cleaned pup and ate placenta	Experimental: permanent	Beginning of third day	Nursing; retrieving; nest building decreased (nest building decreased less)
	Control: no separation	Fifth day	Increase in maternal behavior
At birth	2 days, then foster pups left with mothers for 9 days	First day after introduction of foster pup, then irregular intervals until tenth day after birth	Behavior increased after introduction of foster pups, then decreased to level of mothers with no pups; behavior decreased after separation, more for mothers with 4-day separation
	4 days, then foster pups left with mothers for 1 day		
At birth	4 days	After separation	No maternal behavior
3 days after birth 9 days after birth 14 days after birth	4 days	After separation	Maternal behavior returned; 60% to 75% of mothers nursed
Ninth day after birth	Permanent	Every other day after separation	Maternal behavior declined earlier and to lower levels than controls
Fourteenth day after birth	Permanent	Every other day after separation	Decline in maternal behavior did not decrease—had already begun naturally

*Data from Rosenblatt, J. S., and Lehrman, D.: In Rheingold, H. R., editor: Maternal behavior in mammals, New York, 1963, John Wiley & Sons, Inc.

Table 2-3. Effects of separation on maternal behavior in goats

Source	Beginning of separation	Length of separation	Effects
Collias, 1956	Shortly after birth	2 to 4½ hours	5 of 6 young rejected for at least 1 hour on return
	Shortly after birth	15 to 45 minutes	6 of 6 young accepted
	No separation		8 of 8 young accepted
Klopfer, 1971	Immediately after birth	1, 2, or 3 hours	2 of 15 dams allowed kids to nurse; 15 of 15 dams vigorously rejected alien young
	5 minutes after birth	1, 2, or 3 hours	14 of 15 dams immediately reaccepted kids; 15 of 15 dams vigorously rejected alien kids
Hersher, Richmond, and Moore, 1963a	Experimental: 5 to 10 minutes after birth	½ to 1 hour	*Observation of dam, her own kid, and two other kids 2 to 3 months later* One half of kids did not nurse at all; one half nursed indiscriminately No dam butted own young but frequently butted alien young
	Control: no separation		No kid nursed indiscriminately

A recent series of experiments by Sackett and Ruppenthal (1974) suggests that mother-infant separation may also affect monkey mothers. Because mothering behavior per se was not their focus, these studies are not strictly comparable with those involving goats or rats. Here the behavior measured was maternal motivation, defined as the preference to be near neonates as opposed to monkeys of other ages. These authors used a choice situation consisting of one central compartment surrounded by six others to which other cages containing stimulus animals could be attached (Fig. 2-1). The female monkey was placed in the central compartment, and the cages of two stimulus animals were randomly hooked to two of the six outer compartments. Plexiglass dividers allowed the subject animal to have a clear view of the stimulus animals. The number of seconds spent near a given stimulus provided a measure of relative preference for that stimulus animal. Table 2-4 presents the relevant results of these experiments. Mothers separated from their infants for 1 hour after birth showed a preference for neonates. However, if this separation lasted for 24 hours, the mothers' preference for neonates seemed to disappear.

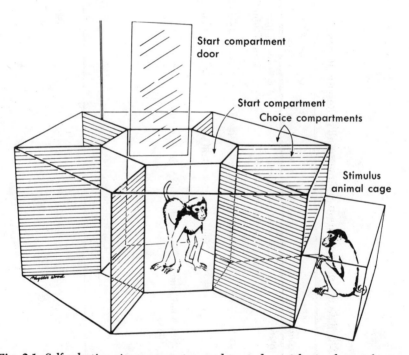

Fig. 2-1. Self-selection circus apparatus used to study social stimulus preferences. (From Sackett, G. P., and Ruppenthal, G. C. In Lewis, M., and Rosenblum, L. A., editors: The effect of the infant on its caregiver, New York, 1974, John Wiley & Sons, Inc.)

Table 2-4. Maternal motivation in pigtail macaque mothers separated from their young[*]

Separation began	Length of separation	Preference (neonate or adult female macaque)
At birth	1 hour	Neonate
2 weeks after birth	1 hour	Neonate
1 month	1 hour	Neonate
2 months	1 hour	Equal preference
6 months	1 hour	Adult
Controls (had not been pregnant or lived with infants)		Adult
At birth	24 hours	Adult
2 weeks	24 hours	Neonate
1 month	24 hours	Neonate
2 months	24 hours	Equal preference
6 months	24 hours	Adult
Controls		Adult
At birth	7 days	Adult
2 weeks	7 days	Neonate
1 month	7 days	Adult
2 months	7 days	Adult
6 months	7 days	Adult
Controls		Adult

[*]Data from Sackett, G. P., and Ruppenthal, G. C.: In Lewis M., and Rosenblum, L. A., editors: The effect of the infant on its caregiver, New York, 1974. John Wiley & Sons, Inc.

Meier (1965) studied the mother's actual acceptance of her newborn after surgical delivery in feral- and laboratory-reared monkeys (Table 2-5). Mothers were delivered surgically and separated from their infants for 2 hours. Although mothers with normal births immediately accepted their infants, none of the laboratory monkeys that were delivered by cesarean section accepted their infants by the third day after delivery. However, four of seven feral monkeys accepted their cesarean section–delivered infants on the first day, and the remaining four accepted theirs by the second day.[*]

[*]Sackett and Ruppenthal (1974) suggest an explanation for the different behaviors by feral- and laboratory-reared monkeys. The latter as a rule are "motherless monkeys" who were reared in cages without their own mothers. Feral monkeys, on the other hand, were typically captured after having been reared by their own mothers. So, in a sense, one is seeing the second generation effects of inadequate mothering in laboratory monkeys, whose maternal behavior is more easily extinguished under stress.

Table 2-5. Effects of separation on maternal behavior in primates

Species and source	Beginning of separation	Length of separation	Effects
Rhesus macaque monkey (Meier, 1965)	Experimental: with cesarean section with local anesthetic	Not specified—approximately 2 hours	Laboratory animals reared in isolation did not accept infants (did not approach, pick up, or hold to ventral surfaces) Feral animals: 3 accepted infants on day of birth, the other 4 accepted infants by next day
	Control: vaginal birth—no separation	None	Laboratory and feral animals: normal maternal behavior
Pigtail macaque monkey (Rosenblum and Kaufman, 1967)	4.8 to 6.1 months after birth	4 weeks	4 of 4 mothers immediately reaccepted infants; enclosure by mothers greater in month after than in month before separation; maternal behavior normally discouraging dyadic cohesiveness (i.e., punitive deference and nipple withdrawing) at this age appeared rarely
Rhesus macaque monkey (Harlow et al., 1963)	7 months after birth	3 weeks	3 of 4 mothers immediately accepted infants; 1 of 4 seemed totally indifferent for over 24 hours, despite infant's efforts

Other studies involving primates have demonstrated that when separation occurs for four weeks when the infant monkey is approximately 6 months old, most mothers will reaccept their young. In all cases maternal behavior regressed to a level appropriate for the care of a much younger offspring. The mother exhibited increased restraining, and she lacked the rejection behaviors that normally foster the independence of a 6- to 8-month-old offspring.

Separation of a newborn or young animal from its mother therefore significantly alters maternal behavior. The sooner after birth the separation occurs the stronger are the effects. For each species there seems to be a specific length of separation that can be endured. If separation extends beyond this sensitive period, the effects on mothering behavior during this breeding cycle are often drastic and irreversible.

ADOPTION

Separation studies are concerned with the stimuli that support maternal behavior, the removal of which causes it to decline in parturient females. Adoption studies, on the other hand, deal with the conditions that promote maternal behavior in nonparturient females toward infants that are not their own. We are interested in whether there is a particularly sensitive period during which a new infant can be introduced, how long a period of time is required for successful adoption,* whether certain environmental conditions are necessary for successful adoption, and species-specific differences in adoption behavior.

> COMMENT: The situation most parallel to the human phenomenon of adoption in which a nonmaternal woman is required to carry out maternal care of an infant is found in several animal species in which nonmaternal females are either presented with newborn young or are exposed to them in a social group. The response of the female in this situation varies greatly in different species: Mice, both female and male, respond almost immediately with maternal behavior, whereas among rats the response develops slowly over five to seven days but can be speeded to two days by forcing the female into close contact with the young. In rhesus monkeys the phenomenon of "aunts" exists, in which young females try to gain access to newborns and exhibit the preliminary forms of maternal behavior when permitted to do so.   J. S. ROSENBLATT

Grota's (1968) experiment with laboratory rats demonstrates that certain conditions facilitate adoption. Pups introduced to a female who has been lactating for one day have a greater chance for survival and rapid growth than pups introduced to a female who has been lactating for ten days. Thus the closer the introduction of new pups is to the female's date of delivery the more successful the adoption will be. When the new pups were introduced after one day, females successfully adopted as many as ten pups. However, when ten alien pups were given to a mother who had been lactating for ten days, significantly fewer survived than when only four pups were introduced.

> COMMENT: The problem being discussed comes under the broad heading of synchrony between the mother and her offspring. Normally synchrony develops from early beginnings at birth and becomes refined (in some mother-young groups) as the two interact in the days that follow. Synchrony exists with regard to many functions, both behavioral and physiological, including lactation and nursing. The greater the discrepancy between the mother's condition and the developmental

---

*"Successful adoption" is the situation in which the female performs the behaviors necessary for the survival of the adopted young.

status of the young the more difficult it is for the two to become synchronized, and of course the greatest discrepancy exists when the female is nonmaternal and the young are in need of maternal care.

J. S. ROSENBLATT

Schneirla and colleagues (1963) found that litter size also affects adoptive maternal behavior in the female cat. Although one new kitten was accepted and nursed whether introduced on the seventh, twelfth, or fifteenth day after birth to a female whose own pups were removed at birth, a litter of three new kittens was only encircled if introduced before the fifteenth day. After fifteen days the introduction of three kittens caused attacking and avoidance behaviors in the mother. It is interesting to note the differences in the time periods during which cats and rats will accept alien young. If a female rat's own pups are taken from her at birth, alien pups are incapable of eliciting maternal behavior four days later; however, if a cat is separated from her kittens at birth, an alien kitten can elicit maternal behavior twelve and sometimes fifteen days afterward.

Under normal conditions dams butt away alien young. However, Hersher's group at the Cornell Behavior Farm in Ithaca, New York, demonstrated that goats can be induced to adopt alien young, provided that the mother and kid are isolated from others but left in close proximity to each other and that the dam is prevented from butting the kid. Once bonding occurs under these conditions, no differences may be observed between dams with foster young and dams with natural young. It is also possible to foster cross-species adoptions, but cross-species mothers often seem more "anxious" (Hersher et al., 1963*b*).

Hersher speculates that the agitation often appearing in cross-species foster mothers may largely result because the young animal maintains the behavior characteristic of its own species, to which the mother is incapable of adjusting. For example, kids wander away from their flocks more than lambs, thus ewes raising kids spend much more time away from the flock and are more often anxious than ewes raising adopted lambs (Hersher et al., 1963*b*).

Schneirla and associates (1963) observed that a cat will usually adopt a kitten not too much older than her own, unless the kitten shows an eccentricity in behavior that causes disturbing encounters.

Harlow and co-workers (1963), while observing rhesus monkeys, noted a female attempting to make contact with an orphan that was placed in her cage. The infant responded by screaming and rolling itself into a tight ball. The female vacillated between approach and avoidance for days but never adequately responded to the strange infant. Harlow also observed a rhesus monkey who had just given birth and been separated from her own infant attempting to adopt a kitten.

The adoption was successful as long as the mother clung to the kitten. However, as the mother gradually began to relax her hold and move about the cage, the kitten, unable to cling, fell from her body. Finally, after several frustrating days of repeatedly retrieving the kitten, the mother abandoned it.

The following principles may be derived from the work just described:

1. There appears to be a sensitive period after birth, distinct for each species, during which females will adopt alien young.
2. In some species, such as goats and sheep, adoption will not take place after the sensitive period without specific conditions (i.e., close contact, isolation, and adequate length of time).
3. Environmental conditions, such as the number of young introduced, influence the success of adoptions.
4. Unusual behavior on the part of the infant may interfere with successful adoption.

MECHANISMS

Our final task is to attempt to understand the mechanisms underlying the reasons why female animals behave the way they do before, during, and after the birth of their young. Why do pregnant females prepare for birth? Why is it that the closer to the time of parturition that alien young are introduced, the greater is the probability of their acceptance? Why is the length of separation of a mother from her young such an important factor in whether she will again behave maternally when they are returned? The studies of both Klopfer (1971) and Rosenblatt (1963-1975) have been designed to answer these questions. Each has asked: Is maternal behavior elicited by characteristics of the young or is it primarily triggered by hormonal changes within the female's body? Each has attempted to answer this question by observing the effects of one variable at a time in a carefully controlled series of studies.

Lott and Rosenblatt (1969) first established that maternal behavior in rats may be exhibited by nonmothers. Both virgin female and male rats, even those who were gonadectomized or hypophysectomized, responded to 5- to 10-day old pups after five to six days with the maternal behaviors of retrieving, crouching, nest building, and licking. Therefore maternal behavior is not completely dependent on hormonal changes, although new mothers respond to pups immediately.

COMMENT: Pup odors that cause females to avoid or perhaps fear the pups at first appear to prevent virgin rats from responding to pups immediately. If virgin rats are prevented from smelling the pups, they act maternally after less than a day of contact, and sometimes immediately. Of course when females give birth, they do not avoid pup odors. This indicates that an important part of the initial attachment involves overcoming avoidance or fear of pups, and this may be one role of hormones or perhaps may be based on experience with similar odors during pregnancy.   J. S. ROSENBLATT

To determine whether pregnant rats behave more like virgin rats or more like newly delivered mothers, Lott and Rosenblatt (1969) compared the latencies of maternal behavior for rats whose pregnancies were terminated at various stages. They found that rats who were delivered before the eleventh day of pregnancy did not behave significantly differently from nonpregnant females. They exhibited maternal behaviors after five or six days of exposure to pups. (In rats the gestation period is usually 22 to 23 days.) However, rats delivered by Cesarean section on the sixteenth or nineteenth days of pregnancy responded to pups almost immediately. Similar results were found when pregnancies were terminated by hysterectomies: Rosenblatt (1971) again found that the latency was shorter for females further along in their pregnancies. This clearly demonstrated that during the course of pregnancy, changes occur within the female which affect her responsiveness to young pups.

After several colleagues had failed to isolate hormones that might account for these phenomena, Terkel and Rosenblatt (1968) attempted to establish whether the humoral substance regulating maternal behavior is carried in the blood plasma. They injected virgin rats with 3 to 4 ml. of plasma taken from mother rats within 48 hours of parturition. Control virgin rats were injected with either plasma from donors who had not delivered or with a saline solution. Virgin rats injected with plasma from maternal rats showed maternal behavior significantly earlier than did rats in the other groups. This experiment therefore confirmed the existence of a plasma-carried substance that influences maternal behavior.

To supplement these findings Terkel and Rosenblatt (1972) developed a technique that allowed for the transfer of larger amounts of blood between two rats while both rats moved about freely. By continuously cross-transfusing, they were able to achieve about a 50% mix of the rats' blood (Fig. 2-2). With this method they studied the effects of transferring blood from female rats at different times centering around parturition. Virgin rats received blood from other virgin rats, or from newly delivered mothers, or from mothers who had given birth 24 hours previously, or from females expected to give birth within 24 hours after the exchange. None of the virgin rats that was cross-transfused with other virgin rats showed maternal behavior within 48 hours, whereas seven of the eight virgin rats that exchanged blood with newly delivered mother rats did. However, significantly fewer rats in the other two groups (virgin rats who exchanged blood with rats 24 hours before

Fig. 2-2. A virgin rat during cross-transfusion from the studies of Terkel and Rosenblatt, 1972. (Courtesy Dr. J. Rosenblatt, Rutgers University, Newark, N.J.)

or after delivery) exhibited maternal behavior within this time period.

Thus, according to Terkel and Rosenblatt (1972), it appears that "Only blood transfused during a limited time at parturition induces maternal behavior. . . . Blood from pregnant females twenty-four hours before expected delivery did not yet have the capacity of inducing maternal behavior in a significant proportion of virgins, while blood transferred in the same amount and for the same duration from mothers twenty-four hours after parturition had already lost this capacity." The authors caution that these are not necessarily the precise limits within which the humoral basis for maternal behavior is established, since they sampled only three intervals and achieved only a 50% blood mix. Nevertheless, this study definitely highlights the importance of the period surrounding parturition. Physiological mechanisms seem to heighten the mother's sensitivity to infants at parturition. This suggests that maternal behavior can be supported by hormones, but only for a brief period. Other evidence suggests that after this the presence of the pup is necessary to ensure the continuation of maternal behaviors.

COMMENT: We have come to interpret these findings differently because at the time we did not know that female rats really become maternal within the 24 hours that precede parturition. That is, the mother herself is not stimulated to maternal behavior by the hormones circulating after parturition but probably by a hormone (estrogen) that was secreted 48 hours earlier. This study therefore showed that the hormone was still present in the mother in sufficient concentration to induce maternal behavior in a virgin rat during at least 6 hours after parturition but not 24 hours later.   J. S. ROSENBLATT

Recently, Rosenblatt and associates have further isolated the hormonal substance involved in stimulating maternal behavior. They had earlier found that ovariectomized and hysterectomized pregnant female rats do not show a decreased latency for maternal behavior, whereas female rats that are only hysterectomized on the sixteenth day of pregnancy and later do show such latency. Therefore they hypothesized that the ovaries play a crucial role in the onset of maternal behavior. To test this hypothesis directly Rosenblatt and Siegel (1975) ovariectomized and hysterectomized rats at various stages of the second half of pregnancy. They found that removal of the ovaries at the time of hysterectomy did in fact result in a significantly longer latency than hysterectomy alone.

In a subsequent study they attempted to restore short-latency maternal behavior in hysterectomized-ovariectomized females (Siegel and Rosenblatt, 1975). At the time of surgery the females were injected with estradiol benzoate. One group also received progesterone 44 hours later. Estradiol benzoate in either a high or low dose restored short-latency maternal behavior typical of females hysterectomized at the same stage of pregnancy. Progesterone did not affect the action of estradiol benzoate. The authors concluded that estrogen is instrumental in stimulating maternal behavior. Their findings receive support from those of Shaikh (1971) that serum concentration of estradiol normally increases slowly between the seventeenth and nineteenth days of pregnancy and more rapidly from the nineteenth day until parturition on the twenty-third day. Zarrow and co-workers (1971) showed that blocking the release of prolactin during the last six to seven days of pregnancy did not interfere with the onset of maternal behavior at parturition. Therefore the effect of estradiol cannot be accounted for by the fact that estrogen releases prolactin.

In an effort to determine whether estradiol was the hormonal stimulant of maternal behavior, Rosenblatt and Siegel (1975) studied whether maternal behavior began before parturition, as would be predicted by Shaikh's 1971 finding that serum concentration of estradiol rises rapidly just before parturition. By testing pregnant females with young pups at 2-hour intervals starting 40 hours before parturition, they found that nest building does in fact begin 34 hours prepartum and retrieving begins 24 hours prepartum.

In summary, virgin and male rats will show maternal behavior if left with pups for a sufficient length of time, but latencies are relatively long. The latency for maternal behavior in female rats decreases after the eleventh day of pregnancy. The finding that a plasma-carried substance stimulates maternal behavior near the time of parturition, coupled with the demonstration of the importance of estradiol, clearly shows that physiological mechanisms are partly responsible for the occurrence of maternal behavior prepartum.

After parturition the presence of pups seems to be necessary to maintain maternal behaviors. If pups are taken away at the time of birth for four days, maternal behavior is permanently extinguished. If, however, pups are left with the mother for at least three days before separation, the mother will exhibit maternal behavior even after a four-day separation. Thus there appears to be a period during the first three days after parturition when a transition occurs from internal (i.e., hormonal) control of maternal responsiveness to primarily external support. Interestingly, a significant fall in progesterone and rise in estradiol have been noted by Turnbull and associates (1974) in the five weeks preceding labor in the human mother (Fig. 2-3).

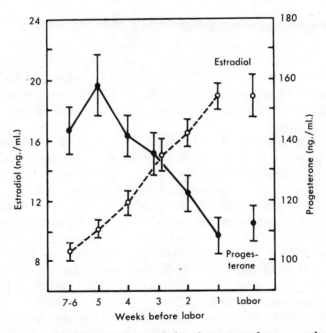

Fig. 2-3. Plasma progesterone and estradiol in human mothers near the time of delivery. (From Turnbull, A. C., Patten, P. T., Flint, A. P. F., Keirse, M. J. N. C., Jeremy, J. Y., and Anderson, A.: Lancet 1:101-103, 1974.)

Klopfer (1971) focused on the characteristics of the young animal that evoke maternal responses in the goat. To examine the effects of visual cues emanating from the kid, he compared the behavior of females who were blindfolded during parturition and the first minutes of contact with their kids with that of females who were not. He found that after a period of separation all goats, whether blindfolded or not, reaccepted their own kids and butted away aliens. Therefore it appeared that visual cues do not trigger maternal behavior in the goat.

He also compared the behavior of goats whose kids had vocalized during parturition with that of goats whose kids had not. Again he found no differences after a period of separation; all females showed maternal behavior when reunited with their kids and all rejected aliens. Auditory cues do not seem to play a crucial role in eliciting maternal behavior.

In a third experiment Klopfer tested the importance of olfactory cues by cocainizing the nostrils of female goats either at the time of parturition or at the time of the acceptance test after separation. Females cocainized at parturition did not reject their young, as would be expected if olfactory cues elicited maternal behavior. Instead, eight of the nine female goats accepted their own young, but six also accepted alien young. Those cocainized at the time of the acceptance test rejected their own young as often as they accepted them. Klopfer (1971) therefore modified his original theory that sensory cues, particularly olfaction, give rise to maternal behavior. He hypothesized instead that olfactory cues must aid the mother's recognition of her young but that "events that transform a female from a rejecting to a motherly animal, events which must be exploited within five or so minutes after parturition (for the goat), must presumably be sought elsewhere than in some kind of external 'releasor.'"

This shift of focus from external releasors to factors endogenous to the female led to a final study. Klopfer reasoned that if endogenous factors are primarily responsible for the appearance of maternal behaviors, females should be receptive to any kid presented immediately at parturition. The results of his study confirmed his expectation. Of five female goats presented with an alien kid for 5 minutes immediately after parturition, all five accepted that alien after a separation of up to 3 hours. Five of the six goats that were presented with their own and alien kids at birth reaccepted both after separation. However, no female accepted an alien other than the one with which she had first been presented at parturition.

Klopfer (1971) concludes that "Something happens in the space of a few minutes after parturition which makes her ready, then and only then, to attach herself to a kid. Once she is attached, she displays many of the human signs of distress on the removal of the kid. Spared the attachment, the removal leaves her as nonchalant as any virgin, despite the fact that she may be lactating heavily." Klopfer suggests a model in which hormonal changes during the final stages of labor cause a temporarily heightened responsiveness to infants.

Rosenblatt (1963-1975) and Klopfer (1971) both present a model in which biological mechanisms are primarily responsible for a mother's receptivity to young at the time of birth but quickly subside afterward. Within the sensitive period, maternal behavior quickly disappears if young are not present to elicit and maintain it. However, if young are present, a smooth transition takes place. Because of her physiological state after parturition, a mother is sensitized to the behavioral cues of her newborn and begins to respond to them. The infant, in turn, responds to maternal behavior, and patterns of interaction quickly develop that establish the bond between the mother and her infant, preventing her from abandoning him. Relatively flexible behavioral mechanisms soon replace more rigid biological mechanisms. From an evolutionary perspective such a model is reasonable, since it provides for the survival of the species in the face of changing and potentially destructive environmental conditions.

> COMMENT: I think your statement of the concept of transition between hormonal and nonhormonal mechanisms regulating maternal behavior is a good one, accurate and spelled out. I think it is a matter of philosophy if one wants to call that period a "critical period" for the formation of the mother-young attachment. I tend to think in terms of developmental stages rather than critical periods. Therefore transitions from one developmental stage (even in mothers) to the following one involve all the events of preceding stages, not just the events occurring during the transition. It may be of practical value to emphasize a critical part of the transition, as you have done, but in the long run I believe it is better to keep in mind that important factors outside the critical period affect the success or failure of transition from one developmental stage to another.   J. S. ROSENBLATT

Chapter 3

Human maternal and paternal behavior

MARSHALL H. KLAUS and JOHN H. KENNELL

> How long does the fire of love in a
> woman endure when the eyes and touch
> are no longer there to kindle it?
>
> *The Divine Comedy*—DANTE

Female mammals of many species exhibit regular patterns of attachment behavior before, during, and after the birth of their offspring. What about the human mother? What triggers, fosters, or disturbs her attachment to her infant? In an attempt to answer this question, we have gathered information from a wide range of sources including (1) clinical observations during medical care procedures, (2) naturalistic observations of mothering, (3) long-term, in-depth interviews of a small number of mothers, primarily by psychoanalysts, (4) structured interviews or observations, and (5) results from a small number of closely controlled studies on the mothers of both premature and full-term infants. As we consider the available information, it is important to remember that the necessary controls possible in studies of animal mothers are not always possible in studies of the human mother. Therefore we must delicately tease out information and integrate observations from diverse sources. All studies must be considered within the framework of the social setting. Cultural influences, the values and expectations of both the mother and the observer, as well as hospital structures and policies all may influence the final outcome.

The mother and the observer of the birth enter into the situation with certain biases, with attitudes that have been subtly shaped throughout their lives. Even in the Western world behaviors and practices surrounding birth vary widely.

> COMMENT: In most of the Western world there is a pervasive attitude on the part of the medical caretakers of mothers and infants which varies little. This attitude is that the birth of a baby must be treated as an illness or an operation—an attitude that creates an atmosphere of

pathology, or of curing pathology at best. The Rosenthal effect of this on mothers' attitudes toward their pregnancy, delivery, and new baby becomes a major issue in understanding how frightened and ineffectual mothers in American culture feel around this event.   T. B. BRAZELTON

Beautifully illustrating this variety in birth practices is the town of Termoli, a small community in an agricultural region of Italy. When a woman is about to give birth in the hospital, according to anthropologist Schreiber (1974), the members of the family congregate outside the labor and delivery rooms. Within 5 minutes of the birth the parents, grandparents, and, on the average, five other relatives will have kissed the baby. Within the first 20 minutes the mother-in-law, who holds the baby first, returns him to his mother. The news of the birth is quickly dispatched to the parents' home, and a pink or blue rosette, depending on the sex of the baby, is hung on the front door. The birth has been officially announced, and visits by all the near and distant relatives, acquaintances, and neighbors begin. Schreiber found that within six weeks, in a town of 1500 people, 80% of the households had visited the home of a newborn with congratulations and usually a small gift for the mother or baby. In Termoli the birth of a baby brings great pride and tribute to the mother.

However, models or practices that seem to work well in one society are not necessarily optimal solutions for another culture. The success of any one system is not an indication of its universal merit, and what seems to be "natural" is not necessarily "good." It is necessary to emphasize, then, that for cross-cultural data to be meaningful, it must be examined within the total context of society.

With this caveat in mind, we will begin piecing together components of the affectional bond between a human mother and her infant and determining the factors that may alter or distort its formation. Since the human infant is wholly dependent on his mother or caregiver to meet all his physical and emotional needs, the strength and durability of the attachment may well determine whether or not he will survive and develop optimally.

Events that are important to the formation of a mother's attachment to her infant are listed:

Prior to pregnancy
  Planning the pregnancy
During pregnancy
  Confirming the pregnancy
  Accepting the pregnancy
  Fetal movement
  Accepting the fetus as an individual

After birth
  Birth
  Seeing the baby
  Touching the baby
  Giving care to the baby

By observing and studying the human mother according to these periods, we can begin to fit together the interlocking pieces that lay the foundations of attachment.

> COMMENT: I would add another to the list of steps. During pregnancy: Doing the "work" of becoming a mother rather than a "girl" or a married but childless woman. After birth: Accepting her role as a mother and seeing the baby as separate and with strengths of his own.
>
> T. B. BRAZELTON

BASIC CONSIDERATIONS
Prior to pregnancy

Experimental data suggest that the past experiences of the mother are a major determinant in molding her caregiving role. Children use adults, especially loved and powerful adults, as models for their own behavior. "Playing house," an activity that dominates the waking hours of girls during the preschool years, appears to be a preparatory rehearsal for mothering a real baby two or three decades later. Mothers who watch their preschoolers are continually surprised to find that their daughters imitate their own actions, attitudes, and facial movements in the most minute detail.

Child development literature suggests that children are socialized by the powerful process of imitation or modeling. They may respond to how they themselves were mothered or what they observed. Thus long before a woman herself becomes a mother, she has learned through observation, play, and practice a repertoire of mothering behaviors. She has already learned whether or not infants are picked up when they cry, how much they are carried, and whether they should be chubby or thin. Interestingly, these "facts" that are taken in when children are very young become unquestioned imperatives for them throughout life. Unless adults consciously and painstakingly reexamine these learned behaviors, they will unconsciously repeat them when they become parents.

> COMMENT: One of the most tragic aspects of the nuclear family culture in the Western world is that many, if not most, young women are never exposed to caretaking of children before they have their own. Very few new mothers in my practice have ever handled an infant or cared for a small child.
>
> T. B. BRAZELTON

A young girl in a developing country such as Guatemala has responsibility and experience with the care of young infants until she delivers her own, which allows her to make fine adjustments in her mothering style and gain a wealth of confidence before she herself becomes a mother. Thus the way a woman was raised, which includes the practices of her culture and the individual idiosyncrasies of her own mother's child-rearing practices, greatly influences her behavior toward her own infant. A striking example is the observation that often mothers who batter their children were beaten when they were young. Frommer and O'Shea (1973) have also noted a significant increase in problems of early maternal caretaking when the mother's parents were separated from each other at an early age (less than 11 years).

By understanding the genesis of maternal and attachment behavior, perhaps we can better envision interventions that will foster change in those cases where such is desirable for mother and infant.

Pregnancy

During pregnancy a woman concurrently experiences two types of developmental changes: (1) physical and emotional changes within herself and (2) the growth of the fetus in her uterus. The way in which she feels about these changes will vary widely according to whether she planned the pregnancy, is married, is living with the father, or has other children. It will also vary according to the age of other children, her occupation or desire for one, her memories of her childhood, and her feelings about her parents (Boston Women's Health Book Collective, 1973). For most women, pregnancy is a time of strong and changing emotions, ranging from positive to negative, frequently ambivalent. With the realization that she will soon have a baby, particularly if it is her first, the woman must adapt to a dramatic shift in her life-style as she changes from an individual responsible primarily for herself to a parent responsible for the life and well-being of a child. There will also be changes in her relationship with the father, since she will now have to divide her time and attention between two people (Benedek, 1952).

Caplan (1960) considers pregnancy to be a developmental crisis involving two particular adaptive tasks.

Acceptance of pregnancy. During the first stage of pregnancy a woman must come to terms with the knowledge that she will be a mother. When she first realizes that she is pregnant, she may have mixed feelings. A large number of considerations, ranging from a change in her familiar patterns to more serious matters such as economic and housing hardships or interpersonal difficulties, all influence her acceptance of the pregnancy. This initial stage, as outlined by Bibring and associates (1961), is the mother's identification of the growing fetus as an "integral part of herself."

Perception of the fetus as a separate individual. The second stage involves a growing awareness of the baby in the uterus as a separate individual, which usually starts with the remarkably powerful event of quickening, the sensation of fetal movement. During this period the woman must begin to change her concept of the fetus from a being that is a part of herself to a living baby who will soon be a separate individual. Bibring and associates (1961) believe that this realization prepares the woman for birth and physical separation from her child. This preparedness in turn lays the foundation for a relationship with the child.

After quickening, a woman will usually begin to have fantasies about what the baby will be like, attributing some human personality characteristics to him and developing feelings of attachment. At this time she may further accept her pregnancy and show significant changes in attitude toward the fetus. Unplanned, unwanted infants may seem more acceptable. Objectively, there will usually be some outward evidence of the mother's preparation. She may purchase clothes or a crib, select a name, and rearrange her home to accommodate a baby.

The production of a normal child is a major goal of most women. Yet most pregnant women have hidden fears that the infant may be abnormal or reveal some of their own secret inner weaknesses.

Brazelton (1973) has clarified the importance of these changes and turmoil that occur during pregnancy for the subsequent development of attachment to the new infant.

> The prenatal interviews with normal primiparas, in a psychoanalytic interview setting, uncovered anxiety which often seemed to be of pathological proportions. The unconscious material was so loaded and distorted, so near the surface, that before delivery one felt an ominous direction for making a prediction about the woman's capacity to adjust to the role of mothering. And yet when we saw her in action as a mother, this very anxiety and the distorted unconscious material could become a force for reorganization, for readjustment to her important new role. I began to feel that much of the prenatal anxiety and distortion of fantasy could be a healthy mechanism for bringing her out of the old homeostasis which she had achieved to a new level of adjustment. The alarm reaction we were tapping in on was serving as a kind of shock treatment for reorganization to her new role. . . . I now see the shakeup in pregnancy as readying the circuits for new attachments, as preparation for the many choices which they must be ready to make in a very short critical period, as a method of freeing her circuits for a kind of sensitivity to the infant and his individual requirements which might not have been easily or otherwise available from her earlier adjustment. Thus, this very emotional turmoil of pregnancy and that in the neonatal period can be seen as a positive force for the mother's adjustment and for the possibility of providing a more individualized environment for the infant.[*]

[*]From Brazelton, T. B.: Effect of maternal expectations on early infant behavior, Early Child Develop. Care 2:259-273, 1973.

COMMENT: This is an excellent example of how physicians would be likely to label a mother as "anxious" or "needing help," when in truth she was undergoing normal anxiety—important to becoming a mother and adjusting rapidly to *any* kind of infant.   T. B. BRAZELTON

An interesting example of the way in which the adjustment may be handled in another culture occurs in Thailand. For centuries Thai mothers have purchased a clay statue of a mother and infant when they became pregnant. At the time of birth the statue is thrown into the river; thus the image of the mother and infant before birth is literally destroyed. Fig. 3-1 shows three of these figures.

To understand better the complex events that occur during the perinatal period, we will direct our attention primarily to the mother-infant dyad. It is necessary to repeat again and again that the father, the other siblings, and the extended family are of vital importance to this dyad. Brazelton (1973) suggests that prospective fathers go through an upheaval that is similar to that of the mothers.

Each young man was forced to reevaluate his role as a provider for the family, as an adult male ready to adjust to the responsibility of a dependent, as a model for the new child's learning about masculinity, and as a major support for his wife as she adjusted to her role as a

Fig. 3-1. Thailand figures that are purchased by the mother at the beginning of pregnancy and destroyed after the birth of the baby.

mother. In the process, he was forced back on self-examination and his experience with being fathered. If he was trying to free himself of ties to his own parents, it was hard for him to identify with them as models for his new role. He may have barely adjusted to being a husband, and the new, added expectations became difficult for him to encompass. In our lonely, nuclear family structure in the USA, the young father was often the only available support for his wife. They had moved away from their families, both in physical distance and in psychological expectations, and were unwilling to fall back on them for moral or physical support. There were rarely other supportive figures nearby—such as family physicians, ministers, close friends or neighbors who could help. The father was expected to assume the major supportive role.*

COMMENT: In these days when fathers are eager to play a more active role with wives and their babies, it behooves us to think of the few supports a new father has to help him make his own adjustment. That there is tremendous, valuable energy for attachment to be captured is reflected in a recent statement by Margaret Mead: "No developing society that needs men to leave home and do his 'thing' for the society ever allows young men in to handle or touch their newborns. There's always a taboo against it. For they know somewhere that, if they did, the new fathers would become so 'hooked' that they would never get out and do their 'thing' properly." In our lonely, nuclear families maybe a father's best "thing" is to become more involved with his wife and new baby.   T. B. BRAZELTON

Bibring (1959) agrees that what was once a transitional period with carefully worked out traditions for support has become a time of crisis with no societal mechanisms for helping expectant parents cope with the profound changes and developmental conflicts. In the past the structure of the extended family permitted a young girl to observe pregnant women and to be present and help during birth. Thus pregnancy and birth were shared experiences in which every girl participated from an early age. This is still true for the majority of young women growing up in rural and semirural areas of developing countries. Fig. 3-2 shows a new mother in an Indian home in the village of Santa Maria Cauqué in the Guatemalan highlands. In isolated, nuclear families in the United States a young woman and even more, a young man, may have had no experience at all with prospective parents and, although expecting a baby, may not be able to discuss or visit with anyone else involved with pregnancy. With modern hospital deliveries there is the additional fear caused by the strange environment.

*From Brazelton, T. B.: Effect of maternal expectations on early infant behavior, Early Child Develop. Care 2:259-273, 1973.

Fig. 3-2. A new mother starting care of her infant under guidance of her grand-mother in the Indian village Santa Maria Cauqué in the Guatemalan highlands.

Since birth has been moved from the home to the hospital to meet better the physical needs of the mother and infant, there has been a growth of a number of organizations that have partially replaced the extended family. These are groups in which both parents learn with other couples about pregnancy, labor, birth, and infant care. Although their stated purpose is to prepare parents for the actual labor and birth, the result is the sharing of hopes, expectations, and fears; they partly substitute for an extended family. The bonds made through shared participation are strong, and couples will often stay in touch with each other for years afterward.

Evidence that women do begin to feel attached during pregnancy comes from a study of Kennell and associates (1970) on women's reactions to the death of their newborns. The design of this study was based partly on the work of a number of investigators who have postulated that the length and intensity of mourning after a loss is proportionate to the closeness of the relationship prior to death. Following this reasoning, it was anticipated that the strength of the mother's attachment to her unborn baby could be measured indirectly by determining the length and intensity of her mourning after the baby's death. If there had been no attachment, there would be no grief.

Using the degree of mourning as a measure of affectional bonding, they noted that affectional ties were present after birth even before tactile contact had been made. In each of the twenty mothers whose infant had died, clearly identifiable mourning was observed. The mothers grieved whether the infant lived for 1 hour or twelve days, whether he weighed 3000 grams or a nonviable 580 grams, and whether the pregnancy was planned or unplanned. The presence of mourning in all the mothers implied that significant affectional bonding had been established by the time of or soon after the birth of the child. Longer and more intense mourning was seen in mothers for whom the pregnancy was a positive experience and in mothers who had tactile contact with their infants, indicating that both pleasurable anticipation of the infant's birth and physical contact with him after birth may be significant factors in the bonding process.

Cohen (1966), however, emphasizes that any stress, such as moving to a new geographic area, marital infidelity, death of a close friend or relative, previous abortions or loss of previous children, which leaves the mother feeling unloved or unsupported or which precipitates concern for the health and survival of either her infant or herself may delay preparation for the infant and retard bond formation. After the first trimester, behaviors that are a reaction to stress and suggest rejection of pregnancy include a preoccupation with physical appearance or negative self-perception, excessive emotional withdrawal or mood swings, excessive physical complaints, absence of any response to quickening, or lack of any preparatory behavior during the last trimester.

Birth

The scanty data relating to birth suggests that mothers who remain relaxed during labor, who cooperate and have good rapport with those caring for them, are more likely to be pleased with their infants at the first sight (Newton and Newton, 1962). Unconsciousness during birth does not cause the mother to reject her infant in an obvious manner, as has been observed in some animals. However, systematic studies in this significant area are lacking. In general, the more difficult the labor the lower is the incidence of breastfeeding.

We have recently begun to study home births. In sharp contrast to the woman who delivers in the hospital, the woman giving birth at home appears to be in control. Immediately after the birth she appears to be in a remarkable state of ecstasy. We have called this *ekstasis*. The exuberance is contagious, and the observers share the festive mood of unreserved elation after the birth and groom the mother. Striking is the observers' intense interest in the infant, especially in the first 15 to 20 minutes of life.

These preliminary studies of home births have been made from video tape recordings and films, as well as from long discussions with perceptive midwives (Mills, 1974; Lang, 1974). One midwife, Raven Lang, has made observations of fifty-two home births. Thirty-seven percent of the deliveries were made in the hands-and-knees position. Some midwives deliver in a lateral position, which allows the mother to watch the birth of her own infant. The observers are also extremely elated during the birth and offer encouragement and support to the mother; in the first 15 to 20 minutes of life there is intense interest in the infant. Lang also noted that the observers of the labor and birth became more attached to the infant than other friends of the family who did not witness the birth. We believe that this is one of the important principles of attachment. In the past, when maternal mortality was high, this served an essential function by ensuring a substitute mother.

These home births that were studied in a select population show a somewhat different pattern of interaction, only fragments of which are visible in hospital births. To summarize the findings in a home birth:

1. The mother is an active participant.
2. She immediately picks up the infant after birth.
3. A striking elevation in mood is observed in association with great excitement of the others who are present.
4. Everyone present is drawn to look at the infant for prolonged periods.
5. The mother is groomed.
6. Breastfeeding starts within 5 to 6 minutes, beginning with prolonged licking by the infant.

COMMENT: In many other cultures the first 30 minutes after birth are devoted to the mother herself. She seems to need and prefer a recovery period of her own before she becomes interested in the infant. This makes a good deal of sense, and I think the ecstasies we see may in larger part be related to her relief at having finally made it to the other end of labor. This euphoria can certainly be mobilized to attach to the infant, and in American culture, where so many roadblocks have been institutionalized, mothers who are experiencing home births may be demonstrating behaviors that are signs of relief at having their autonomy intact.   T. B. BRAZELTON

We have also recently begun preliminary observations in a Guatemalan hospital of the effects of providing a friendly supportive woman (a "doula", as described by Raphael [1973]) who stays with a primiparous mother-to-be during labor and birth. (Women are routinely separated from other family members.) Although it is too early to be certain, there appears to be less crying and possibly shorter labors among women who are not alone. More time will be required to determine the long-term effects of this experience on the process of attachment.

To understand better the attitude and behavior of mothers and the mother-infant interaction in the first hours and days of life, we need more studies on the effects of various delivery procedures and anesthetic interventions. For example, research is now under way on the effects of drugs administered to the mother during labor and birth on the behavior of newborn infants. It seems clear that most anesthetics do depress infant responsivity and thus are likely to influence the first interchanges between mother and child. In our own experience we have been amazed at the differences between large numbers of infants born in other countries with no maternal analgesia or anesthesia and the neonates in the United States delivered under minimal analgesia and conduction anesthesia. The latter infants need to be treated as postsurgical (or postanesthesia) patients for many hours, with head positioned low, repeated suctioning, and close watching (Brazelton, 1961; Richards and Bernal, 1971). If mothers in developing countries received such drugs, one wonders how many babies might be lost due to problems of airway secretions associated with a lessened sensitivity of the cough, gag, and other reflexes.

   COMMENT: Certainly a depressed infant is less likely to be responsive either on initial contact or during feeding situations, and he becomes less stimulating and responsive to a mother who is trying hard to mobilize herself to attach to her new infant.   T. B. BRAZELTON

There is also a need for a comprehensive study of the overall effects of conduction anesthesia and obstetrical practices, such as episiotomies, on mother-to-infant attachment. The relief of pain for a short period of time has to be weighed against the effects of altering this unique experience in the life of a woman, which under unmodified conditions, is reported to be frequently associated with orgasmic sensations and followed by a period of particularly heightened perceptions. In contrast are the sometimes hectic, painful, and awkward maneuvers needed to administer conduction anesthesia as labor progresses rapidly; the relatively common postspinal headaches that keep mothers lying on their backs and limit interaction with their infants for three to five days; and the effects of episiotomy repairs on the comfort, mobility, and ability of the mother to care for her baby. These negative factors must be balanced against the relatively brief period of intense pain associated with natural childbirth. The contrast in the postpartum activity and comfort between mothers who have delivered in the United States with medication and anesthesia and those in the Netherlands and Guatemala who have had none has been impressive. Mothers in Guatemala go home from the hospital to take over full care of their babies one or two days after birth.

Does natural childbirth improve or alter mother-to-infant attachment? Does the presence of the father during birth enhance mother-to-infant and father-to-infant attachment? Does the father's presence during childbirth also affect the closeness of the relationship between mother and father? What are the effects of allowing a mother to choose her position, or allowing her to control the events in the birth?

> COMMENT: The feeling of autonomy, of being in some control over a rather frightening crisis in your life, of *having* a *choice* about what happens may be critical as a force for development in both men's and women's, fathers' and mothers' lives at life crisis.   T. B. BRAZELTON

These questions lead us further into the birth process and the parents' participation in it.

Quite appropriately the research on maternal attachment has stimulated an increased interest in the behavior of fathers. Greenberg and Morris (1974) have used the term *engrossment* (absorption, preoccupation, and interest) to describe the powerful impact of a newborn on the father. They have identified several specific aspects of the father's developing bond to his newborn, ranging from his attraction to the infant, his perception of the newborn as "perfect," to extreme elation and an increased sense of self-esteem (Fig. 3-3).

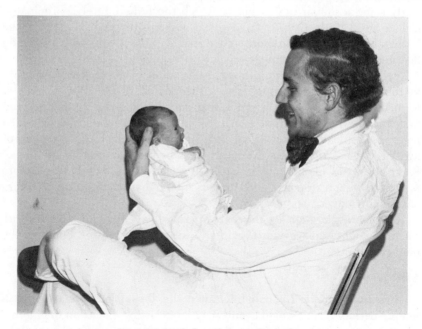

Fig. 3-3. A father enjoying his baby.

Recently Parke (1974) has described hospital practices that exclude the father from the early interaction with his infant as reflecting and reinforcing a cultural stereotype. Both American culture and theories have focused on the maternal role in early infancy, largely ignoring the father. However, recent modifications in hospital practices and the renewed interest in home births indicate a changing view of the father's role.

Parke has observed parents in three different situations: the mother or father alone with the infant at 2 to 4 days of age and the father, mother, and infant together in the mother's hospital room (i.e., triadic interaction).

The most striking finding is that Parke's studies have not revealed any significant behavioral differences between fathers alone with their infants and mothers alone with their infants. In the triadic situation the father tends to hold the infant nearly twice as much as the mother, vocalizes more, touches the infant slightly more, and smiles at the infant significantly less than the mother. The father clearly plays the more active role when both parents are present in contrast to the cultural stereotype of the father as a passive participant. In fact, in this triadic interaction the mother's overall interaction declines. It should be noted that all but one of the fathers whom Parke studied had attended labor and birth, and this could be expected to produce an unusual degree of father-to-infant attachment. However, he recently conducted another study using a similar design but in which the fathers rarely participated in labor and birth. Despite these social and institutional differences, the fathers again played the more active and dominant role with increased holding, vocalizing, and touching.

Parke believes that the father must have an extensive early exposure to the infant in the hospital where the parent-infant bond is initially formed. "There is a lot of learning that goes on between the mother and infant in the hospital—from which the father is excluded and in which he must be included so he'll not only have the interest and a feeling of owning the baby, but also the kinds of skills that the mother develops." Parke reviewed his findings as indicating that the father is much more interested in and responsive toward his infant than United States culture has acknowledged.

Further exploration of this early period may be especially fruitful, since it might uncover further interlocking processes for bonding the mother and infant.

After birth

Sensitive period. Immediately after the birth the parents enter a unique period during which events may have lasting effects on the family. This period, which lasts a short time, and during which the parents' attachment to their infant blossoms, we have named the *maternal sensitive period*. Because we believe this concept is crucial to the understanding of the bonding process, we will examine in detail the evidence supporting its existence. During this enigmatic period, complex interactions between mother and infant help to lock them together. This must be distinguished from the sensitive time during which the infant establishes a stable, affectionate relationship with his mother—from 2 to 6 months of age (Yarrow, 1961; Bronfenbrenner, 1968). In this section we must emphasize that we are focusing on the process of attachment from parent to infant.

The carefully designed experimental animal studies described in Chapter 2, which reveal the drastic and irreversible effects of early separation on animal mothering behavior, are obviously unconscionable in the human being. However, the data from the several clinical observations and controlled studies performed throughout the world strongly support the principle of a unique period in the human shortly after birth that is essential for mother-to-infant attachment.

Clinical support for a sensitive period. In a remarkable accident in an Israeli hospital, two mothers were inadvertently given and consequently took home and cared for the wrong babies. At the time of the two-week checkup, the error was discovered and efforts were made to return the babies to their own families. Each mother had become so attached to the baby she had cared for during the first fourteen days that she was reluctant to give him up. Their husbands, on the other hand, strongly supported correcting the error because of facial and other characteristics unique to the individual families. In other nursery accidents where the wrong baby has been presented to a mother for the first feeding or to be held for a brief period, we have been greatly impressed by her lingering thoughts about that baby. Often, months later, when her own child seems completely satisfactory in every respect, she will refer to that first child and say, "Oh, that was such a lovely baby."

These observations lead to the question of what happens when an infant is separated from his mother during the newborn period. In our clinical experiences we have noted that many mothers who have been separated from their infants are noticeably hesitant and clumsy when they begin to take on their infant's care. It takes them several visits to learn the simple mothering tasks of feeding and diapering that most women pick up rapidly. When the separation is prolonged, mothers report that they sometimes forget momentarily that they even have a baby. After a premature baby has gone home, it is striking to hear how often the mother reports that, although she is fond of her baby, she still thinks of him as belonging to someone else—the head nurse in the nursery or the physician—rather than to herself.

COMMENT: When we consider the mental processes that underlie the beginning of a mother's attachment to her child, the significance of physical closeness to the infant in the postpartum period is highlighted. During pregnancy the mother experiences the infant primarily as a part of herself and invests him with self-love—even when she has fantasties about what kind of an individual he may be. Birth represents a partial loss of self, both bodily and mentally. When the mother has the immediate and continuous opportunity to hold and nurse the infant, she can merge with him, that is, reestablish the bodily unity with him, and can transfer her self-love from the "inside" infant to the "outside" one. At the same time his unique behavior and interactions with her facilitate the beginning of a relationship with the infant as a separate individual.

However, when the infant is physically removed from the mother, instead of effecting a transfer of self-love, she has to detach herself psychically from that part of herself—a process akin to, but not identical with, mourning. When the baby is later restored, the mother's psychic detachment may have proceeded so far as to impair her capacity for accepting him again as a part of herself. Effective "selfless" mothering of, and empathy with, the infant depend primarily on the mother's investment of him with self-love. In caring for him she cares for a loved part of herself. If this process fails, she is likely to treat the infant as a foreign body or even to maltreat him because his demands interfere with the fulfillment of her own needs.   E. FURMAN

The clinical observations of Rose and associates (1960) and Kennell and Rolnick (1960) suggest that affectional ties can be easily disturbed and may be permanently altered during the immediate postpartum period. Relatively mild illnesses in the newborn, such as slight elevations of bilirubin levels, slow feeding, additional oxygen for 1 to 2 hours, and the need for incubator care in the first 24 hours for mild respiratory distress, appear to affect the relationship between mother and infant. The mother's behavior is often disturbed during the first year or more of the infant's life, even though his problems are completely resolved prior to discharge, and often within a few hours. This is one of our principles of attachment—that early events have long-lasting effects. Anxieties a mother has about her baby in the first few days after birth, even about a problem that is easily resolved, may affect her relationship with the child long afterward.

COMMENT: It is not that mothers cannot attach after such separations, it is that it may be more expensive—and unnecessarily so. And in stressed situations, where there is little or no reason to want a baby or to want to attach to him, this difference may be critical.

T. B. BRAZELTON

Studies of the effects of rooming-in have also confirmed the importance of contact during the early postnatal period. At Duke University a number of years ago, an increase in breastfeeding and reduction in anxious phone calls was noted when rooming-in was instituted (McBryde, 1951). In Sweden, mothers randomly assigned to rooming-in arrangements were more confident, felt more competent in caregiving, and appeared more sensitive to the crying of their own infants than mothers who did not have rooming-in (Greenberg et al., 1973).

All these clinical reports suggest that the events occurring during the first hours after birth have special significance for the mother. Nursery practices in the modern hospital in the United States do not generally acknowledge this and, instead, separate mother and infant immediately after birth to monitor the mother in an adult recovery area and the infant in a transitional care nursery. If there were convincing evidence of an early sensitive period in the human being, major changes in hospital care practices would be necessary to ensure that mother and baby remain together.

Many difficulties arise in attempting to determine systematically whether or not there is a sensitive period in the human. Human maternal behavior is determined by a multitude of factors; for instance the intellectual abilities of a mother may enable her to overcome potential difficulties such as an early separation from her infant.

> COMMENT: All mothers are ambivalent to some degree in the beginning. A "sensitive period" in the human would certainly be less rigidly determined by timing, by critical events, and by all of the things that describe a critical or sensitive period in animals. We would all prefer to think of the human mother as more flexible, as able to be more plastic to recover from stress, and so on. But maybe we are expecting a great deal of most mothers under the stress of the present medical system in the United States.   T. B. BRAZELTON

It is assuredly difficult to isolate and demonstrate the effects of the events during a short period of time on maternal attachment. Nonetheless, we believe that the studies available suggest strongly that the immediate postpartum period does have major importance in the development of a mother's bond to her child.

Studies supporting the hypothesis of a sensitive period. In eight studies the amount of contact between mothers and their neonates in the hospital was varied. In one carefully controlled investigation involving primiparous mothers with normal full-term infants, an "early and extended-contact" group of fourteen mothers was given their nude babies in bed for 1 hour in the first 2 hours after birth and for 5 extra hours on each of the next three days of life (Table 3-1). The other group of fourteen mothers received the care that is routine in most

Table 3-1. Clinical data for fourteen mothers in the extended-contact and fourteen in the control group*

	Control group	Extended-contact group
Maternal characteristics		
Age (years)	18.6	18.2
Number of mothers		
Married	5	4
Black	13	13
White	1	1
Mean score†		
A (residence)	6.5	6.7
B (occupation)	6.9	6.7
C (education)	4.9	4.9
Nurses' time (min/day)	14	13
Hospital stay (days)	3.7	3.8
Mean birth weight (grams)	3074	3184
Number of infants		
Males	8	6
Females	6	8

*From Klaus, M. H., Jerauld, R., Kreger, N. C., McAlpine, W., Steffa, M., and Kennell, J. H.: Maternal attachment: importance of the first post-partum days, N. Engl. J. Med. **286**:460-463, 1972; reprinted by permission.
†In this (Hollingshead) scoring system, on a scale of 1 to 7, residence (A) of 7.0 = poorest housing, occupation (B) of 7.0 = unskilled workers, and education (C) of 5.0 = reaching tenth to eleventh grade in high school.

United States hospitals: a glimpse of the baby at birth, a brief contact for identification at 6 to 8 hours, and then visits of 20 to 30 minutes for feedings every 4 hours. The groups were matched as to age and marital and socioeconomic status of the mothers, and they were not significantly different in the sex and weight of the infants. Women were randomly assigned to groups, given the same explanation of the study, and, to the best of our knowledge, were not aware that there were differences in mother-infant contact in the first three days.

To determine if the additional mother-infant contact early in life resulted in altered maternal behavior, the mothers returned to the hospital twenty-eight to thirty-two days after birth for three separate observations. The observations consisted of (1) a standardized interview, (2) an observation of the mother's performance during a physical examination of her infant, and (3) a filmed study of the mother feeding her infant.

Three separate questions related to caregiving were asked and then scored on a scale of 0 to 3. Question 1: "When the baby cries and has been fed and the diapers are dry, what do you do?" A score of 0 was given for letting the baby cry, and a score of 3 was given for picking it up every time. An intermediate score was given for behavior falling between these two extremes. Question 2: "Have you been out since the baby was born? How did you feel?" A score of 0 was given if the mother's answer was "yes" and if she felt good and did not think about her baby while she was out; a score of 3 was given if she did not go out without the baby or if she did go out but thought about the baby constantly. Extended-contact mothers were more reluctant to leave their infants with someone else and usually stood and watched during the physical examination. They showed more soothing behavior when their babies cried during the examination (Figs. 3-4 and 3-5).

To study the mothers' behavior in another situation, time-lapse films were made during feeding of their infants. Feeding was chosen as a measure of maternal performance because of its universality and its central position in the mother-infant relationship. All the mothers knew they were being photographed and were told to spend as much time

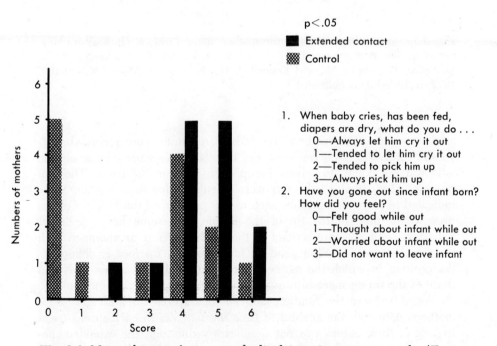

Fig. 3-4. Maternal scores from a standardized interview at one month. (From Klaus, M. H., Jerauld, R., Kreger, N. C., McAlpine, W., Steffa, M., and Kennell, J. H.: N. Engl. J. Med. **286**:460-463, 1972; reprinted by permission.)

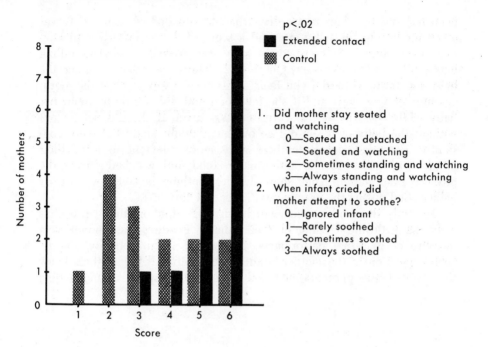

Fig. 3-5. Scored observations of the mother made during a physical examination of her infant at one month. (From Klaus, M. H., Jerauld, R., Kreger, N. C., McAlpine, W., Steffa, M., and Kennell, J. H.: N. Engl. J. Med. **286**:460-463, 1972; reprinted by permission.)

as they wished. The mothers' and babies' reactions were recorded at 1-second intervals. Each frame of the first 600 was scored by analyzers who did not know to which group each mother belonged. The frequencies of particular behaviors were calculated for each mother. Some indicated her caregiving skills, such as the position of the bottle and the presence of milk in the tip of the nipple, and some her attachment behaviors, such as close contact of the mother's chest or abdomen with the infant's trunk, fondling, and *en face* position. *En face* is defined as the position in which the mother's face is rotated so that her eyes and those of the infant meet fully in the same vertical plane of rotation.

Fig. 3-6 shows the fondling and *en face* scores for both groups of mothers. Although the amount of time the mothers in each group spent looking at their babies was not significantly different, the extended-contact mothers showed significantly more *en face* (11.6% in experimental mothers compared with 3.5% in control mothers) and fondling (6.1% compared with 1.6%) than did control mothers. No significant differences

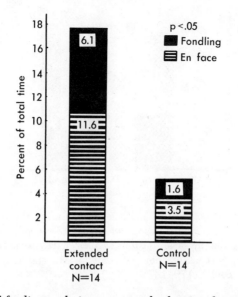

Fig. 3-6. Filmed feeding analysis at one month, showing the percentage of *en face* and fondling times in mothers given extended contact with their infants and in the control group. (From Klaus, M. H., Jerauld, R., Kreger, N. C., McAlpine, W., Steffa, M., and Kennell, J. H.: N. Engl. J. Med. **286:**460-463, 1972; reprinted by permission.)

in measures of caregiving were noted, although the bottle was held away from the perpendicular more often in the control group. By all three measures studied, differences between the two groups of mothers were apparent at one month after birth. These methods were designed to measure attachment and not to evaluate good or bad mothering.

At one year after birth the two groups of mothers again showed significant differences during a 1½-hour observation period behind a one-way mirror (Kennell et al., 1974). Extended-contact mothers spent a greater percentage of time near the table assisting the physician while he examined their babies and soothing them when they cried (Figs. 3-7 and 3-8). We wondered if a few mothers in one or both groups had accounted for the consistency and persistence of the differences over a span of eleven months. However, the ranking of the mothers within each of the two groups showed no significant correlation for the measures at the one-month and one-year examinations.

COMMENT: One could interpret these mothers as being "overprotective"—allowing the babies less than optimal chances for autonomy of their own.   T. B. BRAZELTON

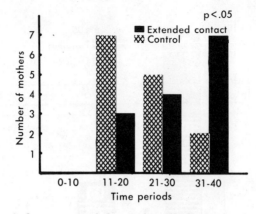

Fig. 3-7. Scored observations of the mothers made during the physical examination of their infants at one year showing number of 15-second time periods spent at table-side assisting the physician. (From Kennell, J. H., Jerauld, R., Wolfe, H., Chesler, D., Kreger, N. C., McAlpine, W., Steffa, M., and Klaus, M. H.: Dev. Med. Child Neurol. **16**:172-179, 1974.)

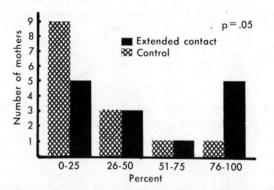

Fig. 3-8. Scored observations of mothers made during the physical examination of their infants at one year showing the number of 15-second time periods spent soothing their infants in response to crying. (From Kennell, J. H., Jerauld, R., Wolfe, H., Chesler, D., Kreger, N. C., McAlpine, W., Steffa, M., and Klaus, M. H.: Dev. Med. Child Neurol. **16**:172-179, 1974.)

At two years five mothers were selected at random from each group, and the linguistic behaviors of the two groups of mothers while speaking to their children were compared (Ringler et al., 1975). The extended-contact mothers asked twice as many questions and used more words per proposition, fewer content words, more adjectives, and fewer commands than the control mothers (Table 3-2). At 5 years we compared

Table 3-2. Characteristics of mother-to-child speech at 1 and 2 years*

	1 year		2 years	
Measure	Extended contact	Control	Extended contact	Control
Number of words per proposition	3.43	4.34	4.62†	3.66
Mean utterance length	2.5	2.7	3.9	3.1
Percentage of				
Adjectives/all words	0.20	0.10	16.00‡	12.00
Content words/all words	62.60	57.60	48.00	62.00‡
Questions/sentences	10.40	25.20	41.00†	19.00
Imperatives/sentences	68.00	49.00	43.00	74.00†
Statements/sentences	15.00	26.00†	16.00	6.00

*From Ringler, N. M., Kennell, J. H., Jarvella, R., Navojosky, B. J., and Klaus, M. H.: Mother-to-child speech at 2 years—effects of early postnatal contact, J. Pediatr. **86:**141-144, 1975.
†p < .05.
‡p < .02.

nine children whose mothers had received early contact with ten in the late group. Children of early contact mothers had significantly higher IQs and more advanced scores in two language tests (Ringler et al., 1976). These findings suggest that just sixteen extra hours of contact within the first three days of life affect maternal behavior for one year and possibly longer, and they offer support for the hypothesis of a maternal sensitive period soon after birth.

It should be noticed that this study does not test the specificity of attachment but only the quality. Also, the experimental groups of mothers and infants were actually separated from their infants at birth. The baby was placed with the mother 1 to 2 hours after birth and did not remain with her constantly from birth as in a natural home birth situation. The amount of anesthesia and drugs given to the mothers in this study would be considered minimal for primiparous mothers in a university hospital in the United States, but the mothers and infants in both groups did receive medication that may have influenced the effects of the early contact.

Seven other studies of mothers and their full-term infants have either been reported since 1970 or are presently under way. Winters (1973) gave six mothers their babies to suckle shortly after birth and compared these with six mothers who did not have contact with their babies until approximately 16 hours later. All had originally intended to breastfeed, and none stopped because of physical problems. Two months later all six mothers who had suckled their babies on the delivery table were still breastfeeding, whereas only one of the other six mothers was still breastfeeding.

In 1974, Klaus, Kennell, Mata, Sosa, and Urrutia started a long-term study in two separate hospitals in Guatemala City, using an experimental design similar to that presented earlier. In the I.G.S.S. (Social Security) Hospital one group of nineteen mothers was given their babies on the delivery table during the episiotomy repair and then allowed to stay with them in privacy for 45 minutes. Each mother-infant pair was nude under a heat panel (Fig. 3-9). The other group of mothers was separated from their babies shortly after birth, which is the usual routine in both hospitals. Except for this difference in initial contact, the care of the two groups was identical. The babies were brought to their mothers to start breastfeeding at 24 hours. All the infants were discharged with free milk at two days. (Free powdered milk was available on demand for

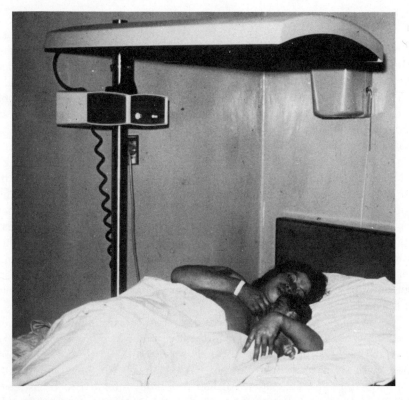

Fig. 3-9. A Guatemalan mother alone with her infant during the first few minutes of life. (A heat panel is above.)

the first year for all infants born in this hospital.) The socioeconomic, marital, housing, and income status of the mothers in the two groups at Social Security Hospital were similar (Table 3-3). Significantly more mothers were still breastfeeding and there were fewer episodes of infection in the early contact group. Six months after birth the mean weight gain of the infants in the early contact group was 761 grams, or nearly 1½ pounds greater than that of the infants in the control group (p <.05) (Table 3-4).

In Roosevelt Hospital in Guatemala City a similar study was carried out, and at twelve months there were no significant differences in weight gain or breastfeeding, but there were more episodes of infection in the control group (Table 3-5). Unfortunately there were differences at entry to the study in the two groups of mothers and infants at the Roosevelt Hospital (Table 3-3). These initial differences in patient population may explain why this study only partly supports the hypothesis of a maternal sensitive period.

Sousa and co-workers (1974) recently compared the success of breastfeeding during the first two months of life for two groups of 100 women who delivered normal full-term babies in a twenty-bed maternity

Table 3-3. Demography and details of two Guatemalan studies

| | Description of sample | | | |
| | Social Security Hospital | | Roosevelt Hospital | |
	Control	Experimental	Control	Experimental
Number	20	20	30	30
Initial contact first hour of life (minutes)	0	45	0	45
First feeding with mother (hours)	24	24	12	12
Mothers' age mean (years)	22	23	20	21
Socioeconomic score	15	14	11	13*
Mean birth weight (grams)	2863	2850	2741	2929*

*p < .05.

Table 3-4. Results of study in Social Security Hospital

	Control		Experimental	
Age (months)	6	12	6	12
Mean weight increase (grams)	3739	5685	4498*	5974*
Number of infants breast-feeding/total	3/18	0/18	9/17*	5/17*
Cumulative episodes of infection	39	68	31	45

*p < .05.

Table 3-5. Results of study in Roosevelt Hospital

	Control		Experimental	
Age (months)	6	12	6	12
Mean weight increase (grams)	4144	5661	4163	5582
Number of infants breast-feeding/total	21/28*	12/27	10/26	5/25
Cumulative episodes of infection	89	144	60	65

*p < .05.

ward in Pelotis, Brazil. In the experimental group the baby was put to breast immediately after birth, and permanent contact between the mother and baby was maintained during the lying-in period. The baby lay in a cot beside his mother's bed. The control group had the traditional contact with their infants—a glimpse shortly after birth and then visits for approximately 30 minutes every 3 hours, seven times a day, starting 12 to 14 hours after birth. The babies were kept in a separate nursery. Successful breastfeeding was defined as the mother's not using complementary feedings other than tea, water, or small amounts of fruit juice until two months after birth. At two months 77% of the early contact mothers were successfully breastfeeding in contrast to only 27% of the control mothers. A weakness in this design is that during the experimental period a special nurse worked in the unit to stimulate and encourage breastfeeding. Although not definitive in itself, this study adds weight to our hypothesis.

> COMMENT: These studies serve to point out how punitive and interfering medical care systems in the United States are in the birth and early attachment process. Anything which regains the priorities of the importance of the mother or of her baby or of their being together will enhance their self esteem and, of course, the importance of their dyadic attachment.   T. B. BRAZELTON

Exciting data have recently been received from De Chateau in Umea, Sweden, that confirm and extend studies described in this chapter. In investigations of a white Swedish population, he observed the effect of early skin-to-skin contact during the first 30 minutes of life on infant and maternal behavior 3 months later. Table 3-6 presents the mothers' responses to interview questions at 3 months. It is of interest that even though mothers with early contact fed their babies at night twice as long as did the controls, mothers in the control group reported more problems with night feeding. Mothers in the control group also had help at home for a longer period after discharge.

Table 3-7 presents data from home observations, also made when the infants were 3 months old, during a 10-minute free play period scheduled

Table 3-6. Maternal interview data at 3 months[*]

	Early contact (N = 21)	Control (N = 19)
Planned pregnancy	12	12
Unplanned pregnancy	9	7
Participation in antenatal program	17	12
Perception of delivery		
Hard	4	1
Normal	3	3
Easy	14	15
Husband visits to maternity ward		
Frequently	16	16
Not frequently	4	2
First week at home		
Difficult	19	15
Easy	2	3
Adaptation to child		
Easy	13	3
As expected	7	14
Difficult	1	2
Problems with night feedings		
Yes	1	6
No	17	10
Mean duration of night feeding (in days)	42	24
Mean number of days the mother had help at home	7.6	19.5
Percentage of mothers still breastfeeding	58	26

[*]Data from De Chateau, P.: Neonatal care routines; influences on maternal and infant behavior and on breast feeding (thesis), Umea, Sweden, 1976, Umea University medical dissertations, N.S. no. 20.

2½ hours after the afternoon feeding. It is interesting that mothers who had early contact spent significantly more time in the *en face* position and kissing their infants, whereas control mothers more often cleaned their infants. The two groups appear to focus on different ends of the baby. One group was busy cleaning up whereas the other was giving love. A striking finding was that infants of early-contact mothers cried less and smiled and laughed significantly more than did infants of control mothers. It should be stressed that the only difference between the control and experimental groups occurred in the first 30 minutes of life, since all mothers had their wrapped infants in a crib near their beds from 30 minutes of age to approximately 2 hours after birth.

The length of breastfeeding in these two groups during the first year of life was an additional and important difference. Mothers given extra contact breastfed longer than did controls (mean: early contact, 175 days; controls, 108). These findings are similar to those we obtained in Guatemala.

Table 3-7. Home observations at 3 months during a 10-minute free play period[*]

	Mean frequency		
Observation	Early contact (N = 21)	Control (N = 19)	p
Infant behavior			
Eyes closed	0	1.1	0.10
Eyes open	10	8.9	0.10
Crying	0.2	1.2	0.02
Smiling/laughing	2.7	1.4	0.02
Looks at mother	7.5	7.3	N.S.
Maternal behavior			
Looks en face	3.1	0.8	0.008
Smiles	5.5	4.5	N.S.
Laughs	0.9	0.5	N.S.
Kisses	1.1	0.3	0.009
Cleans	0.1	0.5	0.05
Gives toy	4.6	4.0	N.S.
Rocking infant	0.1	0.5	0.10

[*]Data from De Chateau, P.: Neonatal care routines; influences on maternal and infant behavior and on breast feeding (thesis), Umea, Sweden, 1976, Umea University medical dissertations, N.S. no. 20.
N.S., Not significant.

In a third study in 1974 at Roosevelt Hospital in Guatemala City, a group of nine mothers was given their infants nude, under a heat panel, after they had left the delivery room. A second group of ten mothers was separated from their infants according to the usual routine. The infants in both groups were sent to the newborn nursery for the next 12 hours, after which they went to the mother in a seven-bed room for the first breastfeeding. At 12 hours each mother's interactions with her infant were observed by an investigator who did not know to which group she belonged. Observations of the mother's fondling, kissing, looking en face, gazing at, and holding the baby close to her were made for 15 seconds of every minute for 15 minutes. The group with early contact showed significantly more attachment behaviors.

In 1975 a similar study was conducted with three groups of mothers (Hales et al., in progress). Twenty mothers lay skin-to-skin with their infants under a heat panel for 45 minutes immediately after they left the delivery room. Another twenty mothers were separated after birth but brought together at 12 hours after birth with their infants under a heat panel for the identical type of contact. A third group was separated after birth. These mothers did not have skin-to-skin contact in privacy but first received their infants at 12 hours (the routine of this hospital). Observations of the mothers in all three groups were made 36 hours after

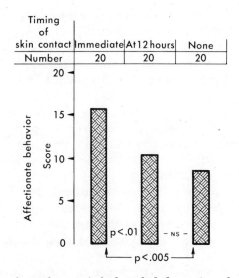

Fig. 3-10. Scores of attachment (which included *en face,* looking at the baby, talking to the baby, fondling, caressing, smiling at the baby) observed at 36 hours after birth in three groups of mothers, two of which received their infant skin-to-skin at either 45 minutes of age or 12 hours. The control mothers received no skin-to-skin contact.

birth by an observer who did not know the previous experience of the mothers. The mothers who had contact with their neonates immediately after birth showed significantly more attachment behaviors (*en face,* looking at the baby, talking to the baby, fondling, caressing, kissing, smiling at the baby) when compared with the mothers who were skin-to-skin with their infants for 45 minutes at 12 hours and the control group (Fig. 3-10). There were no differences in proximity behaviors and none in measures of caretaking. A progression in attachment behaviors is observable from the early skin-to-skin contact group to the two groups of control mothers. This is the first study that begins to define the limits of the sensitive period.

The systematic and detailed studies of mothers who were given early or late contact with their premature infants, described in Chapter 4, are further support for this concept.

In an interesting and significant observation of fathers, Lind (1973) noted that paternal caregiving in the first three months of life was greatly increased when the father was asked to undress his infant twice and to establish eye-to-eye contact with him for 1 hour during the first three days of life. On the basis of this evidence, we strongly believe than an essential principle of attachment is that there is a *sensitive period* in the first minutes and hours after an infant's birth which is optimal for parent-infant attachment. We must now attempt to answer the question of why this period is so important. What happens between a parent and a newborn infant that pulls them together and assures the mother's long-term commitment to the relationship? Again we must consider observations from a number of sources to find our answer.

An important step in understanding this period was made when Wolff (1959) described for the first time six separate states of consciousness in the infant, ranging from deep sleep to screaming. The state with which we are most concerned is state 4, the quiet, alert state. In this state the infant's eyes are wide open, and he is able to respond to his environment. Unfortunately, he may be in this state for periods as short as a few seconds. This made original detection of the state difficult and explains why it was not identified until 1959. Fig. 3-11 shows a 4-day-old infant in the quiet alert state (state 4). However, Desmond and co-workers (1966) observed that the infant is in state 4 for a period of 45 to 60 minutes during the first hour after birth. After this discovery it was possible to demonstrate that an infant can see, that he has visual preferences, and that he will turn his head to the spoken word, all in the first hour of life. After this hour, however, he goes into a deep sleep for 3 to 4 hours. Thus for 1 hour after birth he is ideally equipped for the important first meeting with his parents.

Fig. 3-11. A 4-day-old infant with his father in the quiet alert state (state 4).

Reciprocal interaction

The fascinating question of *why* the development of maternal attachment progresses so rapidly during the early postpartum period can only be answered by minutely examining what happens between the mother and infant during this crucial time. What pulls them together, ensuring their proximity through the many months during which the infant is unable to satisfy his own needs? What are the rewards for the mother's commitment and efforts? In the center of Fig. 3-12 is a picture of a common situation—a mother feeding her infant in the first hour of life. The diagram surrounding the picture, however, belies the simplicity of the scene in a schematic presentation of the multiple interactions simultaneously occurring between mother and child. Each is intimately involved with the other on a number of sensory levels. Their behaviors complement each other and serve to lock the pair together. The infant elicits behaviors from the mother which in turn are satisfying to him, and vice versa, the mother elicits behaviors in the infant which in turn are rewarding to her. For example, the infant's hard crying is likely to bring the mother near and trigger her to pick him up. When she picks

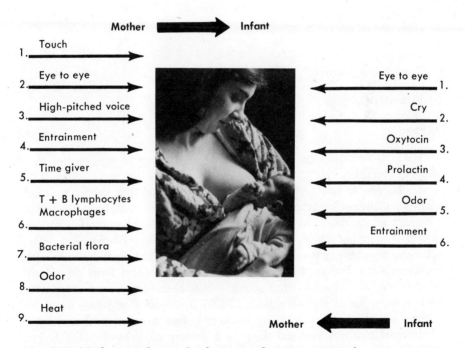

Fig. 3-12. Mother-to-infant and infant-to-mother interactions that can occur simultaneously in the first days of life.

him up, he is likely to quiet, open his eyes, and follow. Looking at the process in the opposite direction, when the mother touches the infant's cheek, he is likely to turn his head, bringing him into contact with her nipple, on which he will suck. His sucking in turn is pleasurable to both of them. Actually, this is a necessarily oversimplified description of these interactions. These behaviors do not occur in a chainlike sequence but rather each behavior triggers several others. Thus the effects of an interaction are more like that of the stone dropped into a pool, causing a multitude of ever-increasing rings to appear, rather than like a chain where each link leads to only one other. In a sense we see a fail-safe system that is overdetermined to ensure the proximity of mother and child.

Because of the limitations of language, the interactions must be described sequentially rather than simultaneously, dispelling momentarily the richness of the actual process for the sake of understanding it. We therefore will have to present each system singly, although it is important to remember that they interlock (Fig. 3-12).

MOTHER ➡️ **INFANT**

1. Touch
2. Eye-to-eye contact
3. High-pitched voice
4. Entrainment
5. Time giver
6. T and B lymphocytes, macrophages
7. Bacterial nasal flora
8. Odor
9. Heat

We will first describe the interactions originating in the mother that affect the infant.

1. _Touch._ A most important behavioral system that serves to bind mother and infant together is the mother's interest in touching her baby. Although no studies have yet defined which neonatal characteristics elicit maternal touching, three independent observers have described a characteristic touching pattern that mothers use in the first contact with their newborns. Rubin (1963) noted that human mothers show an orderly progression of behavior after birth while becoming acquainted with their babies. Klaus and associates (1970) observed that when nude infants were placed next to their mothers a few minutes or hours after birth, most mothers touched them in a pattern of behavior that began with fingertip touching of the infant's extremities and proceeded in 4 to 8 minutes to massaging, stroking, and encompassing palm contact

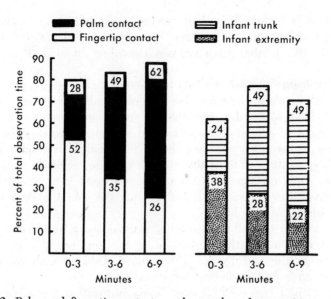

Fig. 3-13. Palm and fingertip contact on the trunk and extremities at the first postnatal contact in mothers of full-term infants. (From Klaus, M. H., Kennell, J. H., Plumb, N., and Zuehlke, S.: Pediatrics **46:**187-192, 1970.)

of the trunk (Fig. 3-13). In the first 3 minutes mothers maintained fingertip contact 52% of the time and palm contact 28% of the time. In the last 3 minutes of observation, however, this was reversed. Fingertip contact had greatly decreased, and palm contact increased to 62% of the total scored time. Rubin (1963) observed a similar pattern but at a much slower rate. In her study mothers usually took about three days to complete the sequence, but the infants were dressed, which may account for the difference. Mothers of normal premature infants who were permitted early contact followed a sequence of touching, but at an even slower rate (Fig. 4-1); even at the third visit mothers of premature infants were not using their palms. Much more progress in tactile contact occurred in mothers of full-term infants in just 10 minutes.

In a study of home births, Lang (1972) observed that almost always the mother rubs the baby's skin, starting with the face. Rubbing is done with the fingertips and is usually a gentle stroking motion. This occurs before the initial nursing and before delivery of the placenta. The baby is usually offered the breast but often does not suck at first. The most common action for the baby when given the mother's nipple is to continually lick it.

Thus we have fragmentary evidence for what we believe is a significant principle—that human mothers engage in a species-specific sequence of behaviors when first meeting their infants, even though the speed of this sequence is modified by environmental and cultural conditions. Is this related to what was described in animal mothers in Chapter 2?

2. *Eye-to-eye contact.* Another interaction that proceeds from mother to child originates in the eyes. The mothers studied by Klaus and associates (1970) expressed strong interest in eye-to-eye contact. Seventy-three percent of the mothers verbalized an intense interest in waking the infant to see his eyes open. Some even voiced a relationship between the condition of the baby and his eyes, for example, "Open your eyes. Oh, come on, open your eyes. If you open your eyes I'll know you're alive." Several mentioned that once the infant looked at them, they felt much closer to him.

The mothers of full-term infants studied by Klaus and associates (1970) showed a remarkable increase in the time spent in the *en face* position from the first to the fifth minute. Table 3-8 shows the percentage of *en face* in mothers of full-term infants.

Lang (1972) observed in most home births that immediately after the birth of the baby, but before the delivery of the placenta, the mother picked up the baby and held him in the *en face* position while speaking to him in a high-pitched voice.

> COMMENT: Eye-to-eye contact serves the purpose of giving a real identity or personification to the baby, as well as getting a rewarding feedback for the mother.   T. B. BRAZELTON

In Fig. 3-14 a mother of a full-term infant is shown in this position, and Fig. 3-15 is from a print by Hans Erni showing the same position.

There seem to be other mechanisms that foster the rewarding eye-to-eye contact. As Robson (1967) so aptly describes, "The appeal of the mother's eyes to the child (and of his eyes to her) is facilitated by their stimulus richness. In comparison with other areas of the body surface, the eye has a remarkable array of interesting qualities such as the shininess of the globe, the fact that it is mobile while at the same time fixed in space, the contrasts between the pupil-iris-cornea

Table 3-8. Percent of total observation time in *en face* position

Initial contact (minutes)	En face (percent)
0 to 3	10
3 to 6	17
6 to 9	23

Fig. 3-14. A mother of a full-term baby in the *en face* position. (From Kennell, J. H., and Klaus, M. H.: Clin. Obstet. Gynecol. **14:**926-954, 1971.)

configuration, the capacity of the pupil to vary in diameter, and the differing effects of variations in the width of the palpebral fissure."*

Brazelton and co-workers (1966) reported that the infant can see at birth. An infant born of an unmedicated mother will easily follow a moving hand at a 12- to 15-inch distance. One would expect the seeing infant to focus on the most interesting visual stimulus, which, as described by Robson, may be the human eye.

In the course of performing the Brazelton Neonatal Behavior Assessment on large numbers of infants, we have been repeatedly struck by the greater appeal of the examiner's face than any inanimate object.

*From Robson, K.: The role of eye-to-eye contact in maternal-infant attachment, J. Child Psychol. Psychiatry 8:13-25, 1967.

Fig. 3-15. Hans Erni print illustrating the *en face* position.

COMMENT: The neonatal data on vision[*] point to the infant's preference for both moving, moderately complex stimuli and those which
are ovoid and have the ungarbled contents of the human face. Goren

[*]Stechler, G., and Lantz, E.: Some observations on attention and arousal in the
human infant, J. Am. Acad. Child Psychiatr. **5:**517, 1966.
Haith, M. M., Kessen, W., and Collins, D.: Response of the human infant to level of
complexity of intermittent visual movement, J. Exp. Child. Psychol. **7:**52, 1969.

(1975) shows that the neonate at birth will follow an ungarbled representation of a face for 180 degrees, but significantly less (60 degrees) and for less time if it is garbled. He is programmed for the human face at birth.   T. B. BRAZELTON

3. High-pitched voice. Lang's (1972) observation that mothers giving birth at home usually speak to their infants in high-pitched voices prompted us to watch for this phenomenon. Interestingly, after hearing about this, we also have observed mothers speaking to their newborn infants in a much higher pitched voice than that used in everyday conversation. They may turn and speak to the doctor or nurse in their regular voice and then abruptly return to the higher frequency speech as they address their neonates. As Brazelton reported, a neonate alerts and attends to a female voice in preference to a male voice because of its higher pitch. The mother's use of a high-pitched voice, then, fits with the infant's sensitive auditory perception and his attraction to speech in the high-frequency range.

4. Entrainment. The microanalysis of sound films shows that human communication is not sound alone but also includes movement. When a person speaks, several parts of his body move in ways that are sometimes obvious and sometimes almost imperceptible; the same is true of the listener, whose movements are coordinated to the elements of the speech. When two people are filmed, the microanalysis reveals that both the listener and the speaker are moving in tune to the words of the speaker, thus creating a type of dance. The rhythm or tune of the dance is the pattern of the speech (Condon and Sander, 1974).

Recent exciting observations by Condon and Sander (1974) reveal that newborns also move in time with the structure of adult speech. "When the infant is already in movement, points of change in the configuration of his moving body parts become coordinated with points of change in sound patterns characterizing speech." In other words, as the speaker pauses for breath or accents a syllable, the infant almost imperceptibly raises an eyebrow or lowers a foot. The investigators demonstrated that live speech in particular is effective in entraining infant movement. Neither tapping noises nor disconnected vowel sounds showed the degree of correspondence with neonate movement as did natural, rhythmic speech. Interestingly, synchronous movements were found with both of the two natural languages tested, English and Chinese. As noted by the authors:

> This study reveals a complex interaction system in which the organization of the neonate's motor behavior is entrained by and synchronized with the organized speech behavior of adults in his environment. If the infant, from the beginning, moves in precise, shared rhythm with the

organization of the speech structure of his culture, then he participates developmentally through complex, socio-biological entrainment processes in millions of repetitions of linguistic forms long before he later uses them in speaking and communicating.*

Although the infant moves in rhythm to his mother's voice and thus may be said to be affected by her, on the other hand the infant's movements may reward the mother and stimulate her to continue. The point is that these areas of contact are interactive.

> COMMENT: By this subtle entrainment of his movements to the rhythm of her speech, the newborn gives the mother feedback that she can hardly resist. We have found that this synchrony becomes the important ambience for their affective communications thereafter. Their communications become a sort of "mating dance" (cf. swans) when they are analyzed on film by frame-by-frame analysis.   T. B. BRAZELTON

5. Time giver. Synchronous movements are part of a much more comprehensive phenomenon of entrainment between a mother and her baby, which has been identified by the intensive and meticulous studies by Sander and associates (1970). We can speculate that while the baby is in utero many of his actions and rhythms are attuned to those of the mother. This is due to a variety of rhythmical influences—her own sleep-wake cycle, the diurnal rhythms of her hormones, the orderly patterns of the mother's day, the regular beat of her heart, and the rhythmic contractions of the uterus preceding the onset of labor and continuing up to the time that the baby emerges from the birth canal. By carefully monitoring the states and activities of normal infants rooming-in with their mothers during the first 2 weeks of life, Sander has confirmed the existence of those behavioral phenomena in the first hours of life that have been emphasized by others, such as an unusually prolonged, alert state following birth. In addition, he has shown that on the second day there is a breakup of the rapid-eye-movement (REM) and non-REM sleep pattern present on the first day. In succeeding days the length of each period of sleep, the total amount of REM sleep, and the total amount of deep sleep decrease progressively. Concurrently there is an increase in crying, which reaches a peak on the third day. Thus the disruption of birth seems to upset the baby's prior rhythms and throw his systems into a state of disequilibrium. He must reorganize and retrain the biorhythmicity of his states and behavior to fit his extra-uterine environment.

By following a steady routine in the early days, the mother helps her

---

*From Condon, W. S., and Sander, L. W.: Neonate movement is synchronized with adult speech, Science 183:99-101, 1974.

infant to reestablish biorhythmicity. As evidence of this, Sander has identified a progressive increase in the co-occurrence of the infant's being in an alert state and his mother's holding him. This increases from less than 25% on the second day to 57% co-occurrence on the eighth day. Cassel and Sander (1975) describe the mother as the time giver *(Zeitgeber)* for the baby for the entrainment of rhythmic neonatal functions. They compare the mother's effect on the infant to the effect of a magnet in organizing and lining up iron fillings.

Sander has emphasized that the alert state in a young infant is extremely stable. He has shown that if the baby is in any state other than the alert state and the mother intervenes, it is likely that he will become alert. However, if the baby is already in the alert state and the mother intervenes, there is only a slight chance of a change in state. The high occurrence of the alert state results from the interaction of a sensitive mother with her infant. When he is alert, he is ready to respond to the mother, to dance in rhythm to her speech or movements.

6. *T and B lymphocytes, macrophages.* New information about breast milk will emphasize the intricate contributions of the mother to the baby shortly after birth. It has been known for some time that breast milk is a rich source of antibodies, particularly in the colostrum. More recently it has been discovered that there are high concentrations of IgA and T and B lymphocytes in breast milk which may line part of the intestinal epithelium and provide protection against the enteric pathogens for which the baby receives little transplacental protection from the mother (Walker, 1973). As an example, if a mother has had a recent enteric infection with salmonella C infection before delivery, cells in the mother's intestinal epithelium will begin to produce antibodies against this organism. Some of these cells will migrate specifically to her mammary gland, where some will be discharged into the colostrum and others will remain in the gland and produce antibodies against salmonella C, which the baby is likely to encounter during his journey through the birth canal. Similar protection is provided against many other potentially dangerous organisms in the mother's gastrointestinal tract. Thus the lymphocytes and antibodies in the colostrum and breast milk may specifically protect the baby against this salmonella infection (Goldblum et al., 1975). This explains partly how a newborn infant who is 100% breastfed is protected in precarious environments from *Shigella,* typhoid, other salmonellas, and pathogenic *Escherichia coli.*

7. *Bacterial nasal flora.* During a period of more than eight years in which the bacteriological status of all the infants in a Guatemalan Indian village was carefully monitored, there was no known baby delivered at home under poor hygienic conditions who developed a staphylococcal skin infection in the first two months of life (Mata, 1974).

During this same period in Guatemala City, a few miles away, many newborns discharged from the hospital nurseries returned with skin infections due to pathogenic strains of *Staphylococcus aureus* (as occurs in hospital nurseries all over the world). The babies in these nurseries were separated from their mothers for the first 12 hours of life. It is our hypothesis that if mother and baby are kept together in the first minutes of life, the mother gives her baby her own mixture of strains of respiratory organisms, such as the *Staphylococcus*. Then these maternally provided strains grow and populate the infant's respiratory and gastrointestinal tracts. Just as a lawn planted with grass will resist the introduction of weeds after the grass has had a good start, these organisms may prevent the baby from acquiring the hospital strains of staphylococci. This principle of bacterial interference has been applied clinically by Shinefield and co-workers (1963), who demonstrated that epidemics of pathogenic staphylococcal infection in newborn nurseries could be stopped by placing a benign strain of *Staphylococcus* into the nares of newborns. A similar protection may be accomplished naturally by the mother.

8. *Odor.* The odor of the mother can also affect the infant. MacFarlane (1975) found that by the fifth day of life breastfeeding infants can discriminate their mother's own breastpad from the breastpads of other mothers with significant reliability. In the future the olfactory system may be found to play an essential part in attachment to the mother.

9. *Heat.* For completeness temperature control should be mentioned. In the past the body of the human mother was a reliable source of heat for the infant, although this is a diminishing function. This has recently been clearly confirmed by the study of Phillips (1974), who found a minimal drop in the infant's temperature when the baby was placed on the mother's chest wrapped and without a heat lamp.

• • •

Other studies have emphasized other aspects of the mother-to-infant interaction. Cassel and Sander (1975) pointed out that the infant has an advanced sensory system when he enters the world, but is greatly retarded in his motor abilities. Motor dependency results in an obvious need for continuous caretaking from a mothering figure. Most important, this dependency serves a second function by involving the infant in interaction, through which the newborn can regulate his circadian rhythms. Although his functions and those of his caretaker are temporarily desynchronized and disorganized in the first days after birth, the baby becomes reorganized by repeated mother-event situations.

Cassel has demonstrated evidence of the newborn's perception of the interaction through experiments in which he has the mother wear a mask and be silent during one feeding on the seventh day of life. The infant takes significantly less milk, scans the room when placed in the crib, and has significant disruption in rapid-eye-movement and nonrapid-eye-movement sleep following the masked feeding compared with the usual feeding.

Meltzoff and Moore (1975) have recently demonstrated the remarkable finding of neonatal imitation of visually perceived stimuli through facial and manual gestures at two weeks after birth. These remarkable findings were obtained by presenting four gestures (tongue protrusion, lip protrusion, mouth open, sequential finger movements) to six infants on four occasions and recording the subsequent performance of the infants. Each behavior occurred significantly more frequently in the 20 seconds after it had been demonstrated to the infant than did other behaviors. Thus the neonate might respond to his mother with a form of mimicry.

Two other observations that demonstrate the "neatness of fit" of maternal and infant behaviors are Salk's (1973) set of tentative findings that (1) neonates quiet when exposed to the natural beating of the human heart and (2) mothers characteristically hold infants on their left side near the heart. Thus if the newborn cries and is picked up by his mother, chances are that her holding will soothe his cries, thus encouraging proximity in times of neonatal distress.

MOTHER ⬅━━━━ **INFANT**
1. Eye-to-eye contact
2. Cry
3. Oxytocin
4. Prolactin
5. Odor
6. Entrainment

Using our simplified system, the following interactions originate with the infant (Fig. 3-12).

1. *Eye-to-eye contact.* The visual system provides one of the most powerful networks for the mediation of maternal attachment. This fact is emphasized by the work of Fraiberg and colleagues (1974) who have described in detail the difficulties that mothers of blind infants have in feeling close to them. Without the affirmation of mutual gazing, mothers feel lost and like strangers to their babies until both learn to substitute other means of communication.

Interestingly, the distance between the eyes of the mother and infant when the mother is breastfeeding or holding him in her arms is about 12 inches, which is the distance at which infants can best focus on an object. These positions provide repeated opportunities for eye-to-eye contact during a mother's care of her neonate.

Robson (1967) has suggested that eye-to-eye contact is one of the innate releasers of maternal caretaking responses. Some of our experiences have shown how powerful it is. For example, three researchers who were participating in a study with us were required to assist with Brazelton Neonatal Behavior Assessments on infants each day. We were distressed to hear all three say that they did not particularly like babies, found newborns particularly unappealing, and planned never to have a baby. They grumbled about learning the behavioral assessments. As they carried out the assessment, each of the women had her first experience with a baby in the alert state who would follow her eyes with his own, and an amazing change occurred. Suddenly each became enthusiastic about "her" baby, wanted to hold him, and came back later in the day and the next day to visit. At night she would tell her friends about this marvelous baby she had tested. In a few weeks all three decided they would like to have and even breastfeed a baby. This anecdote about the three women demonstrates the compelling attraction of a newborn infant moving his eyes to follow an adult's eyes, and the layer upon layer of emotional meaning that the viewer may place on this.

2. *Cry.* The voice of the infant also affects the mother. Lind and colleagues (1973), using thermal photography, have reported on yet another biological level where reciprocal behaviors pull mothers and infants together. After being exposed to the hunger cries of healthy newborns, fifty-four of sixty-three mothers demonstrated a significant increase in the amount of blood flow to their breasts. The infant's cry causes a physiological change in the mother that is likely to induce her to nurse.

3. *Oxytocin.* The infant can also initiate the secretion of maternal hormones. Breastfeeding the infant or having him lick her nipple leads to the release of oxytocin in the mother, which hastens uterine contraction and reduces bleeding. Thus after birth the mother and infant are closely intertwined through complex behavioral and physical interactions.

4. *Prolactin.* Hwang and associates (1971) have shown that serum prolactin concentrations increase during pregnancy and decrease rapidly in the postpartum period. Furthermore, whenever the nipple of the mother is touched, either by the infant's lips or by a finger, there is a fourfold to sixfold increase in her prolactin level and then a decrease after breastfeeding begins. We have made preliminary studies of prolactin levels in three mothers before and after they were given their infants. In two mothers there were significant increases in the prolactin level after physical contact with their infants, which involved no nursing or touching of the breast. Thus licking, sucking, or perhaps even tactile contact alters maternal prolactin levels.

It is intriguing to consider whether these changes in prolactin levels, which are known to induce the alveoli of the breasts to secrete milk, have other effects on the mother. In birds, prolactin is a love hormone; it appears to activate the close attachment between mother and young. Does the great increase in prolactin also enhance the mother's attachment to her infant? If so, its production through the agency of the child is an efficient biological mechanism serving to promote the survival of neonates.

Evidence that gives partial support to this hypothesis comes from observations in Denver, Colorado, where Avery (1973) has developed a method for inducing milk production in women who have never given birth. Women who have been able to breastfeed their adopted babies have reported the development of strong feelings of closeness and attachment while breastfeeding. In these situations skin-to-skin contact, touch, smell, body warmth, and auditory and visual stimuli all operate together to promote attachment.

Up to this point we have attempted to separate the components of this complex system into effects of the mother on the child or the child on the mother. However, we are now able to approach the fact of interaction operationally. For example, one can hypothesize that the mother is rewarded for her touching by the resulting closeness with her infant, through which she can pleasurably experience his warmth and soft skin. In addition, she can look at him closely and observe his responses to her touch.

5. *Odor.* Interestingly, odor is probably also important. Many mothers report that each of their infants has its own scent.

6. *Entrainment.* From numerous clinical experiences we believe that an essential principle of attachment is that parents must receive some response or signal, such as body or eye movements from their infant, to form a close bond. We hypothesize that for most parents this takes place in the first days of life, when the infant is in the quiet alert state and moves in rhythm to his parents' speech. We have abbreviated this principle to: "You cannot fall in love with a dishrag."

Mary Cassat, in a painting of a mother with an older infant, beautifully captures some of the responses that are rewarding to a mother (Fig. 3-16) and at the same time illustrates this principle.

Maternal and infant behaviors complement each other in several sensory and motor systems, thus increasing the probability of interaction occurring. These behaviors seem to be specific and innately programmed to start the process of locking mother and infant together in a sustained reciprocal rhythm. For example, as we have seen, the mother's use of

Fig. 3-16. A Mary Cassat painting that captures the mutual interactions between a mother and infant during a feeding. (Courtesy The Art Institute of Chicago, Chicago, Ill.)

a high-pitched voice appears to fit perfectly with the infant's especially sensitive auditory perception and attraction to speech in the high-frequency range. Thus if the observation that humans characteristically speak to newborn infants in a high-pitched voice is correct, nature has provided a means by which stimulation from humans is especially attractive to the young of the species and will easily evoke a response. Similarly, a mother's interest in her new baby's eyes corresponds to his ability to see, to attend, and to follow. Nature appears to have preferentially developed in the occipital cortex the visual pathways so that these sensory and motor functions are ready for the newborn infant to receive stimulation from his mother and to interact with her.

Kaila (1935), Spitz and Wolff (1946), and Ahrens (1954) have established that one of the earliest and most effective stimuli for eliciting a social smile in an infant is a visual configuration consisting of two eyes and a mouth shown *en face*. Goren (1975) has demonstrated that this is the innate form preference of newborns, minutes after birth, even before there has been any opportunity for the infant to see human faces. Thus mothers tend to look at their babies in a way that increases the chance that their babies will attend and follow and then, a bit later, smile back. Since smiling is an extremely powerful reinforcer, the visual interaction helps to cement the proximity of mother and child.

It should be noted that Condon and Sander's (1974) studies on entrainment to the human voice were done with infants a few hours old and that all of the babies were bottle fed and were in United States hospitals. Would the entrainment progress more rapidly, would the co-occurrence of the mother's holding and the infant's alerting take place more frequently, and would the breakup in the baby's sleep and awake states be less marked and less prolonged if mother and baby were together continuously from birth and if the baby were breastfed?

Hearing and vision assume greatly enhanced importance in Western industrialized nations, where mother and baby are separated for many hours of the day. In some developing nations, where the baby remains on the mother's body from birth on, these state changes might well be different. A woman in Africa who carries her baby on her back or side is identified as a poor mother if her baby wets or soils on her after the seventh day—that is, if she cannot anticipate these elimination behaviors and hold the baby away before they occur. This finely tuned awareness of the movements of the baby is almost inconceivable to those in nations where mother and baby are kept apart much of the day and sleep separately at night.

These observations are especially provocative because they extend the perceptive observations of Bowlby (1958), Ainsworth (1970), and Ainsworth and associates (1974), who distinguished between executive and signal behaviors. Executive behaviors consist of responses such as rooting, grasping, and postural adjustment, which tend to maintain physical contact between infant and caretaker, once established. Signal behaviors, on the other hand, comprise responses such as crying and smiling, which increase proximity or establish physical contact between infant and mother. We suggest that the signal and executive behaviors act in conjunction with the reciprocal interactions just presented. One of the major advantages of the early interaction is that it helps the parents to become more quickly attuned to the individuality of their own infant and therefore to adapt their behavior to his needs and tempo (Brazelton et al., 1974).

Although individual infants differ in their capacity to receive and shut out stimuli, as well as in their ability to exhibit behaviors to which the environment can respond, we wonder whether some of the individual differences described in later infancy might occur partly as a result of whether the mother is permitted early or late contact. Brazelton and co-workers (1974) and Stern (1974) have started to decode the normal intricate mother-infant interaction at 3 and 4 months of age. We suggest that the amazing synchronization of normal mothers and infants found at that time begins in these crucial first minutes of life.

There are other major rules or principles mentioned briefly in Chapter 1 for which experimental data are not available, but which we believe play a significant role in this attachment.

MONOTROPY—A SIGNIFICANT PRINCIPLE OF MOTHER-TO-INFANT ATTACHMENT

During the past five years we have made three critical observations that suggest a basic principle of attachment. Observations of our nurses working in the premature nursery, discussions with the head nurse at the Matera (a large adoption home in Athens, Greece), and clinical follow-up of twin deliveries suggest that the phenomenon of mother-to-infant attachment is developed and structured so that a close attachment can optimally be formed to only one person at a time. In the premature nursery we have learned that each nurse has a favorite, usually liking the other infants but never having more than one special infant at any one time. When the favorite infant leaves the nursery with the mother, the nurse usually is sad, often for two to five days. At the Matera (Fig. 3-17), where the nurses live on the division for four to five months with the children (nine nurses for twelve infants), a nurse has never become attached to more than one infant at a time, although 3000 infants have been raised in the past fifteen years. After the discharge of the infant at four to five months, the nurses at the Matera usually go through a prolonged period (four to six months) of grief and mourning responses similar to those which follow the death of a close relative.

In addition to this phenomenon are clinical observations of a number of sets of twins, where the larger twin was discharged and the smaller twin was left in the nursery to grow, which suggests that there is a much higher incidence of mothering disorders in the second twin. In a short observation period in Lausanne, Switzerland, three sets of twins were discharged, the larger first, and the smaller later. Three months later the smaller twins of two of the sets returned. One infant had been battered, and the other failed to thrive. The second mother mentioned that the larger twin was hers but not the second baby. We have seen similar problems in our own unit. This is apparently an important principle that may explain why mothers of twins prefer to dress

Fig. 3-17. Nurses at the Matera in Athens, Greece, caring for infants who will be adopted at 4 to 5 months of age.

them alike. Optimally they may only be able to take in one image or bond to one infant at the end of each pregnancy. This has obvious clinical significance, and we are now attempting to design further observations to test this. It is interesting that in a paper written by Bowlby in 1958 discussing a child's tie to his mother, he stated, "The tendency for instinctual responses to be directed toward a particular individual or group of individuals and not promiscuously towards many is one which I believe so important and so neglected, it deserves a special term. I propose to call it monotropy." This observation about the tie in the opposite direction, mother to infant, has the obvious clinical implication that twins should be kept together and should be discharged at the same time so that simultaneous attachments may be possible.

Another significant principle which has evolved from many clinical experiences and the work of Evans (1972) is that the processes of attachment and detachment cannot easily occur simultaneously. We have noted in many parents who have lost one of a twin pair that they have often found it difficult to mourn completely the baby who died and at the same time to feel attached to the survivor. The same problem is found when a mother quickly becomes pregnant after losing a neonate. Supporting evidence is the observation of Evans and associates (1972), who discovered that one third of parents who have a failure-to-thrive infant without organic disease have recently suffered from the loss of a close family relative. While mourning the loss of a parent, they are unable to care for their newborn adequately. Thus, whenever feasible, it should be recommended that a new infant not be conceived until the grief is finished (six to twelve months).

COMMENT: The authors introduce the concepts of attachment and attachment behaviors in the context of human mothers' relationships to infants. Using a paradigm derived from observations in other species, Klaus and Kennell also postulate the existence of a sensitive period for the development of species-specific maternal attachment behaviors in humans.

The terms *attachment* and *attachment behaviors* were previously defined with respect to the infant's tie to his mother—the proximity-seeking and contact-maintaining activities of infant to mother that provide protection from danger and satisfaction of physiological needs.[*†] The similarity in terminology invites comparison of the theoretical formulations of attachment in mothers and attachment in infants. Infant attachment is postulated to be the infant's contribution to his survival, and attachment behaviors are interpreted in terms of their survival value in the environment in which the species evolved.[†] If maternal attachment were to be evaluated in terms of such an evolutionary significance, the behaviors chosen to indicate maternal attachment should contribute to survival of the infant and the species. The survival of the individual baby requires the availability of caregiving 24 hours a day for months and years, and the survival of the species requires the child's maturation to reproductive adulthood. Thus, if maternal attachment has survival value, one would expect to find behaviors that provide life support during infancy and that ensure the independent development of the infant. Behaviors considered in this chapter to be indicators of maternal attachment (fondling, gazing, kissing, holding close, looking *en face*), however, seem to correspond to behaviors that might be called "affectionate" in contemporary Western society. Whether these affection-

[*]Bowlby, J.: The nature of the child's tie to his mother, Int. J. Psychoanal. 39:350-373, 1958.
[†]Bowlby, J.: Attachment and loss, vol. 1, New York, 1969, Basic Books, Inc., Publishers.

ate behaviors are crucial to infant and species survival is unclear. They are not specific to the mother-infant relationship and are frequently seen in society as other people interact with infants. Do these behaviors help to explain what it is that allows mothers to tolerate and enjoy the complete disruption of their previous life patterns that infant caregiving entails, to maintain contact in situations frequently associated with avoidance or disgust in human societies (feces, vomitus)? The maternal attachment indicators chosen also do not seem of equal importance in other cultures. For instance, in studies in Zambia and Zinacantan* eye-to-eye contact rarely occurs between mother and infant and is not reliably associated with other social interaction. Can one say that Zambian mothers, who are in constant skin-to-skin contact with their infants, are less attached to them than United States mothers?

The research on a "sensitive period" for maternal attachment indicates some short-term effects of early contact, but long-term data are still being gathered. The accurate detection of such a period requires better determination of relevant maternal behaviors. However, the emphasis on the immediate postpartum period may obscure the importance of prenatal influences and postnatal adaptations. The relative importance and interaction of these different contributions to mother-infant relationships still require further study.

Research reported in this chapter shares a general limitation of most data on human reproductive and nurturing behavior. This group of behaviors, critical to species survival, is relatively stable, and the fundamental patterns probably evolved during the long period when people lived as hunters and gatherers. Yet generalizations about human mothers are based largely on data collected in industrialized societies, which represent a recent and brief phase in human evolution. Some behaviors seen in industrialized countries may be representative of species behavior, but it is unwise to infer so without extensive cross-cultural comparisons in preagricultural and agricultural societies. The so-called "natural" childbirths and home deliveries in the United States are no exception; these are the products of individuals struggling to control their own experience, in reaction against cultural patterns that place control in the hands of specialists.[†] This is certainly not "natural" behavior of a species in its "natural" habitat.

Objective descriptions of the details of mothers' behavior in this and other cultures are necessary to scientific understanding. The research reported in this chapter should encourage definition of maternal behavior in ways truly representative of the species, to seek the components that are specifically necessary for survival, and to delineate the processes that determine different characteristics of mother-infant relationships. B. LOZOFF

*Goldberg, S.: Infant care and growth in urban Zambia, Hum. Dev. **15**:77-89, 1972.
Brazelton, T. B.: Implications of infant development among the Mayan Indians of Mexico, Hum. Dev. **15**:90-111, 1972.
†Lozoff, B., and Misra, R.: Medical control over labour, Lancet **1**:1242-1243, 1975.

CLINICAL CONSIDERATIONS

Until a century ago, events surrounding childbirth had changed little; elaborate customs served to help parents through the period. In the last century, however, increasing emphasis has been placed on the medical and scientific aspects of birth, but less attention has been paid to the equally valid psychological and social considerations. Has the enormous improvement in medical management, which has dramatically lessened the physical dangers to the mother, contributed to a waning concern about the many other problems a mother faces during pregnancy?

When evaluating clinical data, one must appreciate that it depends on the entire environment, including the social values of the system and the regulations of the hospital. In Russia, for example, a high value is placed on the birth of the human infant, and a woman is honored for having more than three children. But the hospital does not permit the father to be present at the birth or even to visit his wife and baby in the hospital. He does not see the infant until discharge. In Denmark, visiting regulations for fathers are exactly the opposite. Therefore it is not possible to compare the effects of mother-infant contact in the first hours on later maternal attachment in these two systems.

It is also necessary to separate one- and two-phase obstetrical delivery systems. For example, Denmark has a two-phase system. A normal healthy pregnant woman is usually examined and followed through the prenatal period by a midwife, with a few examinations by a physician, and then often gives birth in a maternity clinic. A maternity clinic does not contain all the facilities usually found in a hospital but is designed somewhat like a home. It has no blood bank and only minimal emergency equipment to care for sick infants. Five to six hours after the birth the mother assumes full daytime care for her infant. Fig. 3-18 shows a group of mothers caring for their babies in the maternity clinic nursery. It should be noted that a mother can learn not only from the nurse but also from other mothers as she actually begins to provide for her baby's needs; she gains skill and confidence before she takes him home. The nurse does not usually care for the babies or formally teach; she is available for questions and support.

In this system pregnancy is treated as a normal process and not as a disease. Mothers who have diabetes, toxemia, premature labor, or other complications of pregnancy detected from the first prenatal visits up to the time of birth are monitored by obstetricians and deliver in a hospital.

In the one-phase system, in the United States, Germany, and Switzerland, all mothers with or without complications give birth in the same unit; pregnancy is treated as a disease requiring hospitalization. Therefore, when inspecting data on maternal behavior, it is important to note

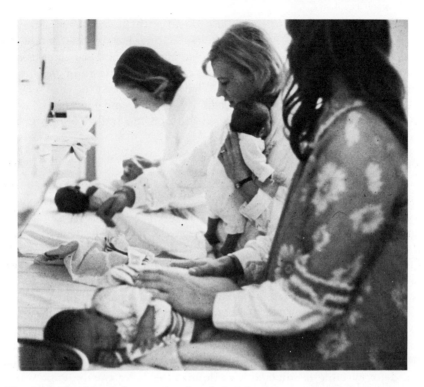

Fig. 3-18. Danish mothers caring for their infants in a maternity care nursery.

in which type of setting the studies were done—a one- or a two-phase system.

To minimize the number of unknowns for a mother while she is in the hospital, she and her husband should visit the maternity unit to see where labor and birth will take place. She should also learn about the drawbacks as well as the benefits of the anesthetic (if she is to receive one), the delivery routines, and all the procedures and medication she is likely to receive before, during, and after birth. Advance preparation increases the parents' confidence by reducing the possibility of surprise. For an adult, just as for a child entering the hospital for surgery, the more meticulously every step is detailed in advance, the less will be the subsequent anxiety. The less anxiety the mother experiences while giving birth and becoming attached to her baby, the better will be her immediate relationship with him.

Preparing for the birth

The mother needs continuing support and reassurance during her labor and birth, whether from her husband, mother, a friend, a midwife, or a nurse. She also must be satisfied with the arrangements that have been made to maintain her home during her hospitalization. In Holland, when a mother gives birth at home, a mother-helper comes into the home at the time of birth and takes over the care of the family and helps the midwife deliver the baby. This gives the mother the freedom to concentrate on the needs of her baby and enjoy her family in the process, and it relieves the pressure on the father, allowing him to reserve his energies for the family.

Birth

To reduce the amount of tension for the mother, she should labor and deliver in the same room, eliminating the necessity of rushing to a delivery room in the last minutes of labor. Once the birth is completed and the mother has had a quick glance at the infant, she usually needs a few seconds to regain her composure and, in a sense, catch her breath before she proceeds to the next task—"taking on" the infant. In standard hospital births this breath catching usually occurs while the placenta is being delivered and while the mother is being cleansed and is having any necessary suturing. It has been our experience that it is best not to give a mother her baby until she indicates that she is ready to take him on. It should be her decision. However, some mothers indicate their desire to hold and nurse their babies within a few seconds. If the delivery table is sufficiently wide and the baby can be kept warm, many mothers will welcome an opportunity for this early contact and nursing.

In many hospitals it is customary to put the baby on the mother's chest for 1 or 2 minutes shortly after birth. Although this is helpful, the lack of privacy, the narrow table, and the short time period do not allow sufficient opportunity for the mother to touch and explore her baby, and maternal attachment may not proceed optimally.

After birth it is extremely valuable for the father, mother, and infant to be together for about 30 to 45 minutes, either in the delivery room or in an adjacent room. Obviously this is only possible if the infant is normal and the mother is well. The mother should have the infant with her on the bed so that she can hold him rather than in a bassinet were she can only see his face. She should be given the infant nude and allowed to examine him completely. We encourage the mother to move over in her regular hospital bed or on a wide delivery table, leaving the other half for her partially dressed or nude infant. A heat panel easily maintains or, if need be, increases the body temperature of the infant. (Fig. 3-19 shows how we manage this situation.) Several mothers have told us of the unforgettable experience of holding their nude babies against their own bare chests, so we recommend skin-to-

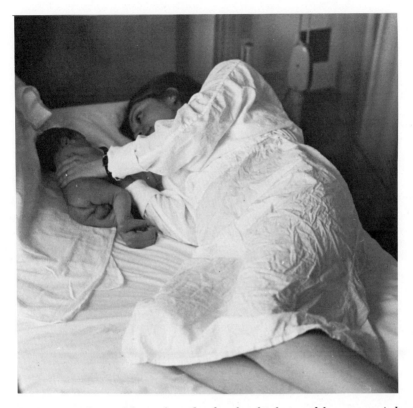

Fig. 3-19. A mother and her infant shortly after birth in a labor room. A heat panel (not shown) is above the infant and is maintaining the infant's temperature.

skin contact. If the mother plans to breastfeed, the first nursing can take place at this time. The father sits or stands at the side of the bed by the infant. This allows the parents and infant to become acquainted. Because of the importance of the eyes in the formation of the attachment, we withhold the application of silver nitrate ($AgNO_3$) to the eyes until after this rendezvous.

We leave the mother, the father, and their baby together for about 30 minutes. After 10 to 15 minutes, when alone, the mother and baby often fall into a deep sleep. In Guatemalan hospitals, where drugs and anesthesia are used more sparingly than in the United States, most mothers are awake after 45 minutes of privacy with their babies. The mother and father never forget this significant and stimulating shared experience. It helps to bond firmly the infant to both parents. We must emphasize that this should be a private session with a minimum of interruptions.

COMMENT: Again, maternity personnel must be aware of the *messages* they are transmitting to parents with such institutionalized procedures. They are saying, "*You* are the important ones to that baby's survival, not we!" "This is an important thing to do, to get attached." People are subtly influenced by medical priorities. For example, we found that many mothers of premature infants hold their babies out in their laps in a seated position to feed them.* On a Brody Closeness Scale the mothers score poorly, until one realizes that they have learned about their babies in premature nurseries where the nurses commonly feed them in this position.   T. B. BRAZELTON

Affectional bonds are further consolidated in the succeeding four to five days through continued close association and interaction of baby and mother, particularly when she cares for him. Close contact with her husband and other children is also important.

First days of life

The arrangement for the mother and her newborn infant vary greatly depending on the culture. In many parts of the world the mother and infant are together in a small hut for the first seven days. In Holland it is common for the mother to have the infant at home in her own room. In Denmark the infant usually stays in the hospital room with the mother for most of the day. One of the authors (M. H. K.) visited a maternity clinic in Horsholm, Denmark, where mothers go when a normal birth is anticipated. We have chosen to describe this clinic because we believe that several of its practices tend to optimize maternal attachment. A mother visits one midwife several times during her pregnancy. All of the women give birth in the rooms where they have labored. The clinic has a homelike living room, dining room, and various kitchens on one floor, and the nursery and mothers' rooms are on another. Sometimes women labor in the living room. At the time of the visit to the unit there were twenty mothers in two- or four-bed rooms. Six hours after birth a mother takes over the care of her infant, and the infant is left next to her bed (Fig. 3-20). Many women describe the value of having their babies at their sides, available for viewing with just a turn of the head. Women mention that they look at their infants over and over again whenever they awaken, continually taking them in. In other Danish hospitals that were visited, the babies are at the foot of the beds, where it is difficult for the mothers to observe them continually (Fig. 3-21). In the Horsholm clinic there is unlimited visiting during the

*From Brazelton, T. B., Koslowski, B., and Main, M.: The origins of reciprocity. In Lewis, M., and Rosenblum, L. A., editors: The effect of the infant on its caregiver, New York, 1974, John Wiley & Sons, Inc.

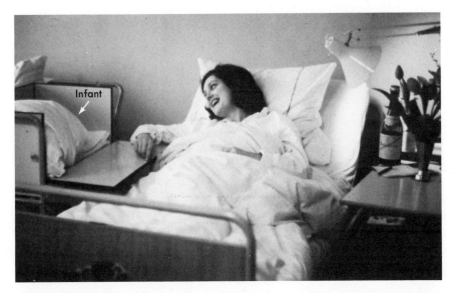

Fig. 3-20. A Danish mother with her infant by her side. Note that the height of the bassinet permits easy viewing.

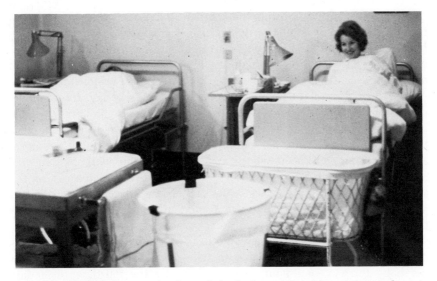

Fig. 3-21. Bassinet kept at the foot of the bed in a Copenhagen hospital, as in many hospitals in Europe.

whole day, and at lunch hours or teatime, mothers come downstairs into the dining room and leave the babies upstairs alone. At night between 8:30 and 10:30 P.M. they take the babies back into the large nursery where they are cared for by nurses overnight, except when they wake and are returned to their mothers for breastfeeding. In the previous year 2100 infants had been delivered in this maternity clinic. Twenty-five were premature infants but none died. The year before there were 1700 births and again no neonatal or maternal deaths. Thus the selection process is effective in picking out high-risk mothers.

One of the most impressive features of this unit can be observed in the morning, when the mothers come to the nurseries to pick up their babies and take over their care. There is much sharing of information about such routine procedures as bathing and diapering between more and less experienced mothers. In this clinic the mother becomes well acquainted with her baby before discharge.

Several features of the birth should be mentioned. There is little anesthesia. The parents are together during labor, there are no stirrups, and the mother's hands are not bound. She has an opportunity to see and hold the baby briefly after birth, and every attempt is made to make it a natural process. Just before birth a general practitioner comes to assist. There is no question that the midwife is in charge, and practitioners usually ask how they can help. The entire birth experience is strikingly different from a hospital delivery in the United States.

At University Hospitals of Cleveland, Ohio, there are a number of different options for housing the mother and infant. The mother can live with the infant continuously, she can have him for a few hours, or he may be kept in the nursery at night and in a bassinet with his mother during the day, from 8:00 A.M. until 11:00 P.M., as in many European and United States rooming-in units. We strongly recommend that the mother have her infant for a long period during the day, for example, at least from 1:00 P.M. until early evening. We also believe that she should see her husband while their infant is in the room and that she be allowed to see her other children. This allows the family to form a new unit around the newborn and decreases the mother's concerns about her other children. This lessens the separation concerns of the siblings, which not only has extremely important preventive benefits for them but also makes for an easier transition when the mother returns home.

In the United States a new mother, particularly a primipara, frequently states that she is unable to take over the strain of caring for her baby for a 3- or 4-hour period until after the fourth or fifth day. In Denmark, where mothers provide total care for their infants in a homelike setting in the hospital, mothers feel able to take over these duties 6 hours after giving birth. How can we account for these differences? Are Danish women healthier? Are they given different drugs? Are the opportunities to care for the baby different? Do the mothers come to the hospital with different expectations?

Almost every physician or nurse who works in a maternity unit comments on the extreme sensitivity of mothers during the early postpartum period. They may become greatly upset over a minor change in their infant and require assurance that he is healthy and that their mothering is adequate. After they have left the hospital, mothers may comment about their unusual and unexpected feelings of hypersensitivity and need for praise. These feelings appear incongruous in a mother with a normal, healthy baby and a smooth postpartum course. It should be noted, however, that these observations have been made of mothers who have, in general, seen their babies only every 4 hours in the hospital. Part of the sensitivity, of course, arises from the mother's concern about her ability to provide adequate mothering care for her baby, but we question whether she would have this much sensitivity and concern if she were in continuous contact with her baby. Perhaps her concern about what happens during the long periods when the baby is away from her—about what the nurses and doctors are doing with him and about his condition—heightens these reactions.

> COMMENT: And about her own importance and adequacy as a mother for this fragile, rather unknown infant. By this time she has been stripped of her autonomy and importance as a person, and also as the important figure to the infant.   T. B. BRAZELTON

The model for the delivery unit of the future should be more than just a facility where continual contact is provided. The policy of the unit should be to give a healthy mother complete responsibility for the care of her infant, with nurses or midwives available as consultants when the mother wishes and asks for help. Homelike delivery units have been started in a small number of hospitals in the United States.

We have noted that male physicians often find it difficult to answer the many small but important questions raised by new mothers. They frequently consider their pressing duties with sick infants more important and give this other responsibility to nurses. Nurses easily manage this task when they are aware of the importance of questions that may be raised.

Postpartum blues

Many physicians and nurses with extensive experience with postpartum patients in the average United States hospital report that well over 80% of mothers have postpartum blues, with crying some time during hospitalization. A number of physiological, psychological, and biochemical explanations have been proposed, but none has been conclusive.

Let us look at three scenes:

1. If you suddenly come into a postpartum division in Russia, you might be impressed with the sad expressions on the faces of the women, their spiritless motions and conversation. Note that husbands are not allowed to visit, that mothers see their babies every 4 hours for feedings, and that they do not participate in other infant care.

2. On a surprise visit to one mother's room on a postpartum division in the United States between feedings, you might find the mother cheerily talking on the phone to her mother, but in the next room the mother is quiet with postpartum blues. Note that fathers visit once a day, that babies are brought every 4 hours for feedings, and that siblings are not allowed to visit.

3. If you come unexpectedly into the maternity clinic in Horsholm, Denmark, you find a quiet, happy, pleasant atmosphere and mutual support as a group of mothers care for their babies and get to know them. Note that babies are with their mothers for the whole day, that the mothers provide all the care, and that fathers and siblings visit freely.

   COMMENT: Also the cultural expectations for not showing one's feelings may dominate a mother's behavior there.   T. B. BRAZELTON

We do not know the etiology of postpartum blues, but our observations lead us to speculate that mother-infant separation, the assignment of most of the caretaking responsibilities to "experts," the concerns about ability to care for the newborn at home, and the limiting of visitors are major factors.

   COMMENT: It is also a cry of helplessness for help in becoming the "ideal" mother that women in the United States have in their fantasies.   T. B. BRAZELTON

RECOMMENDATIONS FOR CARE

1. *Special needs.* The special needs of a mother should be assessed through examining the history of her previous pregnancies, her desires and plans for the birth experience and infant, and the type of mothering she received.

2. *Parent preparation.* Group sessions with provision of information about emotional and physical aspects of labor and birth together with special exercises are of value to the parents-to-be. They help to relieve anxiety and allow the parents to share with others the many problems that arise during a normal pregnancy. This enables the mother to turn

a passive experience into an active one, to become a participant rather than a "victim."

3. *Need for companion.* It is helpful for a mother to have one person (her husband, mother, a friend, a midwife, a nurse, or an obstetrician) with her throughout labor and birth for guidance and reassurance. It has been shown that reassurance makes labor easier and that the more easily labor and delivery progress, the more quickly and happily the mother takes on her new infant.

4. *Enhancing attachment.* To enhance the mother's attachment to her baby the following arrangements should be provided during the birth and the postpartum period:

a. Privacy

b. Extended periods of father-mother-infant contact

c. Complete responsibility given to the mother for the care of her baby, with a nurse or midwife available as consultant

5. *Eye medications.* We recommend delaying eye medications such as silver nitrate for the infant until after the mother has had an extended period with her infant in the first hour after birth.

6. *First hour.* We suggest that the mother, father, and infant have a period alone together in privacy after the placenta is delivered and the episiotomy sutured (5 to 15 minutes after birth). We place a heat lamp or radiant panel over the nude infant, and the mother is instructed not to cover the infant. She may be encouraged to hold him against her bare chest. The period should be long enough so that the mother, infant, and father are able to participate fully in the exciting transformation of three separate individuals into a new family unit.

7. *Rooming-in.* The mother and infant should be kept together continuously or have long periods together in the days after the birth (Jackson, 1948). We suggest that the infant be in a small bassinet at his mother's side for a minimum of 5 hours a day so that she can learn about the infant's needs and activity. During this period it is necessary that she have control over the care of the infant while the nurse acts as consultant. Reversing the usual pattern of "experts" who correct a mother when she deviates from the usual routine is a step in the direction of increased confidence and competence for the mother. The postpartum period should be a time when the mother interacts with her infant so that she may become acquainted with him, learn about his needs, and be thoroughly satisfied with her own ability to meet these needs before she decides on the time of discharge (obviously only if her physical condition warrants this). The average mother in the United States has had so little previous experience with infants that she is unaware that certain characteristics of breathing, color, and bowel movements are normal. She may worry unnecessarily that many normal features and behaviors are a sign

of disease or abnormality. By keeping her baby with her and having the opportunity to talk with other mothers, she will realize that her own infant is normal. Mother-infant contact is particularly important when there has been a separation or an illness in either member of the dyad, for example, after a cesarean section delivery.

> COMMENT: Groups of mothers in hospital can gather, compare their concerns, their inadequacies, as well as their ecstasies. This gives them a great deal of support.   T. B. BRAZELTON

8. *Family visits.* The mother needs close contact with her husband and her other children during this period for emotional support. Sadness about separation from her husband and other children often compels a woman to leave before she is physically ready. The separation may have severe immediate and long-term effects on the siblings, especially those under 3 years of age.

9. *Caretakers.* In the postpartum period, even a perfectly normal woman is extremely sensitive to opinions and statements by the nurse and physician as to health of the infant and her ability to care for him. We strongly recommend that nurses, physicians, and other maternity staff be optimistic and avoid criticism of mothers. Much more will be gained by praising a mother for what she does well. The average mother may look at her infant objectively during the first 24 to 48 hours and then suddenly feel that she has the greatest and most handsome baby ever born. This normal process can be enhanced if nurses and physicians can give every mother the feeling that they, too, think her baby is uniquely grand.

> COMMENT: What about an opportunity just to let off steam—to cry, to show disappointment, to be a baby, etc. This may be more therapeutic for a mother than back slapping. But I doubt that many physicians can tolerate a mother's negative feelings. Most obstetricians, pediatricians, midwives, and nurses are in this racket because of the generally optimistic outcome.   T. B. BRAZELTON

After discharge the physician and nurse can be alert to evidence of the quality of mother-infant attachment. Levy (1951) has provided original and extremely helpful suggestions. For example, he wrote about maternal feelings:

> While questioning a mother and writing on a health record, the pediatrician paused and remarked, "That's a very pretty baby." The mother, who had the baby in her lap, looked at him, said "Thank you," and smiled, but she did not look down at her baby. Accumulation of data in this study appears to corroborate the conclusion that the mother's typical response, after praise of the baby, is to look at it, and that

absence of the glance indicates less than the usual maternal feeling.

Response to the compliment may be as tangible evidence as response of a knee jerk to a tap on the patella. Both must be done in the appropriate manner; although the stimuli will never be exactly the same, the response is forthcoming regardless of the difference in personalities that elicit them.*

COMMENT: As physicians, nurses, and other maternity staff caring for new dyads or triads, why do we not encourage all of this automatically? Why have we allowed such rationalizations as "infection," "sterility," and "optimal medical care" to push out these important aspects of childbirth and caring for the newborn and his parents? Surely, we are not all this insensitive to the vital importance of these issues. I believe that we have allowed it to become institutional practice to separate adults from their infants for three very good *unconscious* reasons:

1. As physicians and nurses, we basically like to help people depend on us. If we allow them too much choice or autonomy, our rewards are minimized.

2. To do this most effectively we must push a pathological model, one in which childbirth and neonatal care are based on treating pathology rather than reinforcing for the strengths that are present in most people and for the odds that are enormously in favor of a good outcome.

3. All adults who care about babies are competitive with all other adults, and each would like to be the primary caretaker of the attractive helpless infant. *Unconsciously* we devalue the role of parents to fulfill our own role as *the* important caretaker of this new infant. No one would ever admit to this drive, but it is universal. Perhaps we could use this same energy to care for the dyad or triad (mother, father, new infant) if we take Klaus and Kennell's advice and change the training of nurses and pediatricians to orient them toward roles of caretaking for cementing rather than splitting families!

T. B. BRAZELTON

Broussard and Hartner (1970) noted that mothers' perceptions of their infants on a simple rating scale given to mothers at one month was strikingly predictive of psychiatric problems in their children at 4½ years and 10 to 11 years of age.

SUMMARY

An assessment of the needs of the human mother makes it apparent that the physical facilities available in the United States are probably inadequate to meet her requirements fully. Her physical needs during

---

*From Levy, D.: Observations of attitudes and behavior in the child health center, Chicago, 1951, Year Book Medical Publishers, Inc.

labor and birth are met adequately, as are the physical facilities for resuscitation and close observation of the infant. However, the standard postpartum arrangements in the United States, which bring the infant to the mother for only 20 to 30 minutes out of every 4-hour period, are probably insufficent for some women to develop a close attachment with their infant. After observing other maternity care systems in the Western world, such as those in Denmark, Holland, and Britain, we have come to believe that there are several other essentials that have been forgotten in the United States. The infant should be near his mother so that she can learn how he reacts and may begin to meet his needs as they arise. This permits her, during her short hospitalization (three to six days in the United States; it is seven to ten days in most European countries), to be prepared to care for the infant completely at the time of discharge (knowing how to feed, clean, soothe, and relax the infant, and how to react to all the little changes such as hiccups, skin changes, burps, and funny noises that appear normally in every infant).

The small amount of time that the American mother has with her infant in the hospital does not give her adequate exposure to him, with the result that she is not fully acquainted with him at the time of discharge. The first days after discharge are described by many mothers as "hellish," or as the most difficult days of their lives. Often the mother's idea of what a good mother should be able to accomplish with her baby has been built up to such an unrealistic level by magazine articles and college courses that she may exhaust herself and then have little tolerance for the many little problems that arise in the course of the early care of her infant. Almost all units in the United States can arrange to keep the baby in a small bassinet at the mother's side during most of the day. We believe that the existing facilities and routines in the United States can easily be adapted so that the conditions are optimal for the development of parent-infant attachment in the first days of life.

COMMENT: One of the most useful techniques I have found for relieving new mothers of their anxiety about their own adequacy in the face of the new infant is to show her the strengths of the infant as a potent individual. When she sees that he has a personality of his own, she no longer feels entirely responsible for this "lump of clay," and it becomes an interaction between them rather than her "action" on him. We have used the Brazelton Neonatal Behavior Assessment most successfully for this.   T. B. BRAZELTON

Chapter 4

Caring for parents of a premature or sick infant

JOHN H. KENNELL and MARSHALL H. KLAUS
with supplemental report by BERTRAND CRAMER

> It is better by far to put the little one in an incubator
> by its mother's bedside, the supervision which she exercises
> is not to be lightly estimated.
>
> PIERRE BUDIN

When the care of the premature infant moved from the fairgrounds to the hospital, most of Martin Cooney's clinical practices were adopted, including the exclusion of the mother from the nursery. The flavor of this period of premature care may best be expressed by quoting from the list of "don'ts" concerning premature infants in Gleich's 1942 report.

1. Don't handle the premature infant unnecessarily.
2. Don't allow anyone except the nurse and the physician into the premature infant's room. Friends and relatives should be kept out.
3. Don't feed the average premature infant oftener than every three hours.
4. Don't make a habit of giving physics to premature infants. Castor oil, for example, causes many of them to vomit and constipates them the next day.
5. Don't leave a bottle of milk in the baby's mouth and walk away.
6. Don't allow premature infants to sleep in the room with other children. Premature infants contract disease easily. The supposedly healthly children may be carriers.
7. Don't depart from a regular schedule of feeding, bathing, and dressing.*

These are a few examples of the prohibitions of this preantibiotic era, which was characterized by strict rules, rigid feeding schedules, and authoritarian control of hospital divisions to prevent the spread of infec-

*From Gleich, M.: The premature infant, Part III, Arch. Pediatr. **59**:172-173, 1942.

tion. In the first premature nursery in the United States, at the Michael Reese Hospital in Chicago, babies remained in the nursery from ten days to three months. Mothers were requested to come to the hospital before the baby was discharged and were taught how to care for their babies and were given written instructions. If the heating facilities at home were inadequate, the mother was loaned a small, electrically heated bed.

Meanwhile, across the Atlantic in Newcastle-on-Tyne, Miller, working with Sir James Spence, was studying the nursing of prematurely born infants in the home. In a comparison of home and hospital nursing in 1945 to 1947, he found that both were equally favorable for premature infants weighing above 3½ pounds at birth. He concluded that home care was safer from the standpoint of infection, more economical, and even more important, served to unify the infant's family. Miller (1948) stressed that everyone in the family should have assigned duties so that "everyone interested is involved and all have a sense of achievement, which gives the child a good start and is far better than if he were taken away to a hospital and returned a month or six weeks later, an unknown infant, feared and strange."

Home care of premature infants did not spread to the United States but was confined to England and Europe. Therefore the first observations of the parents of premature and sick infants in the United States in the 1950s and 1960s were made at a time when parents were totally excluded from the nursery. The reactions of mothers as described by the pioneering investigators may have been extreme because of the total separation from their infants. However, Stewart reports that the general pattern appears to be the same today despite more relaxed visiting regulations (Blake et al., 1975).

BASIC CONSIDERATIONS

In 1953 Prugh made a series of sensitive and insightful observations of the mothers of premature infants. He reported that during the first months of the baby's life the mother is forced into a supporting, peripheral position. Because of her unwanted, involuntary role, the mother, particularly if this is her first child, "often finds herself the prey of disturbing, and at times strongly conflicting, feelings" (Prugh, 1953). Anxiety and guilt were the two most evident emotions in the mother. She was understandably apprehensive about her infant's survival during the early period of hospitalization; however, persistent anxiety often indicated other stresses. Her feelings of guilt heightened her feelings of anxiety. She feared that something that she did or did not do during pregnancy affected the baby and produced the prematurity.

Prugh noted that the mother may have also felt guilty because she could not care for the baby as skillfully as the nurse. Although the mother was grateful to the nurse and physician, she resented the necessity for intervention by a substitute mother. "A mother often became jealous of the capable nurse and this led to an unconscious attempt to handle such unacceptable feelings by projecting the jealous resentment onto the nurse, leading to suspicion and hostility." Although the nurse was the object of resentment, she could serve as a valuable support to the mother during the difficult period of the infant's hospitalization. The mother must proceed emotionally at her own pace. "It is important for the nurse to accept her as she finds her, without judgment or criticism" (Prugh, 1953).

Prugh stressed that it is important that the mother see the premature baby as soon as possible to help "minimize the frightening fantasies which she may develop and help her to begin the process of handling any 'emotional lag.'" He described "emotional lag" as an alienation of feeling that any new mother experiences during her early relationship with her baby. The "difficulty in experiencing the warm, maternal feelings which she expected" is not confined to mothers of premature infants but may be especially intense when mothers are denied close contact with their full-term infants (Prugh, 1953).

> COMMENT: There are times when it is not possible for the mother to see her baby prior to being taken to a special intensive care nursery. We have found in these cases that it is helpful to at least share with the mother some photographs of premature babies. This helps to reduce the dissonance between what she pictures as "the Gerber baby" and what a premature baby actually looks like so that when she does see her baby, the discrepancy between what she expects and how the baby looks is less.   K. BARNARD

Kaplan and Mason (1960) viewed the reactions of mothers to the birth of a premature infant in the context of an acute reaction to trauma rather than in the context of an ongoing pathological process. Their approach is in tune with the crisis theory concepts of Caplan (1965). He defines crises as "time-limited periods of disequilibrium or behavioral and subjective upsets which are precipitated by an inescapable demand or burden to which the person is temporarily unable to respond adequately. During this period of tension the person grapples with the problem and develops novel resources, both by calling upon internal reserves and making use of the help of others. Those resources are then used to handle the precipitating factor and the person achieves once more a steady state." Following Caplan's definition of crisis, Kaplan and Mason recognized that the reactions to a stressful event, such as the birth of a premature infant, could be heavily conditioned by previously existing personality factors. However, they emphasized that hospital practices and the role of health agencies can influence the previously existing personality factors. They delineated four psychological tasks that the mother of a premature infant must master to establish a "healthy mother-child relationship."

1. The first of these tasks should take place at the time of delivery. It is the preparation for a possible loss of the child whose life is in jeopardy. This "anticipatory grief" involves a withdrawal from the relationship already established to the coming child so that she still hopes the baby will survive but simultaneously prepares for its death.

2. In a second task she must face and acknowledge her maternal failure to deliver a normal full-term baby.

3. The third is the resumption of the process of relating to the baby which had been previously interrupted. She has previously prepared herself for a loss, but as the baby improves she must now respond with hope and anticipation to this change.

4. In the fourth task the mother must come to understand how a premature baby differs from a normal baby in terms of its special needs and growth patterns. In order to provide the extra amount of care and protection, the mother must see the baby as a premature with special needs and characteristics. But it is equally important for her to see that these needs are temporary and will yield in time to normal patterns.[*]

We believe that the tasks outlined by Kaplan and his group are in part the result of the hospital setting. It is our impression that a mother need not start to prepare for the death if she is given extra support and early contact with her infant in the first hour of life. We believe that she will have a different set of tasks if the physical arrangements in the hospital and her contacts with the health profession are altered.

COMMENT: Although the mother may be helped to realize that the baby will probably live, she still must face the loss of not having had a full-term infant. Therefore the emotional response as outlined in these four points, although being less profound, will probably still be in evidence, even if the mother has early contact with the infant.

K. BARNARD

Mason (1963) reported a study in which he predicted the quality of the early mother-child relationship from information gathered during interviews with mothers of premature infants during the lying-in period. By utilizing the interview technique once again, an independent judge evaluated the mother-child relationship between six and ten weeks after the baby was discharged. A good outcome was defined as one in which

[*]From Kaplan, D. M., and Mason, E. A.: Maternal reactions to premature birth viewed as an acute emotional disorder, Am. J. Orthopsychiatry 30:539-552, 1960. Copyright 1960, the American Orthopsychiatric Association, Inc. Reproduced by permission.

the mother was moderately successful in meeting the baby's physical and emotional needs; the baby gained weight, or the family seemed pleased with the baby. In the cases judged to have a poor outcome, the mother was hostile or irritable and impatient; the baby was neglected and either lethargic or in poor health; or the family was severely disrupted. The predictions agreed with the outcome ratings in 90% of the cases (seventeen of nineteen cases; $p < .01$).

Mason found that certain aspects of the mother's coping mechanism were extremely valuable in predicting the nature of her subsequent relationship with her child. The interviewers predicted a good outcome if the mother showed and expressed a fairly high level of anxiety, actively sought information about the condition of her baby, and showed strong maternal feelings for the baby, even when she had not yet seen or held him. Strong support by the husband and a previous successful experience with a premature child also indicated a favorable outcome.

If the mother showed a low level of anxiety and activity, chances were that her relationship with her child would be poor. These mothers often denied that they were anxious and focused their concern on matters other than the infant's condition. They often lacked support from husbands and relatives and evidenced little maternal feeling. Mason (1963) concluded that efforts to prevent poor outcomes for mothers and their premature infants should be directed toward increasing "the interaction between the mother and her premature baby."

> COMMENT: The mother demonstrating a low level of anxiety about the child may simply be overwhelmed by other circumstances of her life. For example, in a recent study, when asked what her primary concerns were at one month post partum, about 65% of the sample mothers of premature babies had concerns that related to the child or parenting; 35% of the mothers did not. In looking at circumstances within these 35% of the mothers, there were major circumstances of financial constraint or family problems that were their primary concern. The answer may not always be to increase interaction between the mother and her premature baby; circumstances may require investigation of what may be blocking the mother from having the capacity to interact with her baby.   K. BARNARD

During the same year Blau and associates (1963) examined the possible psychogenic etiology of premature births. They compared the results of psychiatric and psychological tests administered one to three days after birth to thirty women who delivered prematurely and thirty matched control mothers of full-term infants. They did find clinical differences between the two groups. The mother of a premature infant tended to be more immature, uncertain about her role as a woman and mother, and needed more outside emotional support during pregnancy. Blau noted that "though ambivalence is undoubtedly common to all pregnancies, the premature mother has less, in that she tends to become more definitely negative to the pregnancy and hostile to the fetus. She harbors more destructive fantasies about the outcome to herself and to the baby, and is more apprehensive regarding difficulties in labor and delivery." However, it should be remembered that these intriguing observations were made after birth, not before.

Although revolutionary changes in the approach to the diagnosis and management of other infants and children in the hospital were made during this same period, between 1945 and 1960, the premature infant in the nursery remained untouched and unaffected. For example, the scientific approach to fluid and electrolytes of Gamble and Darrow, which required the measurement of a number of blood constituents, had no effect on the care of the premature infant. The premature nursery remained a fortress, protected from innovations, investigations, and parents. It is important to keep in mind that regulations for pediatric hospitals in the early 1950s limited parental visiting to only 30 to 60 minutes once or twice a week.

During the late 1950s and early 1960s the walls of the nursery-fortress began to crumble. It was at this time that the first systematic studies of traditional nursery care procedures such as temperature and humidity control were initiated. Although a few nurseries, such as in the University Hospitals of Cleveland, Ohio, permitted parents into the nursery in the early 1950s, the prevailing policy throughout the United States was to allow parents in the nursery for the first time only a day or two before the infant's discharge, if at all.

The first study to investigate the feasibility of permitting parents into the premature nursery began in December, 1964, at Stanford University, California. Barnett and colleagues (1970) questioned whether parents of premature infants suffered from severe deprivation due to separation from their infants while they were hospitalized. For a two-year period they studied the practicality of allowing mothers (forty-four in all) into the nursery soon after birth, first to handle and then to feed their infants while they were still in incubators. The mothers, because of state rules, wore masks and gowns, and the nurses in the unit instructed them in handwashing procedures. Initially the nurses accompanied the mothers and stood by them while they handled their babies through the portholes of the incubators. On subsequent visits a nurse remained nearby to answer questions. When the babies were able to be fed easily by nipple, the mothers were encouraged to assume this task.

The threat of infection had been a formidable deterrent to permitting parents to enter the nursery. To evaluate the possibility that parents would bring pathogenic agents into the premature unit, cultures were taken weekly for the entire period that mothers were allowed into the unit from the umbilicus, skin, and nares of each infant and from the nursery equipment. These investigators observed that mothers washed more frequently and more thoroughly than both the nurses and house officers. The results of these cultures (Table 4-1) as well as the results of studies done by Williams and Oliver (1969), Silverman and Sinclair (1967), and Forfar and MacCabe (1958) showed no increase in potentially pathogenic organisms. In fact, at Stanford University the number of positive cultures actually declined between 1964 and 1965. It has been speculated that the infant may pick up nonpathogenic bacteria from his mother, which provide him with protection against pathogenic hospital organisms, and hence the number of positive cultures decreases. "A chart review showed no occurrence of staphylococcal, hemolytic streptococcal, or upper respiratory viral disease in the infants during the time when mothers went into the nursery. From these data it would appear that the presence of mothers in the nursery did not increase the risk or the occurrence of infection" (Barnett et al., 1970).

A series of orientation meetings with the premature nursery staff preceded the introduction of mothers into the nursery. Although many of the nurses were originally skeptical of the program, they soon became wholeheartedly enthusiastic. Bringing parents into the nursery did not disrupt the organization or interfere with medical procedures in the unit.

Table 4-1. Culture results of infants and equipment by years[*]

Nursery population	1964	1965	1966
Number of infants in unit	38	48	49
Number and percent of mothers allowed to handle infants in incubators	2 (5%)	27 (56%)	12 (25%)
Infant data			
Total cultures of nares and umbilicus	680	718	694
Number of potential pathogens isolated and percent of positive cultures[†]	146 (21%)	102 (14%)	119 (17%)
Equipment data			
Total cultures of equipment[‡]	390	420	489
Number of potential pathogens isolated and percent of positive cultures[†]	44 (11%)	20 (5%)	24 (5%)

*From Barnett, C. R., Leiderman, P. H., Grobstein, R., and Klaus, M. H.: Neonatal separation: the maternal side of interactional deprivation, Pediatrics **45**:197-205, 1970.
†Includes coagulase-positive staphylococci, beta hemolytic streptococci, *Pseudomonas*, *Proteus*, pneumococcus, yeast, *Clostridium perfringens*.
‡Weekly cultures of incubator gaskets, water reservoirs, oxygen masks, suction bottles, and sink handles.

The nurses readily included the mothers in their babies' caretaking routines, and they often remarked how helpful it was to have parents watching and caring for their own babies. This is not to say that all parents are a joy; there are overly demanding parents just as there are variations in the personalities and abilities of physicians and nurses.

From this group thirteen mothers were selected for detailed study both during their infants' hospitalizations and after discharge. All but two of the thirteen mothers invited into the nursery reacted positively to the experience. These two mothers refused to enter the nursery. Each thought that close contact with her baby would increase her feelings of attachment, making the baby's possible death more difficult to endure. These two families delayed a month before naming their babies and suffered from "anticipatory grief" for a period well beyond the time that the infant was declared out of danger.

The admission of parents to the premature nursery took place so smoothly that it is easy to forget the grave concerns of the physicians and nurses who had received their training and had years of experience in a parent-free, premature nursery-fortress. The spectre of a disastrous and disgraceful epidemic or increase in death rate haunted those who broke with the long-established routines of the past.

The mothers who did enter the nursery typically touched and explored their infants' bodies repeatedly during their early visits. As the mothers assumed more caretaking tasks, such as feeding and diapering, this exploratory behavior decreased. Despite the plastic barrier of the incubator, the mothers would often talk and coo to the baby spontaneously.

The investigators observed differences between the mothers allowed into the nursery and those who were excluded. Those who had entered the nursery showed increased commitment to the infant, more confidence in their mothering abilities, and greater stimulating and caretaking skills.

When mothers are first permitted to touch their premature babies, they begin by circling the incubator and touching the baby's extremities with the tips of their fingers (Klaus et al., 1970) (Fig. 4-1). Their reactions are quite different from those of the parents of full-term infants. At the end of the first visit parents of full-term infants are stroking the trunk with the palm of their hand. Often a mother will align her head with her baby's in the *en face* position. Fig. 4-2 compares the amount of time mothers of full-term infants spend in the *en face* position with the amount of time that mothers of premature infants spend in this position. Fig. 4-3 shows a mother in this *en face* position. It is unclear whether these differences are due to what the mother has been told about the baby, the physical barrier presented by the incubator, or the baby's small size and appearance.

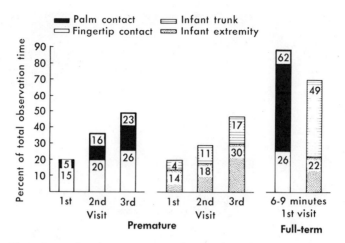

Fig. 4-1. Fingertip and palm contact on the trunk and extremities at the first three postnatal visits in nine mothers of premature infants compared with the sixth to ninth minute of twelve mothers of full-term infants at their first visit. (Modified from Klaus, M. H., Kennell, J. H., Plumb, N., and Zuehlke, S.: Pediatrics **46**:187-192, 1970.)

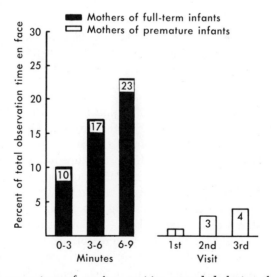

Fig. 4-2. The percentage of *en face* position recorded during the first visit of twelve mothers of full-term infants and the first three visits of nine mothers of premature infants. (From Klaus, M. H., Kennell, J. H., Plumb, N., and Zuehlke, S.: Pediatrics **46**:187-192, 1970.)

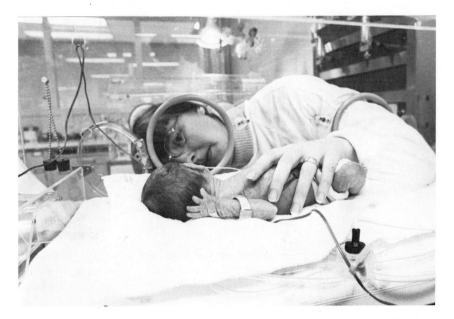

Fig. 4-3. A mother of a premature infant in the *en face* position. (From Klaus, M. H., and Fanaroff, A. A.: Care of the high-risk neonate, Philadelphia, 1973, W. B. Saunders Co.)

COMMENT: *En face* is an important position for mothers and infants, since it is the one position assumed during caregiver-infant contact that increases the chances for social interaction between the mother or caregiver and the infant.   K. BARNARD

In Russia the mothers take a limited part in the care of the premature infant. They live either at home or in the hospital. One of the authors (M.H.K.) had an opportunity to observe the care of premature infants in Russia. In one hospital there were 150 premature infants, and every day about sixty mothers came from home in the morning to spend the whole day with their babies. They showered, changed into clean smocks, had breakfast, and breastfed their babies. Fig. 4-4 shows a group of mothers waiting to breastfeed their infants; Fig. 4-5 shows a mother preparing to express milk for a night feeding. They were able to spend time with their babies, had a chance to talk with the physician, and believed that they were doing something positive to help their babies. In the Leningrad Obstetrical Institute mothers were not discharged after a few days but stayed in the hospital until their premature babies were discharged—often as long as sixty to ninety days—and breastfed the entire time. Sadly,

Fig. 4-4. A group of Russian mothers waiting to breastfeed their premature babies.

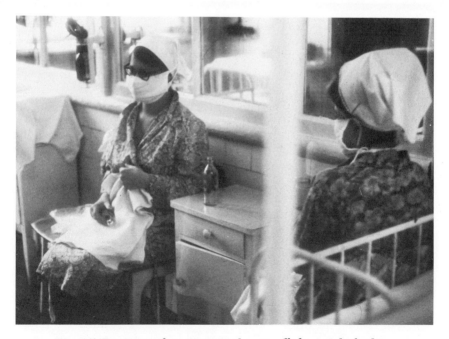

Fig. 4-5. Russian mother expressing breast milk for a night feeding.

their husbands were unable to visit, and they were able to communicate only through letters. These mothers tended to look depressed. In all the Russian hospitals visited, whether the mothers came in the morning to take care of their premature babies or lived in, they did nothing but breastfeed. The babies were brought to them wrapped, and mothers were not allowed to change the baby or participate in other caretaking tasks (Fig. 4-6).

In an attempt to evaluate this practice, we tried to learn about the incidence of battering or failure-to-thrive syndrome (Helfer and Kempe, 1968). All Russian physicians completely denied that battering occurred. In each hospital visited this one question led to a long discussion. The physicians could not believe that infants in the United States were battered. We also questioned Russian physicians about wife battering, which is known to occur. The answers to these questions were confusing. Because they denied both practices, the answers to the question of child battering are difficult to interpret. They explained that battering probably did not exist because Russian women are permitted unlimited abortions. If a woman has a child she does not want, she can also place him in an infant house, which will care for him on a 24-hour basis through the third year. Usually the mothers visit once or twice a week. It is the right of every Russian mother

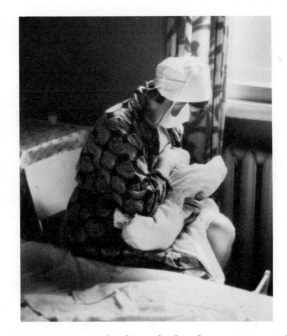

Fig. 4-6. A Russian mother breastfeeding her premature infant.

to admit her child to an infant house; however, only one out of every 150 Russian infants is sent there. In an effort to evaluate the effect of Russian obstetrical caretaking practices, one of the authors (M.H.K.) calculated the rate of admissions for full-term and premature infants in several units and found that the percentage of infants in infant houses who are premature is eight to ten times greater than the percentage of infants delivered prematurely. When the child is 3 years old, his mother decides whether he is to be adopted or taken home. Interestingly, Russian premature infants are given up for adoption twice as often as full-term infants. Thus Russians also have problems with maternal attachment when infants are born prematurely. From this brief look it would appear that permitting mothers only to breastfeed will not eliminate or prevent these problems of attachment in premature infants.

Baragwanath Hospital in South Africa provides another model of premature infant caretaking. There mothers of premature infants live in a room adjoining the premature nursery, and at each feeding time enter the nursery to feed and handle their babies. Dr. Kahn instituted this arrangement because of a shortage of nurses. However, his solution appears to have multiple benefits. It allows the mother to continue producing milk, permits her to take on the care of the infant more easily, greatly reduces the caretaker time required for these infants, and allows a group of mothers of premature infants to talk over their situation and gain from mutual discussion (Bell, 1960; Kahn et al., 1954).

> COMMENT: We have found that parent-to-parent groups are extremely effective in helping parents deal with some of their questions, and they provide the support that helps them handle this crisis. Our experience suggests that contact both with other parents going through the crisis and with "graduate" parents who made it through are helpful. There seem to be three periods of time when a contact with another parent is important. The first is at birth or soon after, the second is when the parents are ready to take their baby home, and the third is when the infant is about 5 or 6 months old.   K. BARNARD

Special mention should be made of the work of Tafari and Sterky (1974) in Ethiopia. They increased the number of babies cared for in a unit fivefold when they permitted mothers to live within the crowded unit 24 hours a day. Mother-infant pairs were discharged when the infants weighed an average of 1.7 kilograms, and most of the mothers breastfed. Previous to this most of the infants had gone home bottle feeding and often died of intercurrent respiratory and gastrointestinal infections. Tafari's procedure is probably appropriate for 80% of the world. Policies in premature nurseries have a direct relation to infant mortality when the cost of prepared milk amounts to such a high proportion of the weekly income.

Two long-term studies on the effects of early mother-infant separation as a result of special care nursery policies, one at Stanford University and the other at Case Western Reserve University, Ohio, have nearly been completed (Table 4-2). The hypothesis in each study was that if human mothers are affected by this period of separation, one might see altered maternal attachment and mothering behavior during the first weeks and months of life in separated as opposed to nonseparated mothers, and as a consequence of this, differences in later infant development.

In the Stanford University study three groups of mothers from similar socioeconomic backgrounds were observed. One group of mothers was given "contact" with their premature-infants in the intensive care unit in the first five days of life, a second group of mothers was "separated" from their premature infants with only visual contact for the first twenty-one days, and a third group of mothers of full-term infants had routine contact with their infants at feedings during a three-day hospitalization. When the separated infants reached 2100 grams, at ages ranging from 3 to 12 weeks, they were transferred to a discharge nursery where their mothers were allowed to be with them as much as they desired for the seven to ten days until discharge at a weight of 2500 grams.

The interactions between the mothers of these three groups and their own infants were observed three times: just prior to discharge and a week and a month after discharge. The behavior of the mothers of full-term infants was not the same as that of the mothers of premature infants. The former group smiled at their infants more and had more ventral contact with their infants. No striking differences were found between the behaviors of the separated and contact mothers of premature infants.

Table 4-2. Studies of early and late maternal contact in the premature nursery

	Stanford University*	Case Western Reserve University
Early contact	22†	27 (1537 grams)‡
Late contact	22†	26 (1428 grams)‡
Number of married mothers	44	42
Socioeconomic status	Middle class	Wide range
Hollingshead Index	3	1 to 5
Length of follow-up (months)	22	42

*Also included 24 full-term infants and mothers.
†Range of birth weights: 890 to 1899 grams.
‡Mean weight.

However, the primiparous mothers in the noncontact group showed significantly less self-confidence in their ability to care for their infants (Seashore et al., 1973). Sameroff (1975) interpreted this as suggesting the following:

> The previous successful childbirth experience of multiparous mothers seemed to insulate them from the debilitating effects of being separated from the premature offspring of their current pregnancy. In the group of mothers who were allowed to visit in the intensive care nursery, the initial deficits in self-confidence were reduced by the time the infant was ready to go home. Only one of the mothers in the separated group showed such a positive change. It would appear from this data that allowing mothers, especially primipara, to be in contact with their premature infants reduces their feelings of inadequacy.*

> COMMENT: Early contact may be more crucial for mothers who, because of their previous life circumstances, are at high risk for attachment, in addition to the prematurity.   K. BARNARD

Leifer and associates (1972) also reported an important set of clinical findings that had not been anticipated. Only one of twenty-two mothers in the contact group became divorced during the period of the study, whereas five of twenty-two mothers in the separated group were divorced. It is worthy of note that a prerequisite for admission into the study was that the parents planned to keep and raise their babies. Surprisingly, in two cases in the separated group, neither parent wanted custody of their baby, and so the baby was given up for adoption.

In the Case Western Reserve University study fifty-three mothers of premature infants were assigned, on the basis of when the baby was born, to two groups, "early contact" and "late contact." Mothers in the early contact group were allowed to come into the premature nursery to handle and care for their premature infants one to five days after birth. The late contact group of mothers was not permitted to enter the nursery until twenty-one days after birth. For the first three weeks these mothers had only visual contact with their infants through the nursery windows.

Time-lapse movies of both groups of mothers feeding their infants were obtained just before discharge and one month later. Fig. 4-7 shows a posed mother illustrating four of the many behaviors that were analyzed from the 10-minute feeding films. In addition, to determine whether early contact influenced maternal behavior, which then affected infant development, Bayley developmental examinations were performed just before discharge and again at 9, 15, and 21 months of age, and a Stanford-Binet test was administered at 42 months of age.

*From Sameroff, A.: In Avery, G. B., editor: Neonatology, Philadelphia, 1975, J. B. Lippincott Co.

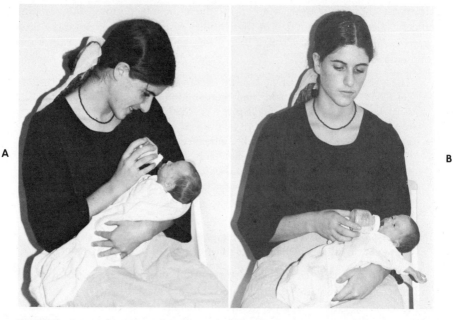

Fig. 4-7. A posed mother showing two different caretaking positions. **A,** Infant is held in close contact (mother's body touching infant's), mother is looking at infant *en face,* bottle is perpendicular to the mouth, and milk is in the tip of the nipple. **B,** Infant's trunk is held away from mother, mother is looking at infant but not *en face,* and bottle is not perpendicular to the mouth.

The mothers who had early contact spent significantly more time looking at their infants during the first filmed feeding. Similarly, there was a correlation between the amount of time mothers looked at their babies during the second filmed feeding and the infants' IQ on the Stanford-Binet test at 42 months of age. That is, mothers who had early contact with their infants spent more time looking at them during feedings, and these children had significantly higher IQs ($r = .71$) and significantly a mean of 99 for early contact children compared with a mean of 85 for late contact children ($p < .05$).

> COMMENT: Mothers who in the hospital period and early first months of life look more at their infant generally tend to be more sensitive to the infant's cues and provide more appropriate stimulation to the infant than mothers who look less at their infant.   K. BARNARD

Interestingly, Bayley developmental scores for the two groups of infants were not significantly different for the first twenty-one months of life (Kennell et al., 1975).

Several problems associated with each of these studies should be mentioned. Both investigations were continued for two years, during which there were changes of procedure and personnel. Eighteen patients were lost from the Case Western Reserve University study during the long follow-up period. Had these patients been included in the testing, the final results may have been altered (Moss, 1965).

Studies of premature mother-infant dyads are especially difficult because of problems that occur during the long and stressful period of hospitalization, combined with the almost impossible task of obtaining a homogeneous population for both groups with respect to parity, sex of infant, birth weight, gestational age, religion, cultural background, and socioeconomic status. It is also impossible to control for the early life experiences of the mother, as well as for stresses that occur at home. Neither group of investigators found it possible to run the early and late contact groups in the nursery simultaneously. Each study had a three-month period of late contact followed by a three-month period of early contact to prevent late contact mothers from observing early contact mothers in the nursery. Eventually both studies were discontinued because they were too painful for the nurses, who thought that it was unfair not to permit all mothers to have early contact with their infants.

As part of the Stanford University study, the parents were interviewed seven times before the infant was discharged. This would tend to pull both the early and late contact mothers into the hospital, possibly increasing the number of visits the late contact mothers made to the hospital. It is surprising that in this study the early contact mothers visited only an average of once every six days. Fanaroff and co-workers (1972) studied the visiting patterns of mothers in a nursery where they were allowed unlimited telephone calls or visits. They determined that 25% of those mothers who visit or phone on an average of less than three times in a two-week period will exhibit significant mothering disorders (Table 4-3).

Table 4-3. Visiting frequency and outcome in the intensive care nursery[*]

	> 3 visits/2 weeks	< 3 visits/2 weeks
Number	111	38
Follow-up	108	38
Disorders of mothering	2 (1.8%)	9 (23%) p = < .001[†]
Abandoned	1	1
Battered	0	2
Failure-to-thrive	0	5
Fostered	1	1

*From Fanaroff, A. A., Kennell, J. H., and Klaus, M. H.: Follow-up of low birth-weight infants—the predictive value of maternal visiting patterns, Pediatrics **49:**288-290, 1972.
†Chi square.

As recently as 1970, only one third of premature nurseries permitted parents to enter the nursery. Barnett and colleagues mailed questionnaires to 2729 premature nurseries. Sixty-one percent, or 1644, of the nurseries responded but only 1444 questionnaires provided usable information. Thirty-four percent, or 486, of the responding nurseries allowed mothers to visit and handle their babies. Of these nurseries, 60% also allowed the father to enter and touch the baby. It is of special interest to explore the reasons governing these nurseries' change-of-visiting practices. Thirty-five percent of the nurseries reported that they first learned of parent visiting practices at workshops in other local hospitals, 25% learned from a visiting nurse or physician, and 22% learned while attending national or pediatric meetings. Of the small group that mentioned literature as a source, 20% listed the *Reader's Digest,* various women's magazines, or a local newspaper. Of the 486 nurseries that offered parental visiting, only eight, or 1.6%, reported having based their decision on research (either bacteriological or psychological). Eighty-one percent of the nurseries gave common sense as their reason for allowing mothers into the nursery. Grobstein strongly believes that there is an urgent need for a far more scientific approach to nursery care, which assigns high priority to the psychological and social needs of the parents and infants. "If the social organization of nursery care ignores these, the trend will continue toward avoidance of professional, institutional care—as evidenced by the increase in home births and similar 'natural' practices which defeat the application of modern obstetrics and pediatrics" (Barnett et al., 1972).

While these changes in visiting policies have been taking place, remarkable strides have been made in improving both the survival rate and quality of the survivors. Stewart and Reynold's (1974) observations reveal that if all the modern techniques, which include early fluid administration and close and detailed monitoring of oxygen, environmental temperature, pH, respiration, and heart rate, are employed in treating the premature infant, he has only a slightly greater chance than a full-term infant of being disabled. It is especially important to note that the studies of Stewart and colleagues include only the very small infants with birth weights under 1500 grams, infants who are usually considered high risk for developmental disorders.

> COMMENT: There should be some caution, since Stewart and Reynold's findings are not widely duplicated as yet by others. The data only represent follow-up before school entry.   K. BARNARD

Recently a burst of studies of infant stimulation has appeared that provides a connection between the many studies of mothering and the future development of the infant. Table 4-4 summarizes some of the observations of infant stimulation. These studies reveal that if a small premature infant is either touched, rocked, fondled, or cuddled daily during his stay in the nursery, he has fewer apneic periods, increased weight gain, a smaller number of stools, as well as an advance in some areas of higher central nervous system functioning, which persists for months after discharge from the hospital. With a shortage of personnel to provide this care, it seems logical to allow parents to provide this special mothering, this additional stimulation that helps a small premature infant to thrive.

Parents need encouragement so that they will continue to provide this stimulation. The premature infant normally has prolonged sleep periods with only short intervals of wakefulness, which is disconcerting to the parents. Mothers often sit beside their babies' incubators for long periods waiting for them to awaken. Since the parents' affection and enthusiasm are stimulated and sustained by seeing the baby's open eyes, it is helpful to explain to them that as the premature baby develops, he is awake for increasingly longer periods of time. Parents are often persistent and ingenious in arousing their babies to "send a message" to them; for example, parents will stroke or pat the baby who responds by opening his eyes. If the mother is able to stimulate and meet his special needs, the baby she will take home will be more responsive and closer in behavior to the full-term infant she had hoped to deliver.

> COMMENT: The whole business of stimulation should not be thought of as just providing additional or more stimulation to the premature infant. More thought should be given to the appropriate types of stimulation and its timing; in fact, many infants are bombarded with stimuli either in the hospital nursery or in the early home situation, when their capacity to deal with stimulus overload is less. They may even develop irritability and crying behavior because of stimulus overload, which is then difficult for the family.   K. BARNARD

In their detailed follow-up study of infants weighing 1500 grams or less, Blake and colleagues (1975) have noted that many English mothers go through three phases in the first six months after the baby's discharge from the hospital.

At first there is a "honeymoon" phase. Excitement prevails, and the parents are usually euphoric at the time of the first visit to the clinic seven to ten days after discharge. A period of exhaustion follows, when the euphoria has waned and the mother has many minor complaints about the management of the baby, particularly about feeding. The mother not only looks exhausted but is exhausted. The feeding problems are often genuine. This phase will last until the baby begins to smile and respond to his mother, which can take anywhere from a few days to several weeks.

Table 4-4. Effects of stimulation in newborn period

Number of patients	Premature or full term	Type of stimulation	Outcome		Reference
			Experimental group	Control group	
60	Premature	Sensory, tactile Kinesthetic (experimental handled) 2.73 times more than controls for 14 days	Greater incidence of morbidity involving genital area conditions* / Longer in state of quiescence‡ / Passed less feces*	Greater incidence of morbidity involving eye, mouth, body rash† / Cried more‡ / Cried more before feeding§	Hasselmeyer, 1964
10	Premature	Tactile, stroked 5 min./hr./day for 10 days	Regained birth weight in 10.8 days, active and healthy 7 to 8 months after discharge / On Bayley developmental test 7 to 8 months after discharge 1 infant showed poor gross and fine motor development‖	Regained birth weight in 15.4 days; 3 infants more than standard deviation below growth mean; 2 of 4 infants suspicious for cerebral palsy; 4 infants below mean for age in motor development‖	Solkoff et al., 1969
32	Full term	Rockerbox	Faster rocking speed (60 times/min.) less distress‡ / After rock, decreased activity level¶ / Distress declined*	Slower rocking speed (30 times/min.) less reduction in activity†	Van den Daele, 1970
18	8 premature 10 full term	Rockerbox White noise	Rockerbox quieted down infant* / Sound and rockerbox quieted down infant more than rockerbox alone‡		Van den Daele, 1970
62	Premature	Auditory-recorded mother's voice 6 times/day, at 2-hour intervals until gestational age is 252 days	Higher motor score on general maturation scale score of Rosenblith test at 36 weeks‡ / Greater auditory response to bell or rattle‡	Lower tactile adaptive score‡ / Lower visual response to red rattle‡	Katz, 1971

N	Infant	Stimulation	Results	Reference
15	Premature	Kinesthetic-rocker bed; Auditory-recorded heartbeat 15 min./hr.	Higher muscle tension responses‡; Greater average daily weight gain†; Greater mental scale score† and expressive language development†; Less time in quiet sleep*; Less time in active sleep†	Barnard, 1975
60	Premature	Recorded female voice; White noise 30 min./day	If quiet, increased heart rate at hearing white noise§; If crying, decreased heart rate at hearing recorded female voice†	Segall, 1972
36	Premature	Handled 20 minutes twice a day until 72 hours of age, then 20 minutes a day	4-month mental score 13.5 higher†; 4-month motor score 16 points higher†; Regained birth weight slower†; 6-month infant behavioral record lower†	Freedman et al., 1972
30	Premature	Visual—suspended nursery birds; Tactile—extra play periods	Higher developmental status at 1 year†; Lower IQ (10 points)§	Scarr-Salapatek and Williams, 1973
18	Premature	Rubbed extremities 5 min./ 15 min./3 hr.	Decrease in frequency of apnea‡	Kattwinkel et al., 1975
21	Premature	Gently oscillating waterbed	Decreased apneic episodes‡	Korner, 1975
20	Premature	Waterbeds gently rocked; Auditory stimuli	Increased weight gain‡; Increased head circumference‡; Increased biparietal diameter*	Kramer and Pierpont, 1976

* = $p < .001$.   ‡ = $p < .01$. || = sample too small for statistical significance test.

† = $p < .05$.   § = $p < .02$.   ¶ = $p < .0001$.

COMMENT: We have found that mothers are physically tired at one month after discharge, and the babies are often irritable, which is in contrast to our evaluation of their behavior in the hospital nursery. In addition, on the Brazelton Neonatal Behavior Assessment the infant more frequently gives ·good responses to the orientation items while in the hospital, but at the one-month examination after discharge it is more difficult to obtain responses to the orientation items. Parents need counseling about the behavioral changes they might see and how to interpret them.   K. BARNARD

A baby born at 28 weeks' gestation does not really interact with his mother until he is 18 weeks old. Suddenly the problems disappear, and the mother's pleasure and confidence return.

Blake and colleagues observed a specific pattern of behavior among mothers during the first few weeks that their babies are home, suggesting that the emotional conflicts are not completely resolved until the baby leaves the hospital. "These mothers are inefficient at recognizing signals from the baby immediately after the baby goes home, they are anxious and probably react indiscriminately to everything, consequently becoming exhausted." This exhaustion leads to inefficiency in practical tasks, and then to resentment. And "then the mothers feel guilty at their resentment." In addition to having anticipated the baby's death, most mothers have already suffered from feelings of guilt and failure. Such emotions can be induced by the birth of a small premature baby alone, but Blake and colleagues (1975) make the following observation:

> Previous infertility, pregnancy failure or termination, abnormalities of pregnancy, denial of pregnancy and unwanted pregnancy, particularly when there have been attempts to terminate it, all tend to intensify these feelings. In addition, many of the mothers experience horror and hate at the sight of their babies, which must lead to even more guilt, especially as our culture dictates that babies are "beautiful" and that mothers automatically love them on sight. The mothers, however, cannot rationalize sufficiently to explain their problems. Instead, they complain of physical difficulties in the baby, such as feeding, vomiting or constipation.*

Over many years we have gained the impression that the earlier a mother comes to the premature unit and touches her baby the more rapidly her own physical recovery from the pregnancy and birth progresses. Interestingly, Budin (1907), the first neonatologist, commented that it is important to keep the mother involved with the care of her infant.

*From Blake, A., Stewart, A., and Turcan, D.: In Parent-infant interaction, Ciba Foundation Symposium 33, Amsterdam, 1975, Elsevier Publishing Co.

As a result of our observations and experiences, we have begun a study to evaluate the effect of a supplemental early intervention program to maximize the attachment of mothers and fathers to their premature infants. The study was designed to determine if mothers who (1) follow a pattern of stroking their infants, (2) are involved in caretaking such as feeding and changing diapers, and (3) are given special guidance on how to understand their infant's needs and responses, will develop a closer attachment to their infants than will mothers who are not given these three experiences during the first two weeks of life. Mothers in both groups were allowed to come into the nursery and were given a description and an explanation of all treatments such as monitors, catheters, and incubator hoods. Only the experimental group was given the special experiences during the first two weeks after the baby's birth. After this the special program was ended, and both the control and experimental groups received the same care.

There were three main differences in the experiences of the control and the experimental groups. First, the experimental mothers were encouraged to visit six times during the first two weeks after the birth of their babies. In the first hour of each visit they were asked to touch and stroke their babies four times for 5 minutes each time with a 10-minute break between touching periods. Second, these mothers were encouraged to help with the caretaking of the baby, for example, diaper changes for small babies and feeding and holding for larger ones. Third, after receiving special instruction about the capabilities of their babies, the experimental mothers were encouraged to develop an interchange with them, communicating by way of the infant's sensory systems. Because most mothers believe that seeing the baby's eyes is so important, bilirubin eye patches were removed and phototherapy was stopped during the mother's visit. An initial pilot feasibility study was carried out with ten mothers in each of the two groups. Analysis of a 15-minute standardized videotaped feeding at the time of discharge showed a significant difference between the two groups. The mothers in the experimental group kept their eyes on their babies significantly more than the mothers in the control group ($p < .02$). A previous study, described earlier, showed a significant correlation between the amount of time the mother's eyes were on her premature baby at an early feeding and the baby's IQ at 42 months of age. The supplementary measures that the experimental group experienced appear promising, since they seem to be enhancing the attachment of mothers and fathers to their babies. Therefore this study is now formally under way.

COMMENT: Many parents have observed that there are no rules or procedures for "how you should act to be a good parent to a premature infant when you visit in the hospital." Therefore the direction the experimental procedure provides in terms of the number of visiting times and the type of touching should give them some security that they are doing what hospital personnel perceive to be an appropriate role for a parent of a premature infant.   K. BARNARD

CLINICAL CONSIDERATIONS

We believe that the rigid visiting rules in nurseries must be changed. Inflexible regulations isolate the mother from her infant, drastically increasing her anxiety about her baby's condition. The nursery should be open for parental visiting 24 hours a day. Studies have shown that infections will not be a problem, providing proper precautions are taken (informing parents that they can only enter if they are feeling well, have no upper respiratory problems or other infectious diseases, and wash their hands thoroughly for 4 to 5 minutes). The boxed material presents our suggestions concerning parental visiting.

Health professionals have six tasks in their work with parents:
1. To help the mother adapt her previous conceptualized image of an ideal normal infant to the small infant she has produced
2. To help relieve the mother's guilt about producing a small infant
3. To help the mother begin building a close affectional tie to her infant, developing a mutual interaction so that she will be attuned to her baby's special needs as he grows
4. To permit the mother to learn how to care for her infant while he is in the hospital so that after her child's discharge, she will be competent and relaxed while caring for him
5. To encourage the family to work together during the crisis of the premature birth, helping the father and mother to discuss their difficulties with one another as they attempt to arrive at satisfactory solutions
6. To help meet the special needs of individual families

COMMENT: I would add a seventh task, which is: To assist the families in the transitional period that occurs after the infant is discharged from the hospital unit. This may involve working with other community agencies involved more directly in home care.   K. BARNARD

Care of the parents

To accomplish these tasks one must begin talking with both the mother and father immediately after the birth. The choice of words will have far-reaching effects. The entire medical and nursing staff should be particularly cautious about suggesting that the infant is not

NEONATAL INTENSIVE CARE UNIT
GUIDELINES FOR PARENTS

1. The nursery is open 24 hours a day for you to visit with your baby. We would like to welcome and encourage all parents to come into the nursery. You may touch your baby now and help to care for him or her.

2. The safety of the baby depends on everyone's thoroughly washing their hands before picking up any baby. You must wash your hands for a period of at least 4 minutes, using the large sinks at either end of the nursery. The outline for the hand-washing technique is above the sink. After hand washing please put on a gown. It is important to tie the gown snugly at the back.

3. If you have any questions about your baby, please do not hesitate to talk to the nurse or the doctor. We find it helpful to chat with you each visit, telling you about the progress of your baby. We may be busy when you call or visit and may find it necessary to ask you to call back later. At times we might be unable to talk completely at every visit.

4. Your observations about your baby are important, so if you notice something that has changed or if you are concerned about something, please be sure to discuss it with the nurses or the doctor caring for your baby.

5. At certain times the nursery appears a bit busy, sometimes hectic; even at these times there is always room for you to come into the unit. Once in a while we may have to ask you to wait a few minutes.

6. If you have any concerns in the evening when you are home, please do not hesitate to call. The nurses enjoy talking with you, even at 2:00 A.M. in the morning. Someone is always here. Call directly to the floor.

7. Please do not come into the nursery if you have any disease that your baby might catch from you such as diarrhea or a cold (this includes a sore throat, cold sores or water blisters on your lips, a runny nose, cough, and temperature). While they are young and in the nursery, premature babies are more susceptible to infectious disease, and so we do not permit anyone into the nursery unless they are feeling well. Please check with the doctors and nurses if you have questions about whether it is safe for you to visit, and after an illness, when it is wise to resume your visits.

normal. Parents never forget early remarks, such as, "Oh, it's very blue . . . It's so small . . . Do you think it will live? . . . Look, it's grunting . . . Why won't it breathe?" Obstetricians must remember that because they have a close tie with the mother, their words will have particular weight. Parents have often remarked long after the birth that they will never forget the physician's remark, "I doubt if the baby will live. It looks too small and immature." Statements such as these reflect the belief of many physicians that if a mother is prepared for a death, she will go through the experience with less emotional upheaval. (The latter has been proved incorrect in studies of parents who have lost newborn infants, which will be discussed in Chapter 6.)

The physician who uses this approach is attempting to be helpful. Although on the surface this approach appears to be reasonable (sharing all concerns with the patient), it is contraindicated in this situation. At present most premature infants do survive. If a woman is to mother her child adequately throughout the rest of his childhood, she must begin by building a firm and close tie with him at birth. Pessimistic remarks in the first hours of life cause a premature infant's mother to hold back, stifling this bond at its inception, and to embark on the process of anticipatory grief. Once this process is fully under way, it is very difficult to reverse its course. If by the end of the second or third day, the obstetrician and pediatrician feel optimistic about the premature infant's survival, they may have already begun to lose the mother. It may be several days before the mother will believe that her baby will live, and she may not be completely convinced for years. The physician must be frank, and if the situation warrants it, must state that in some cases it is extremely difficult to predict how a small premature infant will do. Unfortunately, this situation often leads to a suspension of communication with the mother, adding to her concern. We have found that it helps to describe how we visualize the baby, leaving out some of the negative factors. We do not give the mother any statistics about the baby's chances. If, however, the child has been home for some time, has successfully elicited his parent's attachment, and then returns with meningitis or some other acute disease, physicians should share their worries with the mother from the beginning.

In the previous chapter we discussed how the mother of a normal, healthy newborn must adjust her idealized image of her infant to the actual infant before her. Naturally, the adjustment is much more difficult for the mother of a premature infant. She must realign her idealized mental picture with a thin, scrawny, feeble infant. Because the mother of a premature infant is usually unable to visualize that her tiny baby will ultimately grow into a normal, husky, vigorous, healthy youngster, her adjustment to his appearance is far from easy.

The anxieties of a parent about to enter the nursery for the first time, whether in the 1950s or today, are much greater than those of the physician. The average mother who comes to visit her infant (let us say a daughter) was not prepared physically or emotionally for the early birth, and she is still shaky from it. She is extremely anxious about the health of her daughter, wonders about any abnormalities, worries about whether she will be criticized for producing an unfinished, feeble, imperfect product, and fears that she may carry germs which will harm her daughter. She enters the brightly lit stainless steel and glass citadel, filled with unfamiliar sounds and smells, densely populated by intense young men and women who rush from incubator to incubator, manipulate complicated equipment, and spend long periods of time hovering over individual babies with serious expressions on their faces. These activities appear ominous and suggest an air of great tension—even after several visits. It is not until she has been told that her daughter is definitely progressing well or, far better, until she has touched and seen for herself, that she can begin to relax. But there are usually frightening surprises at the early visits. Complicated wires, fine tubes, large tubes, bandages on the head, arms, or legs, and bright lights and bandages on the eyes cover the baby. She is so tiny, so different from a normal baby. Her head is large, her extremities thin, her movements jerky, and her respiration irregular and labored. Fig. 4-8 pictures what

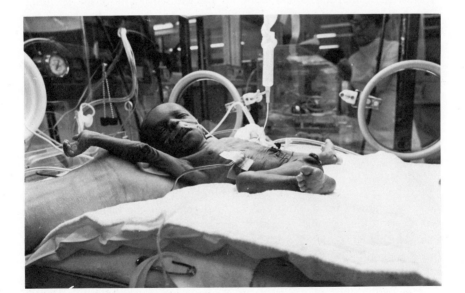

Fig. 4-8. A picture of what a mother sees when she first visits her premature infant.

a mother may see when she comes to visit her baby in the first days of life. At each visit a new problem may be discovered or announced, and with every problem the mother feels a sharp visceral pain. "Do babies with jaundice live?" "How will she ever stand the strain of breathing so hard when she is already so small and fragile?" "Does such a tiny thing ever grow up to be a full-sized child or adult?" "Are they really telling me the truth? What have I done to my poor daughter?"

Although we do not believe that the words can be written into a script, we offer the following conversation as an example. If the 1500-gram infant is grunting but pink at 30 minutes of age, we find it helpful to say, "Mrs. Jones, you have a fine, strong baby, even though he is small. He is showing some of the adjustments to life outside of you that we commonly encounter. We believe he is going to do well after he gets through this early period of adjustment over the next few days. He is pink, active, and beautifully formed. He looks perfect to us except for some difficulty in fully expanding his lungs, but we often see this during this period. There have been many developments recently, and we have many new techniques. We will undoubtedly be using some of these to help your baby, and we'll let you know about them as they are used. I am pleased by his progress and will be seeing you later in the day. If you're feeling well enough, I think you'd enjoy coming to see your son."

It is also important at this point to ask the mother how she is doing and what her concerns are. If she has had a chance to see her baby, we might ask, "How did the baby look to you? What did you notice? How do you feel about the baby and what we just told you? What questions do you have?" Each woman has individual needs, and if we are not careful, we run the risk of overwhelming a mother with unnecessary descriptions—she may well be concerned about something entirely different from what the physician imagines.

To some readers a recommendation for optimism at this point may seem dishonest or misleading—not playing the game "fair and square" with the mother. A physician should never deceive a mother if the baby is expected to die, and we do not intend to imply that deception should be carried out. It is important for the physician first to determine what the chances for a baby will be, and then, on the basis of the current expectations, adjust what he or she says accordingly. Physicians who have had experience with the high mortality rate of the past may find it difficult to be optimistic and may want to have someone else talk to the parents during the period of intensive care.

The father must be involved as well. The physician should discuss with him how his infant is doing and allow him to see the baby at close range. Because the mother may still be foggy from her delivery, it is important to talk with both parents together. Many physicians believe in sparing a woman from the stress of hearing about her sick infant soon after the birth, but it is clear that a mother's worries are far worse than reality warrants and often are not the same as the physician's. At the time of the first discussion, the physician would be wise to reassure the parents that there will be no secrets, that they will be informed about the baby's course, and that both will be told about the developments together whenever possible. (The physician may talk directly to the mother for convenience and have her in turn tell her husband, but the physician must be certain that she is confident that no developments are being kept from her by her husband.)

Today in the United States many small or sick infants are transported from the hospitals where they are born to a hospital with an intensive care unit. At the time of transfer, even if the infant is only being moved for observation of a slightly elevated bilirubin level, most mothers are worried about their infant's survival (Benfield et al., 1976). This is important to remember, since the mother and father will require additional help (Fanaroff and Baskewicz, 1975). Before the infant is transported, we show him to his mother and attempt to describe to the parents, in simple terms, the care their baby will receive. We ask the father to help us care for his infant, impressing on him that he has a very special role to play. There are really two sick individuals in his family—his wife, in one part of the hospital or in another hospital, and his baby in the neonatal center. In addition, he sometimes has other children at home. We have observed that by bringing him into the situation early, he can better master his anxieties. We suggest that he come to the intensive care nursery and discuss the baby's condition with the doctors and nurses and familiarize himself with the routine before visiting his wife. This way he can report current information and help to allay her fears. We encourage him to talk with his wife at least once a day.

Before the mother comes to the nursery, the physician should clearly describe the baby's appearance to her. She should know that he is in an incubator wearing only a diaper, has a small fine plastic tube in his navel through which small blood samples are drawn to regulate his treatment, has another fine tube in his arm through which he is receiving some nourishing sugar solutions, has a small plastic hood over his head to permit precise oxygen control, is pink, active, and moving around, and is waiting for his mother to put her hands into the incubator so he can feel her touch. At this time we also explain to her that a number of recent studies demonstrate that simply touching the infant improves his breathing, physical development, rate of weight gain, and relaxes him. Thus the visit is important not only to the mother but to the baby as well. Frequently, a mother will say that she does not want to touch her baby for fear that she will hurt or infect him. This may stem from her belief that she is an inadequate or "bad" mother because she has not been able to produce a normal baby. It is beneficial to the mother to let her express these feelings, but it is equally important to be encouraging, accepting, and confidence restoring. By telling the mother, "You can come in," we are essentially relaying to her that we consider her a good person and a wholesome influence on her baby. It has been and still is common for a mother to have too much respect for the expert nurses and to feel inferior to them.

The longer the mother must wait before she can see her baby the more time she has to imagine that her worst fantasies are true. However, the sooner she sees her baby the more rapidly she can reconcile her image of him with his true physical condition. The first sight and first handling of the infant are not easy for the mother. We suggest that a chair (preferably a high stool with a back) be placed near the incubator in case she feels faint.

Each mother comes with a different set of worries, problems, and past history. Some can move faster than others. For those who are extremely hesitant about coming in, we say, "How are things going? How have you slept? How are you managing these days? How is your husband managing? How are both of you getting along?" Encouraging her to talk about her thoughts is most helpful. She should neither be forced to put her hands into the incubator nor be pressured to enter the nursery if she is not ready or willing to do so. Many people believe that the mother who denies the illness, withdraws, and is passive has a much more difficult time adjusting. The mother who is able to face the difficulties of the small baby and wrestle with her guilt feelings copes more quickly and easily. Once these feelings are verbalized, the family is on the road to becoming attached to the newborn.

The care of the mother and her baby during the period in the intensive care nursery will influence their relationship throughout the child's life. We have been impressed with the ingenuity of the nurses in developing techniques that allow a mother to hold her baby in her arms while he is being fed by nasogastric tube. They attach the burette to the mother's gown, which permits her to hold her baby until all of the feeding has run into his stomach. We have found notes tacked to the baby's bed: "Please hold my 1:00 feeding for my mother. She will come to give me this feeding. Boy, will I be glad to see her! Signed, Susie." We often find three or four mothers chatting in a room with a single nurse.

The mother must not be given a task if there is the slightest possibility that she will not succeed. She should not bottle feed unless a nurse or a physician has fed her baby several times and knows he can take the feedings easily. During the period when he is being tube fed, the mother should have other tasks, such as changing the diaper and giving him sensory stimulation. Fig. 4-9 is a pictorial essay of a family with a small premature infant. For contrast, Fig. 4-10 shows a premature nursery before parent visiting was permitted.

Early studies of infant development suggest that contingent stimulation (stimulation related to cues from the infant) may optimize development. Therefore we suggest that mothers fondle and talk to their babies as they would normally if the baby were not in the hospital. Fig. 4-11 shows a mother in the intensive care nursery playing with her baby just after a feeding.

The case of Benjamin G., the 900-gram infant of white parents, is an example of the importance of contingent stimulation. Benjamin was extremely immature, was fragile in appearance, and had frequent apneic

The mother began touching the infant hesitantly while he was on the respirator.

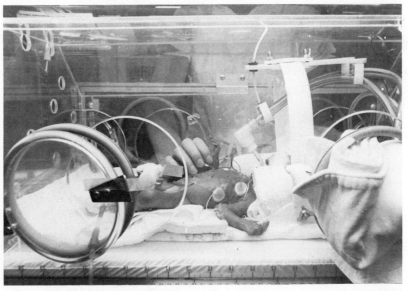

Continued.

Fig. 4-9. A pictorial essay of a family in our nursery who were actively involved with the care of their infant for many days before the baby could be removed from the respirator and incubator. (From Alderman, M. M.: Patient care, Feb. 1, 1975. Copyright, 1975, Miller & Fink Corp., Darien, Conn. All rights reserved.)

During the first weeks of life, the mothers are often anxious and "shaky."

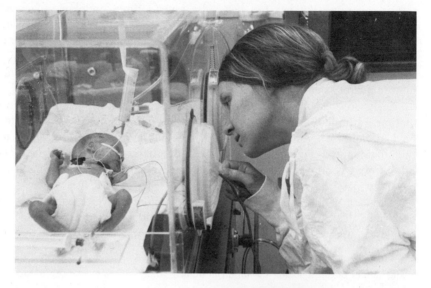

For some period of time, mothers touch mainly the extremities of the infant.

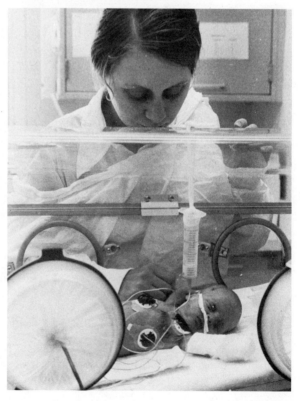

Fig. 4-9, cont'd

The mother and father assisting in tube feeding.

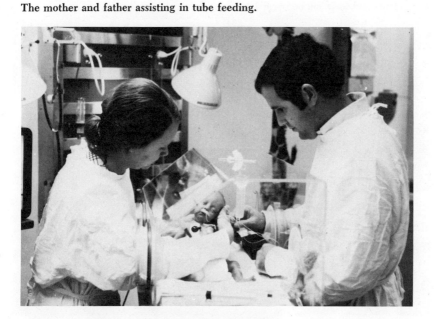

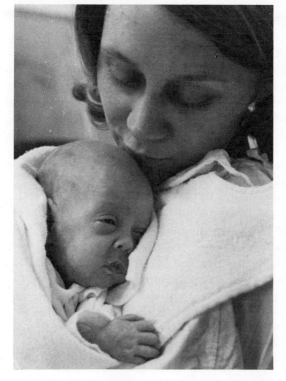

Mothers find it much easier once the infant is out of the incubator. He went home the day after this picture was taken.

Continued.

Fig. 4-9, cont'd

The parents and their son one year later.

Fig. 4-9, cont'd

episodes. His mother, after being informed of the importance of stimulation, came to the hospital early each morning and stayed until noon, returned after lunch and stayed until 6:00 P.M. when her husband finished his work. Her efforts with the baby were sensitively adjusted to him and consisted of considerable talking and stroking. Gradually she assumed more and more responsibility for his feeding and care. Her infant's significant decrease in apneic episodes, his unusually rapid weight gain, and developmental progress in subsequent months as well as in the hospital were remarkable. The staff repeatedly told her that the baby was doing extremely well "due to her efforts." This was a sincere statement because the baby's progress was viewed as well above the normal expectations. There were several reasons for this. The mother was allowed to help care for her baby and consequently believed that she was making an important contribution. On several days the number of apneic episodes were frequent during the night and almost absent when she was present. Most importantly, this mother was able to establish a reciprocal interaction with her baby. She could send messages to him by stroking and talking and could receive messages in return, such as a change in activity level or an opening of the eyes.

Fig. 4-10. A cartoon by Annette Tison made for her sister, Claudine Tison, showing the premature nursery before parent visiting was permitted. (Courtesy Claudine Amiel-Tison, Hospital Port Royal, Paris.)

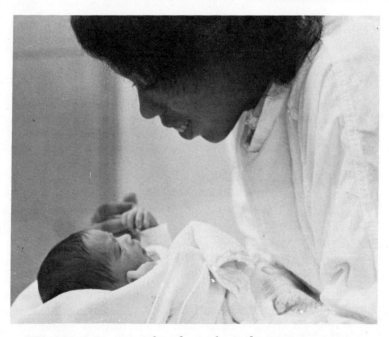

Fig. 4-11. A common sight today in the modern premature nursery.

Early interaction may limit the advancement of anticipatory grief, which in turn would modify the first task of Kaplan and Mason (1960). Their studies were carried out fifteen years ago, at a time when there was no parental visiting. Separation therefore was complete and prolonged, and the mother only handled her baby just before discharge.

Other approaches have been taken in the hope of normalizing the interaction between parents and their premature infant. Crosse (1957) suggested that "Whenever possible the mother should be admitted for several days before the baby is discharged so that she can take over complete charge of her infant under supervision." She provided small rooms for mother-infant dyads so that the two would truly become acquainted before discharge. James (1969) described the successful introduction of a care-by-parent unit to provide a homelike caretaking experience. Nursing support was available for parents of premature infants prior to discharge if they needed it. Other units have tested early discharge. Berg and associates (1969) and Dillard and Korones (1973) discharged premature infants when they weighed about 2 kilograms. Dillard found no deleterious effects associated with early discharge. Actually, these authors had followed Miller's (1948) suggestion to manage large premature infants in the home. However, they did not follow his additional recommendation that experienced personnel should visit the home to organize the families and supervise infant care. Recent studies of early discharge have not revealed any adverse effects on the physical health of the infants, but there have been no systematic observations of maternal behavior or later infant development.

> COMMENT: Early discharge is appropriate as long as the parents are given the support they need. There should be someone to talk to about their questions and someone who can give them reassurance about the baby's condition and their parenting. Even though there are no apparent physical adverse effects of early discharge, the tremendous anxiety some parents experience when taking very young or relatively unstable babies home in terms of feeding, temperature, and respiratory status may have profound adverse effects on the parent-infant interaction and later developmental outcome.　　　　K. BARNARD

We have done a small feasibility study permitting mothers to live in with their infants before discharge, which we have termed nesting. As soon as babies reached 1720 to 2110 grams, each mother, in a private room with her baby, provided all caretaking. Impressive changes in the behavior of these women were observed clinically. Even though the mothers had fed and cared for their infants in the intensive care nursery on many occasions prior to living-in, eight of the first nine mothers were unable to sleep during the first 24 hours. Most of the mothers closed the door to the room, completely shutting out any chance of observation, often to the consternation of the nurses, who felt a strong responsibility for the well-being of the infant. It was interesting to observe that the mothers rearranged the furniture, crib, and infant supplies, resembling in some ways the nesting behavior observed in animals. However, in the second 24-hour period the mothers' confidence and caretaking skills improved greatly. At this time, mothers began to discuss the proposed early discharge of their infants and, often for the first time, began to make preparations at home for his arrival. Several insisted on taking their babies home earlier than planned. The babies seemed to be quieter during this living-in period. In some mothers there were physical changes, such as increased breast swelling accompanied by some milk secretion. The mothers were not satisfied with the living-in nesting procedure until we established unlimited visiting privileges for the father and provided him with a comfortable chair and a cot (Kennell et al., 1973, 1975).

Initially we had difficulties in clearly defining the role of the nurse in the living-in unit. It soon became clear that the mother should be the responsible caretaker, and the nurse must function as a consultant. The role of the nurse and the mother must be clarified, or there will be resultant tussles over who makes the decisions, similar to those when more than one person writes orders for a single patient. Once the safety and feasibility of early discharge of premature infants has been fully confirmed, we suggest that early discharge, preceded by a period of isolation of the mother-infant dyad, may help to normalize mothering behavior in the intensive care nursery. Early discharge must be in conjunction with early parental visiting in the intensive care nursery. Encouraging the development of interaction and total caretaking may sharply reduce the high incidence of mothering disorders among the mothers of small premature or sick infants.

> COMMENT: The role of the hospital nurse in preparing the parents, particularly the mother, for caretaking is consistent with the traditional role that the community nurse has when she provides consultation to parents in home care.   K. BARNARD

Adaptations of the hospital

Each division, wing, or unit of a hospital is a social entity. The whole social milieu changes when parents are permitted to enter the nursery and call 24 hours a day. Before shifting to a new scheme the personnel must be thoroughly prepared. To each of the personnel in a unit, whether a nurse or physician, the job fulfills an individual need. Once the mothers enter the unit, their orientation must change. It has been our experience that nurses usually develop a close attachment to the babies they intimately care for day by day. Therefore they must adjust to the mother's presence in what used to be their domain. The mother and nurse often are jealous of one another, and these feelings must be discussed and resolved before the new nursery setup can run properly.

In the era when mothers and fathers were not permitted into the nursery, the nursery was like a home with the head nurse as majordomo. As mothers and fathers enter the nursery and begin to assume their parental roles, nurses must realize that parents share responsibility for their infant and his small portion of the nursery with the nursing and medical staff.

Meetings in the intensive care unit

We have found in our unit that it is most important to have a staff meeting at least once every two weeks. At this time nurses discuss the problems they have had, both with interpersonal relationships and the deaths inevitable in any unit. Some of the nurses' questions are, "Is it true you don't tell us why babies die because you don't want to hurt our feelings? We think we produce some deaths." In response to the question, "How do you feel about this baby?" one nurse volunteered that she felt as if she were his mother and that she felt terrible when he died. She had an empty feeling that lasted for several days. One nurse mentioned how quickly she became attached to an infant when she was asked to give him cutaneous stimulation and almost felt that he was her own for a moment. In many premature nurseries specific assignments are not made. Nurses usually favor specific babies and often there will be one surrogate mother for each. This nurse can often give the richest reports about the baby and his mother.

Mothers, when they are allowed in the unit, note every little change and deficiency in care. Wet diapers or a little bit of spilled milk do not go unnoticed. They also have many questions. When the infant's condition changes, it is often the mother who is most sensitive to modifications in color, tone, or breathing. When nurses resent implied or actual criticisms, these feelings need to be discussed.

Anyone who has been associated with an intensive care unit for high-risk infants knows that there are acutely ill babies who demand a disproportionate amount of the physician's and nurse's attention. Group meetings provide an opportunity not only to discuss these cases but also the other babies whose progress is more satisfactory, but whose parents may have presented evidence of personal problems. During this crisis period, parents may bring many of their most intimate and immediate problems to the nurse or aides. Consideration of the nurse's intuitive observations about a mother is extremely valuable while making plans for the infant. Nurses are especially sensitive to the needs and adequacy of the mother. Heeding their observations permits problems to be recognized early in the course of hospitalization so that social work and psychiatric intervention may begin at an early stage of the crisis, if necessary.

To enable the nurses and physicians to feel more at ease while discussing their difficulties with parents, some units have someone who is not connected with the unit to lead the group meetings.

Discussions with parents (when the health of the infant is not in doubt)

The possibility of brain damage troubles physicians and nurses while a small premature infant is in the hospital. Usually these concerns are not borne out by difficulties in the future. In a follow-up study in our unit we found that predictions made by pediatricians and neurologists with electroencephalograms and other tests were accurate only 50% of the time—one half of those for whom dire predictions were made proved to be normal. It is our strong belief that disturbances of the brain should *never* be mentioned to parents, unless the outcome can be accurately predicted, as in a case of Down's syndrome. Parents can erase questions that are raised about other organ systems in the baby, but once the possibility of brain damage has been mentioned, it cannot be easily forgotten. Many concerned parents have read about the brain and a closely related organ, the eyes. The physician should be aware of their concern and open to answer any questions. When questions are raised about the future development of a premature infant, the physician can quote the recent optimistic reports. The physician should indicate that although it is never possible at such an early age to predict conclusively the outcome for any baby, full term or premature, the parents have no reason for worry. The existence of eye problems such as retrolental fibroplasia should be acknowledged, but it should be pointed out that babies are monitored closely, which greatly diminishes its potential occurrence. The parents should be further reassured that the baby's eyes will be checked in the hospital and after discharge to make certain that all is as it should be.

Harper and associates (1975) have questioned whether or not encouraging close parental contact in the neonatal period for infants in the intensive care unit has some harmful results. Harper found that parents believe that the opportunity to have contact with their infant in the neonatal intensive care unit is valuable, despite their anxiety. Ninety percent of the parents questioned would have been opposed to restricted contact with their infants; 85% believed that holding their infants made the infant feel more loved and secure; and 44% thought that the quality and quantity of care rendered improved when they were present. Harper states that although "frequent parental-infant contact may build long term relationships, the parental emotional price tag is high." She recommends more psychosocial education for perinatologists and perinatal nurses and the establishment of discussion groups for parents.

Milestones and worrisome signs

As the days progress and the small premature infant begins to grow, the mother realizes that he will most likely survive. As she starts caring for him, she once again readjusts her previous image to one which is closer to her own infant before her. It is remarkable to notice that a mother may comment on how much bigger her baby appears, when in fact he has not gained any weight. Mothers watch closely for any evidence of improvement, whether it be a slight weight gain, a feeding taken by nipple, or a decrease in the use of monitors or other support equipment. Most parents consider the removal of catheters or monitors, the onset of weight gain, and the change from feeding by tube to feeding by nipple to be major milestones in the development of the infant, whereas the staff takes them as routine. We have always found it helpful to present the positive developments to the mother. If the infant loses a few grams of weight (something seen often in the premature nursery), we do not emphasize it. If the mother expresses concern, we point out that this is normal, that weight gain is not a straight line but rather a slow process containing brief plateaus or drops. If a mother is prepared for these fluctuations ahead of time, she will worry less.

Most mothers have mentioned that they do not feel close to their baby until they actually have him in their arms during a feeding (and not really close until they are feeding him at home) and that the glass-walled nursery is a barrier to their feelings of attachment. The more privacy they have the warmer they feel toward their infant. (This is important to remember when building new units for the premature and sick infant; small rooms should be provided for mothers so that the mother will have privacy while interacting with her infant.)

It is important to recognize as soon as possible the mother who is not becoming attached to her infant so that she can receive help. The longer she delays in attaching herself to her infant the greater will be her difficulty in finally achieving a close and warm relationship. During the hospitalization it is therefore wise to assess continually not only the infant's physical progress and clinical care but also the progress of the other patients—the mother and father.

One of the best indicators of the parents' progress is their visiting pattern. For example, is the number of visits decreasing or increasing? Is the mother beginning to consider the baby a member of her family? We try to keep track of the length of time the mother visits, her actions during the visits (does she hop from one incubator to another looking at all the babies, or does she spend the time with her own?), the comments she makes about her infant, and the skill she shows during her visits. There seems to be a correlation between a poor outcome and a mother who travels from incubator to incubator, looks out of the window when she puts her hands into the incubator, or actually turns the baby's face away from hers. Are the parents starting to make plans at home for their infant—painting the room or buying new curtains and equipment they will need? Are they preparing the nest?

The overly optimistic mother who appears unconcerned about her baby's clinical state, who does not ask any questions, and who is very passive presents a worrisome sign. In other words, we are concerned about the mother who denies. The mother who grapples with the problem seems to get through much better. For example, throughout the hospitalization of her twins. Mrs. B. was outwardly extremely confident about her ability to care for her infants, not concerned with the infants, and frequently telling the nurses to change their way of managing and handling the twins. Because Mrs. B. ignored their suggestions, it was difficult for them to communicate with her and to learn how much she understood. After she took her babies home, she was unusually anxious and made many frantic phone calls to the nursery.

> COMMENT: In cases such as the mother who incubator hops or appears unconcerned, care should be taken to detect the pattern of behavior the mother establishes rather than the isolated incident, since all parents' behavior shows a great deal of variability. It is the consistency of a worrisome response that is most important.   K. BARNARD

Discharge requirements

There are two patients in the nursery—the mother and the infant. When discharging the infant, it is necessary to know not only about him but also about the home situation. In some nurseries the infant's attainment of physical milestones (feeding ability, weight gain, and temperature control) determines discharge dates. However, before discharge we attempt to measure the degree of maternal confidence and attachment. Previously, these assessments were made from observations of feeding and caretaking. Now several techniques allow more accurate predictions. The following seem reasonable:

1. Noting the nurses' observations of the mother
2. Inquiring about preparations the mother has made at home
3. A visit (with the mother's permission) if any question about the home situation arises
4. Determining whether the mother feels she is prepared for the discharge

5. Keeping a notebook in which to record every mother's phone calls and visits so that we can assess if she is likely to be a high-risk mother

Follow-up—what to watch for after discharge

After discharge we are alert to situations in which the mother feels inadequate and disturbed. Key signs are frequent telephone calls and more than one visit to the emergency room at a strange hour with a completely normal infant. If the mother appears in the emergency room more than once, or if she appears to be signaling for help, we readmit the baby.

From our own studies we have found that the following may be helpful for the pediatrician: At three to four weeks after discharge we ask the mother whether she has gone out, and if so, who stayed with the baby. We also ask how everything worked out. We have found that the mother's answers fall into one of two categories. She is concerned either about the baby or about herself. The best attachment seems to be associated with replies which indicate that the mother is concerned about leaving her baby and thinks about him while she is away.

During the physical examination a physician can make important observations. Does the mother stand close to the physician, watch the handling of the baby, and soothe him when he cries, or does she appear detached and look around the office and concern herself with other matters? These latter can be important warning signals.

If possible, the physician or nurse should observe a mother feeding her baby. In general, positive features are eye-to-eye contact, close contact with the baby during the feeding, and fondling, kissing, stroking, and nuzzling. Evidence of disturbances in attachment and caretaking are a loose, distant hold on the baby, a propped bottle whether the baby is held in her arms or not, and a failure to hold the bottle so that milk can flow out of the nipple.

Thus it is possible to make semiobjective measurements of mothering behavior with a few questions and simple observations during the physical examination and the feeding. None of these requires additional time.

The surge of interest in perinatal and neonatal care, coupled with the desire to apply these latest ideas to benefit premature infants and their families, has unleashed a flood of innovative, humanistic changes in premature nurseries. The absence of innovation between 1945 and 1960 was almost complete; all the ideas of care were ossified in the pattern derived from Martin Cooney. New procedures, developed to humanize the nursery and promote parent-infant attachment, have sprung from exchanges of ideas at national and regional meetings.

INTERVIEW

The following interview with the parents of a premature infant highlights some of the concepts already discussed in this chapter. The experiences of the parents and their reactions are representative of many parents with an acutely ill infant in a neonatal intensive care unit, transferred from another hospital. Kimberly Dixon* was born after 34 weeks of gestation, required assisted ventilation with continuous positive airway pressure (CPAP) provided in a negative pressure transparent box within an isolette for moderately severe respiratory distress syndrome. The pulmonary disease improved, and she appeared to be progressing well when a delay in her recovery occurred. A patent ductus arteriosus with mild congestive heart failure was diagnosed, so she was digitalized. After this setback her subsequent course was satisfactory. This interview with Mr. and Mrs. Dixon was obtained one month after discharge.

Mrs. Dixon. I was really shocked. I was really tired out and I hadn't seen my baby, and all I could think of was "My baby's very sick and they're going to take her away." I was really afraid she wasn't going to be with me very long. I was ready to run down to the nursery. You know they don't want you to get out of bed right away and you're supposed to take it easy after delivery. I got out of bed, and the nurse came in and said, "You can't get out of bed, dear," and I said, "Well, then, you'll have to get me a wheelchair because I'm going down there and I'm going to see my baby because they're taking her away." So they took me down there, and she looked terrible. I thought, "Oh, my poor little baby."

Mr. Dixon. The doctors that came with the ambulance to pick her up brought her into Ann's room and said, "The baby is sick, but we've seen babies that are a lot sicker than this one." I was somewhat reassured.

Mrs. Dixon. The next thing I knew they were wheeling her in, and the doctor was very nice and explained everything to me. He said, "I'm sure that you're worried about this tube and that tube, and we're going to do this to her and give her more oxygen." He was very reassuring. It was raining that night, and I said, "Please don't let her get wet—she'll get a cold." All I could think of was "That's all she needs—to get a cold on top of all of this." He was very reassuring and told me not to worry and told me he would arrange it with the nurse so that after my husband saw her here, no matter what time it was, he could call back and tell me what they were doing.

Mr. Dixon. That was good. Usually the husband feels kind of left out in a normal birth because he's not allowed in at some hospitals and is not allowed with the mother and child as much as probably a lot of fathers would like to be, but in this situation it's just reversed. I'm here all the time with the baby and trying to get back to my wife once or twice a day and relate to her what I'm seeing.

---

*The family's name has been changed.

COMMENT: Our experience has indicated that many fathers express the feeling that they are closer or more attached to their premature infant than their other children. They relate this to the fact that they had more involvement with the infant in the hospital during his early period of life.   K. BARNARD

Mrs. Dixon. I was still worried. I don't think until I got over to the premature nursery and got to hold her and make sure that she was still really a baby, that she was really OK, that everything was put together right, and that you were doing everything so she would be all right—I still had this empty feeling. I felt very bad. I called over here all the time—almost every hour.

A large percentage of mothers separated from their premature infants describe this empty feeling either while they are still hospitalized in the maternity unit or after they have gone home. The mother's uterus has been physically emptied, but there is no baby for her to hold. In contrast, the mother whose full-term infant remains with her in the maternity unit does not mention this type of feeling.

Mr. Dixon. Probably the biggest thing that helped was when she could actually get over here. She can trust me, but she wanted to see the baby.
Mrs. Dixon. I felt very empty because with all the other mothers and the other mother in my room—she'd get her baby every 4 hours and it was terrible in the hospital—at 6:00 in the morning they would come in and say, "Would you please wake up, Mrs. Dixon, your baby's coming in," and I was there for six days. Every day they'd come in and say, "Please wake up, Mrs. Dixon, your baby's here—it's time to feed her." I'd say, "My baby isn't here." The nurse said, "Honey, you're just asleep—your baby's here." I said, "I know my baby is not here—please don't wake me up." That was very hard. The girl next to me got her baby and fed her baby and she sort of felt bad. She said, "Do you want me to pull the curtain because I have my baby and you don't?" When I went home, there was another mother who had her baby all huddled in her arms—and I just left with my flowers. That was bad. I went to church a lot. I lit every vigil light you could name—I lit them all.

The large staff required for the operation of a modern hospital combined with the efforts to achieve maximum efficiency may result in impersonal care unless strong and repeated efforts are made to discuss the needs of mothers with every member of the hospital staff. Because the nursing and medical care of the baby is separated from the care of the mother, unfortunate situations of this sort do happen. However, if the mother-infant pair is cared for as a single unit, these situations do not occur. Mothers whose babies have died or have been transferred to a nursery for premature or sick infants have repeatedly told us that it would be best to transfer the mother to a separate room or another division so she would not be caught up in the routine care for the normal, healthy newborn infant. Mrs. Dixon's report also makes it clear that if a woman has the mother of a sick infant as her roommate, some of the bloom is taken off her exciting postpartum period.

Mr. Dixon. At that hospital I would change the hours that a father could be there. I had to wait until 7:00 at night after being here during the afternoon or morning, then I could not get into the hospital to see my wife until 7:00 at night, and then only from 7:00 until 8:30. There were so many things I was trying to relate to her—show her the pictures, trying to explain to her what was going on, what they were doing, how the baby was doing. Not that the telephone isn't convenient, but you just want to *be* there, and there isn't enough time. That's kind of a bad situation.

Mrs. Dixon. If you had your baby, the father could be there from 3:00 till 8:30—*if* your baby's there.

Every hospital has a multitude of rules and procedures that are written and unwritten. Although at one time there may have been a good reason for establishing a rule, that reason may no longer exist. Often personnel have failed to consider the overall consequences of a rule that focuses just on the hospital care of the mother or the baby. It is difficult to see why a hospital would allow the majority of fathers to be present with their wives from 3:00 until 8:30 P.M. *but not allow the husband of a woman who has been separated from her baby.* Most of the restrictive regulations in maternity hospitals were originally established to protect the mother and baby, and they must be reconsidered! But with the infant absent, the reason is even less evident.

Mr. Dixon. But in our situation the baby wasn't there so the father is just another visitor. I was angered—they stood like a guard at the door and said you can't go up there till 7:00. They have regulations, and I guess we have to live with them, but I think in certain instances the regulations should be bent a little. I'm sure this is harder on the staff, but it's nicer for the people—and I think that's what hospitals are supposed to be for—the people.

Hospitals are built and operated for the benefit of sick people, and most have been built from funds contributed by lay people. It is easy to see why parent groups, as well as some professional groups, are working toward making hospitals less like military installations and more like home for patients and their families.

Mr. Dixon. But I found the way that we operated in terms of coming and going to the premature nursery whenever we wanted was very beneficial to me, and once my wife got out of the hospital, it was very beneficial to her. Because a couple of nights we stayed here till 11:00.

Mrs. Dixon. I hated to leave.

Mr. Dixon. I felt like an ogre, saying, "Come on, I've got to work in the morning."

Mrs. Dixon. He was so tired, one night he went into the lounge and fell asleep.

I just didn't want to go home. I wanted to sit there and hold her and rock her. I read all these articles about premature babies—if they don't get enough oxygen to their brain or there can be too much oxygen . . . it can hurt her eyes or she could be mentally retarded. Or I thought, "If she has a heart murmur, then she'll never be able to run around and play with other children." I'm going to have to say, "Kimberly, sweetheart, you can't do that— you can't jump on the bed, you can't climb up on the stairs, you've got to sit down and play quietly." I wanted her to be normal, and all I could think about was "What next?"

It is interesting to note that this is the first time either parent has mentioned the baby by name. Parents of premature infants often delay selecting a name for their baby for many days or even weeks. During the hospitalization and sometimes during the first weeks at home, they may not use the baby's name, referring to her as "it" much more than will the parents of a normal healthy infant.

Mrs. Dixon. The digitalis scared me to death. When I was in the hospital, I didn't want to think of it, but it did run through my mind—what's going to happen if this baby doesn't live? When I was over there and she was over here in the nursery, and I didn't really see her, and all I had was second-hand information from everyone, I kept thinking, "If my baby dies, they're not going to tell me and I never held her. I don't want her to die." I kept saying to her, "Now, Kimberly, you wanted to come early, you were so impatient— you're not leaving. Now remember that. I'm going to be very mad at you if you decide to leave." I talked to her all the time—I think the nurses thought I was crazy.

No matter what the parents' level of education, intelligence, or experience, it is not unusual for them to resort to magical thinking in times of stress. Many physicians can remember occasions when parents talked to a baby in this manner when they had been told he may not live.

Pediatrician. When you came in and she had the digitalis, what did you begin to think about?
Mrs. Dixon. Well, I didn't think she was going to die—I thought, "She's going to have a heart problem all the rest of her life." So many things can happen with heart problems . . . and digitalis—that's what they give older people when they have heart attacks.

The parents of every premature infant have different previous experiences with physicians, illnesses, and medications. Any diagnosis, symptom, or medication may bring back memories. It is not unusual that the Dixons believed that since Kimberly received digitalis, she would be on lifelong therapy. This emphasizes the importance of easy and free communication between the parents, nurses, and physicians. The physician should be sensitive to the reactions of overconcerned or under-concerned parents. Fortunately, Mr. and Mrs. Dixon were able to bring up their question so that an explanation could be given promptly. Many parents are too frightened to do this.

Mr. Dixon. The first thought when I found out about the digitalis—I don't know much about medicine—but that is what they give heart attack patients for the rest of their life. I must have been a classic example of worry. My parents had driven in from Detroit. We were waiting. Christ, it was my first baby. You know the old thing about whether you want a boy or a girl. I really didn't care, honestly, as long as it was healthy.

Mrs. Dixon. You know I never thought, and I've never known a baby that was born sick or with anything like that. It never crossed my mind. I'd read articles when I was pregnant about birth defects. It never crossed my mind that my baby would be born and they would have to take her and she would be sick. I was just going to have my baby, and I was going to bring her home, and grandma and grandpa would come and see and say, "Oh, how cute." Everything was going to be typical, stereotyped, having a baby, if that's what you want to call it. But everything was quite different.

Pediatrician. You mentioned you had some fears the first night?

Mr. Dixon. I would have done anything. There really wasn't anything that I could do at that point, but I said, "What can I do?"

Mrs. Dixon. That's the thing. I felt very helpless. It was like you go and visit this baby, and they're taking care of her. They put her monitors on her, and I could talk to her through her isolette, and they did most everything for her. It was like their baby.

"It was like their baby" echoes the words of hundreds of parents of premature infants. This statement by these parents in the nursery and after discharge contrasts vividly with the attachment of parents of normal full-term infants, and it started us searching for the factors that led parents to feel this way. Mrs. Dixon had lived with her baby for thirty-four weeks. Now she felt as if the baby belonged to someone else. This raises the question whether her attachment would be different had she played a larger role in the care of her premature infant. Even though the baby was ill and surrounded by monitors and tubes, a mother like Mrs. Dixon would benefit from contributing something that was uniquely her own to the baby's recovery.

> COMMENT: Occasionally, even parents of full-term babies express that they only felt that the baby really belonged to them a week or so after they got home from the hospital.   K. BARNARD

Mr. Dixon. She didn't want to go home, and that was one of the reasons—"This is my baby. If she can't be at home with me, I want to be with her as much as I can."

Mrs. Dixon. I guess I was very jealous. I know that they're taking care of her and I could have never done that, but yet I was very jealous because here she is, my baby, and I felt very empty because I couldn't do anything for her. There was nothing I could do for her. And so I sat and cried.

This is a criticism of the arrangements for the care of the baby. Although Mrs. Dixon had been welcomed into the nursery and had been allowed to touch and talk to her baby, she had not been given a definite role in the infant's care. Probably optimal mother-infant attachment cannot be achieved until the mother feels she is making an important contribution to the care of her baby.

Pediatrician. Were you jealous of one nurse specifically, or of all of them?
Mrs. Dixon. The entire hospital.
Mr. Dixon. I didn't feel that as much as I did the fear part of it. Babies are small and men are supposed to be somewhat clumsy, but I think that fear kind of carried over, because even afterwards, when she was coming along much better and you said it was just a matter of time before she came home, I was still very much afraid to even hold her. I'd get cramps in my arms after holding her for just 5 minutes because my arms would be clenched so tight. Now I feed her. I change her—I'm still probably not as much at ease with her as Ann is, but that fear part of it is gone.
Mrs. Dixon. Now she's a real baby.
Pediatrician. When did she become a real baby?
Mrs. Dixon. When she got out of her isolette and got into that little bassinet.
Mr. Dixon. Ann says she's got rid of her plastic house—now she's a real baby. When we realized that was coming up, we'd say, "Come on, Kimberly, let's get into your own little bed instead of that isolette. You can be a real baby then."
Mrs. Dixon. I know it's silly, but I thought perhaps it was my fault that she was born early, and I kept thinking, "But I did everything I was supposed to do—I took my vitamins and I took the iron and I did everything the doctor said."

For the Dixons, Kimberly did not seem real until she was in a bassinet where she could be handled as a normal baby. It is a universal and normal reaction of mothers to wonder what they did that resulted in the early birth, even though they may have the education and intelligence to appreciate that it was not their fault. Later on, Mr. Dixon clarifies how perplexed he was, and Mrs. Dixon comes closer to the heart of the matter. She felt that there was something the matter with her, something bad about her that resulted in her baby's premature birth. It is helpful to discuss the mother's fears. It is also important to demonstrate to the mother that we do not consider her responsible for the prematurity of her baby, that she must play an important role in the baby's care, and that she must touch him because it will be helpful to his progress.

Mr. Dixon. She did all these exercises the doctor said, and I'm not sure the exercises didn't contribute to it in a way.

Mrs. Dixon. But they tell you to do these to prepare for delivery.

Mr. Dixon. We'd gone to these Stork Club classes, and I guess in a way they're good and in a way they're a waste of time.

Mrs. Dixon. I don't think I'd recommend them to anyone.

Mr. Dixon. They tell you the classic symptoms of labor. I went to bed one night and she said, "I have a bad backache." As I woke up, I saw that she was crying and I said, "I don't understand what's going on, so I'm going to call the doctor." So we called her obstetrician, and the doctor talked to her and got me back on the phone, and he said, "It sounds as if your wife may be in labor." But the Stork Club classes make everything seem so regimented— Ann didn't feel any of that—it seemed to come on so quickly. Of course you're not expecting it 6 weeks early, so maybe it happened and we didn't recognize it.

Mrs. Dixon. I felt great that day until about 11:30 that night, when I got this horrible backache.

Pediatrician. You said that after the baby came you wondered what had happened or what you might have done. What sort of thoughts went through your mind?

Mrs. Dixon. I didn't know. I wanted to know why she was early. Was it my fault—did I do something wrong? Was there something the matter with me?

Mr. Dixon. She asked me that question one time on the phone: "What did I do that made the baby come early?" The doctor said she could still drive a car— she was still 6 weeks away.

Mrs. Dixon. I'd go to the grocery store at the corner of the street.

Mr. Dixon. That's about it, but that's what I couldn't understand. I couldn't understand why she felt maybe it was her fault. I said, "That happens sometimes."

Mrs. Dixon. But I wanted to know why. For a while, and when she got so sick, I thought, "Maybe there's something the matter with me and that's why she was born so early." Everything wasn't ready for her to be born so early.

Mr. Dixon. Especially with the first one. I think if it were to happen again, it would be a little easier to take. It was a very frightening experience for both of us. She kept saying, "What did I do? Is it something that I did? Aren't I right because the baby came early?" That was difficult for me to comprehend because I kept thinking to myself, "We conceived the child and carried it for almost nine months, almost full term." Six weeks early isn't eleven weeks early. You didn't have a miscarriage in the first month or something, so maybe it's a biological thing. I don't know, but I couldn't comprehend why she would tend to think it was her fault.

This lengthy discussion about Mrs. Dixon's guilt feelings illuminates the mother's intense and persistent preoccupation with her guilt about the premature birth. Also highly significant is her statement, "Everything wasn't ready for her to be born so early." Parents of a premature infant are deprived of about six weeks of psychological preparation.

The changes that occur in the last six weeks are usually impressive. The parent prepares for the birth of the baby, both physically and psychologically. The parents of a normal full-term infant experience a labor that is not associated with concern for the welfare of the baby. In contrast, the entire experience of labor, birth, and attachment for the mother of a premature infant takes place under a cloud of fear.

Mrs. Dixon. I just felt that she's my baby and I'm supposed to be taking care of her while she's there and maybe I didn't do that. I don't know—I thought I did everything.

Mr. Dixon. The biggest thing we felt at that time was fear. Fear for the baby, and I guess in a way, fear for ourselves. What happens? You plan for a baby and if the baby doesn't make it, what do you do? How do you pick up the pieces and keep going? But I think the biggest thing that really helped us was the staff at the hospital, yourself, and all the other doctors.

Pediatrician. How did they help?

Mr. Dixon. Reassurance.

Mrs. Dixon. Being so kind and answering all of my questions and talking to me at 2:00 and 3:00 in the morning and not saying, "Oh, it's Mrs. Dixon again."

Mr. Dixon. It's the whole atmosphere.

Pediatrician. You mean they still kept their sense at 2:00 in the morning?

Mr. Dixon. Well, of course 2:00 in the morning to them may be 2:00 in the afternoon for some people; they're more awake than we are, but we've called at 2:00 in the morning, 11:00 at night, just before they're changing shifts, and nobody ever rushes you and says, "Call back in 10 minutes." Somebody always takes the time to talk to you and explain things. That's the biggest thing. I learned more while Kimberly was in the hospital here about medicine and different things, equipment and pieces of equipment, how you use it, blood transfusions—they had to give her blood.

Mrs. Dixon. That scared me too. I thought, "Oh, poor baby—she doesn't have enough blood."

Mr. Dixon. But after that, the change. It was remarkable. It seemed the day after she got that blood there was such a rapid improvement. Her color and activity. She became much more active and cried.

Pediatrician. Could we go back to the first time you handled her? When was that?

Mr. Dixon. She was still in the incubator. She was only in 40% oxygen—no, lower than that. I think it was 30%. So they said we could hold her for a few minutes.

Mrs. Dixon. Everybody knew that I wanted to hold her. Everybody knew me when I walked in. I didn't know them, but they all knew me. "Oh, you're Kimberly's mother!"

Considering the intense pressure on the staff of an intensive care nursery, it is remarkable how warm, welcoming, and thoughtful the staff in this nursery has been. The staff nurses, nurses' aides, and secretaries have been welcoming mothers into the nursery to touch and hold their infants since the early 1950s. In any nursery it may at times be difficult to show enthusiasm about the visit of parents, particularly when the work load and pressures are heavy. It has been helpful for us to put ourselves in the place of a mother. She comes to the incredibly frightening nursery, fearful that her baby is dead or dying. There are new sounds, tubes, machines, and other sick babies. Combined, these are often enough to cause beginning nurses or medical students to feel faint, particularly if blood or unusual odors are evident. Because she has been separated from her infant, the mother's imagination has pictured a baby who may be much sicker in many respects than her baby. Her tremendous guilt and overpowering belief that something bad about her has injured her baby and caused the infant to come early and be sick heightens her anxiety. The best remedy for the mother is for the staff of the nursery to recognize her, welcome her into the nursery, tell her what a fine baby she has, tell her how much the baby benefits from her visits and touch, and impress on her the importance of the care and feeding she will provide for her baby.

Mr. Dixon. That's how they knew her, as Kimberly's mother.

Mrs. Dixon. But I got to hold her, and I just felt like all these thoughts I had about her dying completely were gone because there was no way. I was very determined there was no way. "You're going to fight. You wanted to come early, you're not leaving now. You're staying."

Mr. Dixon. We told that to her—"You can't leave now. You've fought too long."

Mrs Dixon. "You were so impatient, you couldn't wait, you're staying here, not leaving."

Pediatrician. Do you remember when you felt the baby was yours?

Mr. Dixon. I think we felt that from the beginning, but in a way the jealousy comes back up. I didn't really feel that as much as I did the fear.

Mrs. Dixon. I didn't feel that she was my baby until I got to stay with her— when you said I could live with her those three days in the hospital. I took care of her, I did everything for her, I carried her, and I did everything for her. I fed her. Then she was my baby.

Pediatrician. It wasn't when she came out of the incubator and you held her that first day, then?

Mrs. Dixon. I was still scared then. I knew she was my baby, but I didn't know for keeps, and I didn't feel she was a real baby.

The mother's fear about the survival of her baby may inhibit the normal attachment process. The opportunity for this mother to care completely for her baby did much more than the previous visits to assure her about the value of her contributions to Kimberly's well-being.

Mr. Dixon. Had anything happened after that so the baby couldn't come home, Ann would have been very upset.

Pediatrician. So something changed when you had the baby down at the end of the hall in the room.

Mrs. Dixon. She was a real baby. She was mine.

Mr. Dixon. And she was going home. We were going to be together as a family.

Mrs. Dixon. Finally we were going to be a family. I wasn't going to have to run back here and run back home and fix dinner and run back to the hospital. I was so tired of doing that. It's not that we resented coming here at all —I wanted to be here. It was just so much, going back and forth, and I hated to leave here. I really did. I thought, "I have to leave my baby now." I always told the nurse, "Please turn her head the other way so that when I walk out she won't see me leave." One night she cried and I had to go back. I felt like, "She knows I'm leaving her, and I can't leave her." So I went back in and she stopped crying and I finally left.

Mr. Dixon. I don't think Ann and I have ever really talked about that. But as soon as the baby was born, of course you know it's my first child and I was so excited. The doctor said, "There is a slight problem, but don't be concerned." I didn't really become that concerned until we went back to the hospital. But that baby was mine from that moment. I was petrified, especially when we came here and saw all these incubators and here's Kimberly. But I got to put my hand in (the isolette). I was scared. I really was. You encouraged me and said, "Put your hand in." You said, "Touch her leg." If anybody could have taken a picture—I put my hand in almost hesitantly. I was frightened. But that baby was mine—or ours—in my mind anyway. The baby was sick; there were some problems. Everything that could be done was being done. I was very reassured by you and the staff. Your people are fantastic. That was what pulled me through.

Mrs. Dixon. Everyone was so kind, and no one gives you, "Oh, Mrs. Dixon—again."

Pediatrician. Could we go back to the last three days when you stayed in the room? Did you feel the baby was yours right away or was it the second day?

Mrs. Dixon. When the nurse left, she was mine. I had to take care of her; I had to do everything for her, and that was great. I felt like, "She's my baby now, and I have all the responsibility for her."

Pediatrician. Did you think about her a little differently?

Mrs. Dixon. There was no nurse there. Before there was always a nurse around so I could say, "Hey, come here. What's this, what's that?" Here I am, right here, she's my baby and I have all the mother responsibilities now. There's no nurse here who can pick her up and say, "Well, it's time for this now."

Pediatrician. When you lived in with your baby, you were on a division where the babies weren't just getting bigger, the babies there were sick. Did the mothers talk to you or try to include you?

Mrs. Dixon. Well, at night we'd go into the lounge and sit and talk. There was a mother of a girl who was six weeks early also. She is now 2 years old and has had twelve operations on her head in two years. She doesn't think that she will live beyond 6 years old. I thought, "My baby was six weeks early too!" And they didn't know this when she brought the baby home. Her baby was in the hospital for a month also, and they told her, "Oh, your baby is fine."

Pediatrician. So all the old worries quickly came back?

Mrs. Dixon. Yes, they all came back. I thought, "Why is he putting me here—to make me realize how lucky I am that my baby is well? Because I know—I feel like I'm the luckiest woman in the world."

Mr. Dixon. Now that the baby is home I sometimes forget she was sick. She's so well—she screams and she hollers. And I love to hear her cry—except at 3:00 in the morning.

Mrs. Dixon. I think it was good that while I was in the hospital he was here with the baby. I thought that was very good because whenever he would come and talk to me about her, he was so proud. He would say, "I was touching her and I was rubbing her leg. They told me to hold her hand, and you know, she gripped my hand—just pulled on really tight." I thought that was very good because usually the father just sits there and watches.

Mr. Dixon. Here it was just the opposite.

RECOMMENDATIONS FOR CARE

1. *First hour.* When a premature infant weighing between 4 and 5 pounds is born and appears to be doing well without grunting and retractions, we have found it safe for the mother to have the baby placed in her bed in the first hour of life with a heat panel above them. We do not recommend this unless the physician feels relaxed about the health of the infant.

2. *Accommodations.* A mother and her infant should ideally be kept near each other in the same hospital, on the same floor. When the long-term significance of early mother-infant contact is kept in mind, a modification of restrictions and territorial traditions can usually be arranged. Ideally a mother appears to develop a closer attachment if she can have some privacy with her infant in a separate room near or connected to the unit.

3. *Transport.* In our transport system we have found it helpful, if the baby does have to be moved to a hospital with an intensive care unit, to give the mother a chance to see and touch her infant, even if he has respiratory distress and is in an oxygen hood. The house officer or the attending physician stops in the mother's room with the transport incubator and encourages her to touch her baby and look at him at close hand. A comment about the baby's strength and healthy features may be long remembered and appreciated. The infant must be pink and adequately ventilating before we take him to his mother. If he is gasping and blue, resuscitative measures are taken in the referring hospital, and our transportation team stays in the hospital until we can be sure of a safe trip.

4. *Father's participation.* We encourage the father to follow the transport team to our hospital so that he can see what is happening with his baby. He uses his own transportation so that he can stay in the premature unit for 3 to 4 hours. This extra time allows him to get to know

the nurses and physicians in the unit, to find out how the infant is being treated, and to talk with the physicians in a relaxed fashion about what we expect will happen with the baby and his treatment in the succeeding days. We allow him to come into the nursery, often offering him a cup of coffee, and explain in detail everything that is going on with his infant. We ask him to act as a link between us and the members of his family and the hospital by carrying information back to his wife so that he can let her know how the baby is doing. We suggest that he take a polaroid picture, even when the infant is on a respirator, so that he can describe in detail to his wife how the baby is being cared for. Mothers often tell us how valuable the pictures are for keeping some contact with their infant even while being physically separated.

5. *Initial visit to nursery.* A mother should be permitted into the premature nursery as soon as she is able to maneuver easily. In all our contacts we tell her that the staff of the nursery looks forward to her visit and that we know her baby will make better progress once she is able to visit. When the mother makes her first visit, it is important to anticipate that she may become faint or dizzy when she looks at her infant. We always have a stool nearby so that she can sit down, and a nurse stays at her side during most of the visit describing in detail the procedures that are being carried out, such as the monitoring of respiration and heart rate, the umbilical catheter, the feeding through the various infusion lines, and the functioning of the incubator.

6. *Cesarean section mother.* We have found it exhausting for mothers who have had a cesarean section to visit more than once a day after discharge from the hospital. The single visit a day can be extended, but it is best that it not last more than a few hours in the first week after the mother has had a cesarean section birth.

7. *Family visits.* We also encourage grandparents, brothers, sisters, and other relatives to view the infant through the glass window of the nursery so that they will begin to feel attached to the infant.

8. *Discussions with parents.* At least once a day we discuss how the child is doing with the parents; we talk with them at least twice a day if the child is critically ill.

It is necessary to find out what the mother believes is going to happen or what she has read about the problem. We try to move at her pace during any discussion to ensure that she understands everything we say.

9. *Telephone communications.* While discussing the infant's condition by telephone with the mother who is still in the referring hospital, we ask the father to stand nearby so that we can talk to them

both at the same time and they can hear the same message. This group communication reduces misunderstandings and usually is helpful in assuring the mother that we are telling her the whole story.

Parents are encouraged to call our unit 24 hours a day. This permits them to get an immediate report of their baby's status, activity, and color. This practice has occasionally led to confusion because several nurses may report the same infant's condition within several hours and use slightly different words. Ideally, only one nurse should talk with the parents. However, this is not practical, since shifts last 8 hours. Confusion can be avoided if the nurse writes down her message to the mother on the care record. However, this may be impossible in an extremely busy unit.

The day secretary has the daily weights of the infants available at her desk. Therefore she can at least quickly report this information to the mother who calls and is waiting to speak to the nurse.

> COMMENT: In our nursery there is generally a nurse assigned to each baby, and the parents would know who was taking care of their baby during a particular shift. Thus when they call in, they either ask for or are referred to the nurse who is taking care of their baby, and the information given may be highly personal and specific to their child's progress. This has helped to develop rapport and very good communication between the parents and the nursing staff.   K. BARNARD

10. *Optimistic attitude.* If there is any chance that the infant will survive, we are optimistic in our talks with the parents from the beginning. If the infant is receiving 70% oxygen and assisted ventilation with continuous positive airway pressure, and if he has a P_{O_2} of 55 mm. Hg at 24 hours and a reasonable pH, we will say, "We're pleased by your infant's progress. He's active and pink. Although we're not in the clear yet, if we went to see Jimmy the Greek at Las Vegas or any other gambler, he'd certainly be betting with us and with good odds." The next day, when the blood gas values are about the same, we might say, "The baby's had an awfully good 24 hours; you have made a strong baby with good stamina. We're really pleased that everything is remaining the same. Now after going another day the baby's condition is obviously improving." There is no evidence that if a favorable prediction proves to be incorrect and the baby dies, the parents will be harmed by the early optimism. There is almost always time to prepare them before the baby actually dies. If he lives and the physician has been pessimistic, it is sometimes difficult for parents to become closely attached after they have figuratively dug a few shovelfuls of earth. We recognize that this recommendation is contrary to many old customs and places a heavy burden on the physician. It is our belief that if the

infant does die, we must still work with the mother and help her with the mourning period.

11. *Possible brain damage.* Once the possibility that a baby has brain damage has been mentioned, the parents will never forget it. Therefore, unless we are 100% sure that the baby is damaged, we do not mention the possibility of any brain damage or retardation to the parents. On many occasions we have had neonates who have appeared to be brain damaged, but who later were obviously perfectly normal. Of the premature and full-term infants in our hospital suspected to be brain damaged, only *one half* were correctly diagnosed as normal or brain damaged in spite of multiple diagnostic studies and skillful neurological evaluations. If we had told the mother and father that we were concerned about damage to the brain, we might have indelibly inscribed on both parents' minds a concern which might have continued for many years. After the possibility of brain damage has been mentioned early in infancy, we have had these children return years later and tell us how much it has affected their lives. Even after 20 years of normal progress some tell us they are still concerned that they are subnormal in mental ability and that they avoid competitive situations and worry excessively about examinations.

12. *Explaining findings.* It is important to emphasize that if we have a clear, objective finding, such as a cardiac abnormality or a specific congenital malformation, we see no reason to hide this from the parents. We would never lie to a parent. It should be remembered, however, that in overwhelming situations some parents can only assimilate a small amount of information every day. Explanations can be kept as simple as is appropriate to the situation. There is no need to add a wide variety of diagnostic possibilities or potential complications that may never develop.

13. *Touching.* As soon as possible we describe to both the father and the mother the value of touching their infant. It helps them get to know him, reduces the number of apneic episodes (if this is a problem), increases weight gain, and hastens the infant's discharge from the unit.

14. *Feedback from infant.* We are presently testing the principle that the human mother must receive feedback from her baby in response to her caretaking for her to develop a close attachment. If the infant looks at her eyes, moves in response to her caretaking, quiets down or shows through any behavior that he appreciates her efforts, he will provide fuel for his mother's feeling of attachment. Practically speaking, this means that the mother must catch the glance of the baby's eye and be able to see that some maneuver on her part, such as picking him up and soothing him, actually quiets him. We suggest to our

mothers, therefore, that they try to send a message to the baby and pick one up in return. Usually when we say this to the parents, they laugh. They think we are joking. We then explain that small premature infants do see, being especially interested in patterned objects, and that they can hear as well as adults. Because the baby often sleeps for 2 to 3 hours, waking up for only short periods of time, the parents need to stay in the nursery for long periods to be able to see one of these short periods. This usually requires special help from the nurse or some other caretaker.

It is important to remember that feelings of love for the baby are often elicited through eye-to-eye contact. Therefore if an infant is under bilirubin lights, we turn them off and remove the eye patches so that the mother and her infant can really see each other.

15. *Breastfeeding.* It is especially helpful for the mother to make some tangible contribution to her infant, such as providing breast milk. At the present time it appears that breast milk may be very helpful in reducing the number of infections and other complications in the premature nursery. Therefore we are presently suggesting to all obstetricians referring patients to our unit that they enthusiastically suggest that the mother supply some of her milk to meet the nutritional needs of her infant.

16. *Recording parental performance.* From our previous observations we have found that keeping a book in which to record parental phone calls and visits is useful in determining which mothers are likely to require additional help from a social worker or extra discussions about the health of their infant. If a mother visits fewer than three times in two weeks, the probability of occurrence of some sort of mothering disorder, such as failure to thrive, battering, or giving up the baby increases. Therefore, if the visiting pattern of a mother is less than that of most mothers, she is given extra help in adapting to the hospitalization.

17. *Staff meetings.* Nurses should feel comfortable in reporting any worries or problems that they have about a mother's and father's behavior. To accomplish this there must be a good working relationship between the physicians and the nurses. Meetings with the nursery staff in the intensive care unit should be held every two weeks. This provides an opportunity for them to express their very real concerns and problems.

COMMENT: The necessity for team work is as great in the high-risk nursery as anywhere, and it is important that the staff have the opportunity to develop knowledge of each other's skills and abilities and thereby gain a respect which will enhance the working relationship and the team work which is required in caring for the infant and the family.

K. BARNARD

We are including the following report because it describes the reactions of mothers of premature infants in a nursery that has been a leader in the development and application of intensive care. At the time of this study this nursery was beginning to allow mothers to enter and touch their premature infants. The circumstances and reactions present at the time of this study are quite different now, a few years later. This is a psychological study of the reaction of mothers to the birth of a premature infant; it was conducted by a psychiatrist who was attempting to gather clinical information in the area of mother-child attachment. We would like especially to thank Dr. Bertrand Cramer, who submitted this manuscript to us.

A mother's reactions to the birth
of a premature baby

BERTRAND CRAMER, M.D.[*]

Many studies have shown that both the psychic development and the ultimate emotional stability of the child depend on the nature of the child's relationship with his mother. Although maternal actions influence the child throughout his development, the early patterns of a mother-child relationship play a particularly decisive role. In fact, this relationship has already begun before birth and has been influenced by the mother's attitudes, both unconscious and conscious, toward her feminine role and by her fears, desires, and preconceptions of pregnancy, childbirth, and child rearing.

Just as the child develops from stage to stage, his mother must go through a series of developmental phases. Each presents the mother with new challenges and psychosocial tasks that she must master, using her own internal and external resources. As Caplan (1964) has stated, these challenges represent "developmental crises," which can be described in terms of the demands they place on a woman's inner psychological forces, and which may precipitate healthy or unhealthy outcomes.

Prematurity is an "accidental" psychosocial crisis that lends itself well to study. It occurs frequently, and its onset and severity can be easily determined. Caplan and co-workers (1965) have successfully documented the major tasks facing the mother of a premature infant. First, she must face the possibility that her child might die. Second, she must cope with a feeling of inadequacy, since she has been unable to produce a "normal" baby. Third, after the initial days of uncertainty

[*]At the time of the study, Dr. Cramer was "medecin adjoint" at the University of Lausanne Pediatrics Department, Lausanne, Switzerland.

she must renew her relationship with her child, a child who thus far has been separated from her. Fourth, she must adapt to the specific characteristics of a premature infant's development.

When mothers of premature infants are studied closely, it is apparent that they must put forth an enormous psychological effort to cope adequately. Caplan and co-workers have stated that the parents must have the following capabilities to cope effectively with the crisis: They must have the capacity to understand the problem realistically (a cognitive coping mechanism); they must be aware of their feelings and able to verbalize them (an affective coping process); and they must be able to elicit help from others (a social coping mechanism). By studying these methods of coping, Caplan and co-workers made predictions concerning the future emotional stability of the mother and most importantly the future emotional health of the child, from which they were able to predict the nature of her maternal behavior.

Whereas Caplan's pioneering studies have documented that premature birth causes a major psychological crisis for the mother, with the tasks and coping mechanisms that he described, my colleagues and I were interested in eliciting clinical material that would describe the mother's behavior and, particularly, the subjective experience during the crisis.

We anticipated that such a clinical study would enable us to determine the following:

1. Psychological reactions commonly found in mothers who have given birth to a premature infant
2. Individual variations in responses
3. The impact of the staff's attitudes and hospital practices on the mother's feelings
4. An improved preventive and therapeutic approach by identifying the main areas of stress and suffering

For this purpose I interviewed mothers of premature babies in a semistructured interview, encouraging the mother to express thoughts and feelings freely, while asking leading questions about the reactions to the premature birth, the first sight of the baby, the separation from him, fears for the baby's health and survival, the hospital routine, the first encounter with the baby in the incubator, the homecoming, and finally caring for a small infant.

The mothers were interviewed twice, once during the ten days after the birth and then again approximately two months later. All the mothers were interviwed for 1½ hours each time.

The sample consisted of thirteen mothers. A mother was chosen if her infant was born prematurely, weighed less than 2500 grams, and was predicted to be in the premature unit for at least two weeks. Each of the mothers was told that she was part of a larger, ongoing research project on prematurity. If it was acceptable to her, a physician would ask her questions about the birth of her child. None of the mothers refused to participate. However, three mothers broke their second interview appointment.

CLINICAL FINDINGS
Self-esteem problems

The most frequently found feeling was a sense of failure. A typical comment by a mother was, "I am not even able to carry it through to the end like other mothers." Mothers explained their infant's premature birth on the basis of a personal defect, often believed to be a physical one. One mother thought that the prematurity was due to a hormonal deficiency; another requested an examination of her kidneys. The mother who had the most severe problem in accepting her feminine identity explained the prematurity on the basis of a psychological defect, "It is as if I were not maternal enough . . . I rejected the child." She accused herself of being too manlike and revealed serious anxieties about the integrity of her reproductive organs.

Several mothers expressed this sense of failure in the maternal role by declaring that they would never want to become pregnant again. They thought that it would be better to avoid pregnancy, since they might not be able to carry it through properly.

The separation of the infant from the mother heightened the feeling of failure. To these women such an experience served as proof of their inadequacy as mothers. Not only had the mother delivered prematurely, but she felt inadequate—she was not capable of caring for her own infant.

The infant was a profound wound to the mother's self-pride. The mother saw the child, an extension of herself, as defective or an inferior quality product, since he had a low birth weight, a disappointing physical appearance, and frequently accompanying pathology.

Mrs. N. could hardly hide her disappointment, "I always hoped to have big babies weighing at least 3500 grams. If the baby had been that big, they would not have taken him away from me. I feel inferior to my girl friends. In my family they produce big babies. It was always the joy of my family to have big bundles. I told myself that the baby was not complete." Insufficiency was a common theme. The pregnancy was not complete, the baby was not complete, and hence many mothers drew the irrational conclusion that they too were not complete.

The mother's concern for the future normality of her child, especially in the intellectual sphere, is a result of her initial feeling of her child's incompleteness. "Will he be like other kids?" "Will he be able to keep up in school?"

The blow to the mother's self-esteem is even more dramatic when her child is afflicted with a congenital defect or a chronic disease. If parents of children born with multiple congenital defects do not receive help, they can have such a lowered self-esteem that they totally withdraw interest in and concern for the child, whom they perceive as a sign of their own badness. The results can be dramatic, with total maternal deprivation or battered child syndrome as the outcome.

To understand the dynamics of these blows to the mother's self-esteem and the tremendous impact they can have on the evolution of the mother-child relationship, we have to borrow from the psycho-analytical concept of narcissism. Narcissism is the investment of love and interest in the self-image, the body and its contents. Although this form of love is centripetal, directed toward the self, other currents of love are centrifugal, directed toward people and the external world. This is object love. To understand the mother's relationship with her child it is necessary to examine the relationship between narcissism and object love in the mother. Such a study was done by Bibring and associates (1961).

In early pregnancy the embryo is enveloped by the mother's body, and hence the mother views her unborn infant as part of herself, incorporating it into her own narcissism. This total fusion, where the embryo is viewed merely as a content of the body, is disrupted at the first signs of quickening. The mother then begins to perceive the fetus as a separate entity and therefore begins to invest it with increasing amounts of object love. By the time of birth the mother's transition from narcissistic to object love is more nearly complete. Now the mother is able to tolerate the anatomical separation and to consider her newborn as a complete person, well separated from herself. However, the infant remains encapsulated by his mother's narcissistic love, and it is only the slow development of the child into an adult that allows the mother to become increasingly aware of her child's separate existence.

However, in a premature birth there is an abrupt eviction of the fetus before the mother has been able to invest it with enough object love. We may therefore hypothesize that in a premature birth the fetus is the recipient of too much narcissistic love—as if he were still perceived as part of the mother's inner organs. The birth becomes an insult to the mother's bodily integrity and is a narcissistic injury. As one mother said when her child was taken from her at birth, "It was as if they ripped a piece of my guts out."

A clinical finding clearly illustrates the mother's inability to perceive the baby with enough object love because of premature eviction from the narcissistic mother-fetus unit: The majority of the thirteen mothers described a feeling of inability to believe that their child was real. The mothers made comments such as, "I just can't believe it, it is as if *nothing* had happened." "For me to believe it, I would have to see the child." This dreamlike unreality indicates that to the mother the child is still a part of her, not an independent real object. This feeling of unreality, heightened by the lack of object love, is strengthened by the enforced separation between the mother and her child. All the mothers thought that the real birth occurred weeks later, when they could touch and feed the child, and mainly when they could take him home.

None of the mothers had prepared a crib or clothing for her child. To these mothers their infants were not yet real, independent people who would need to be cared for once outside their protective body.

In view of these various findings, we propose the following hypothesis: The birth of a premature infant is a severe blow to the mother's self-esteem, mothering capabilities, and feminine role. It is conceived of as a loss of a body part, an insult to her bodily integrity, and a sign of inner inferiority. The premature birth enforces a feeling of unreality about the child, who is perceived as alien, thus more easily rejected.

Three mothers did not have a self-esteem problem. Of these three, two started into labor very soon after the death of a close relative (a mother, a brother). They explained that the newborn was called on to replace the lost relative. One of these two mothers said, "I had the little one for Mother. It will help me to cope with the loss of Mother. It fills up a void for my father too." The other mother, whose brother died in an automobile accident, said, "When the baby was born, my mother said, 'It is through your brother's death that we got the baby.'"

In these cases the premature child, far from revealing a defect, helped the mother to cope with another narcissistic blow, the loss of a loved one.

The third mother previously had numerous spontaneous abortions, which had severely undermined her husband's respect for her. When she finally had a 1390-gram infant, it was experienced as a victory, despite its poor appearance. It was a great achievement, compensating for the severe blows dealt to her maternal pride by the previous miscarriages.

The deterioration of the mother's self-esteem, as just described, confirms Caplan's (1965) finding that the mother must overcome the narcissistic blow of the premature birth and the deficiencies of the infant before she can accept her child. The lowering of the mother's self-esteem, coupled with the early separation of the mother-child dyad, inhibits the establishment of the mother-child relationship.

Guilt problems

Almost all of the mothers of the premature infants expressed guilt feelings. They accused themselves of being bad mothers, of having exposed their child to great stress by forcing him out of the protective womb. "If he were still in me, he wouldn't have to suffer with all those needles and tubes."

To the mothers the premature birth was a punishment for some misdeed. When asked to explain the cause of the prematurity, they expressed varied irrational interpretations. Although there may have been some grain of reality in their explanations, the issue was blown out of proportion. For example, they attributed the prematurity to the following: engaging in sexual activity too frequently, drinking three glasses of cognac, smoking, enjoying a job, or feeling inadequate. Several mothers thought that they would never be able to forgive themselves if the child were to be damaged or to die. Some mothers were concerned that their child might later accuse them for having given birth prematurely. Often mothers attempted to transfer the guilt onto doctors, nurses, or their husbands—accusing them of some misdeed that caused the prematurity.

These feelings of guilt interfere, often severely, in three areas:

1. In the establishment of a relationship with the child. The mother believes that she is dangerous and incapable of protecting the child. As a result, when finally in contact with the child, she does not dare to touch him unless given permission by the nurses. The greatest fear occurs when the child comes home. The mother is afraid to feed the baby by herself or to bathe him. "I am afraid he might choke to death." "He will slip out of my hands and drown." "I am afraid he might break in my hands." Considering themselves as potential dangers to the child, the mothers may not enter or even visit the premature unit.

Often mothers think that the nurses can offer better maternal care to their infant than they can. To them the premature unit is a surrogate womb, more successful in protecting the child than they are. These feelings of gratitude, however, are accompanied by a feeling of inferiority. The mother's feelings of maternal paralysis can be greatly increased when the staff considers the unit to be an air-tight, totally aseptic area where visiting mothers are essentially thought to be a bother and a source of infection.

2. Guilt feelings interfere with the mother's ability to ask the hospital staff medical questions. The mother's lack of information fosters the perpetuation of guilt-centered explanations and increases the mother's belief that she is a potential harm to her child. One mother clearly indicated that she did not want to know too much about the causes of the prematurity because she was afraid her "faults" would be revealed.

3. The mother's feelings of guilt determined whether the interview had positive or negative therapeutic results.

For several mothers the interview provided an opportunity to verbalize and neutralize their guilt feelings. By providing the mother with a straight forward medical explanation and relocating the sense of guilt, we were able to neutralize her guilt feelings. For example, one mother was afraid of approaching her newborn until she was able to acknowledge her rejection feelings. She believed that she had rejected her son in the same way she had rejected all of her feminine functions. After the interview she "reestablished" the relationship with her son and said, "My maternal instinct has come back." She was grateful for the opportunity to express her negative, guilt-ridden feelings and have them "neutralized" by rational, medical explanations.

Mothers who could not cope with their guilt were cautious during the interviews and could not benefit from them. These mothers refused to come for the follow-up interview. They had been exceedingly guarded during the first interview and had minimized their concern for their infant. They were unwilling to explore their feelings further or express a desire to learn more about the medical causes of prematurity. One husband called after his wife had been interviewed and accused the interviewer of asking indiscreet questions, of accusing his wife of having wished to abort the child. This was not true, but it revealed the mother's own guilt, since she had conceived before marriage. When this mother had been asked to explain the reasons behind the prematurity, she had replied, "I rather avoid thinking about a precise reason." She was so burdened by guilt, so ashamed of harboring wishes for an abortion, that she could not freely experience or reveal her emotions. She refused a second interview.

These guilt reactions are also present in all the parents of children born with defects or congential conditions. This guilt can be severe enough to dissolve a marriage, each spouse unburdening his or her guilt by accusing the other of carrying a "bad gene" or being the cause of the illness.

Just as the success of the interview depended on the mother's ability to tolerate guilt, it is probably the guilt factor that determines the outcome of the physician-parent relationship in cases of premature birth and congenital defects.

It was interesting to note that certain characteristics of the newborn influence the mother's ability to handle her guilt. One mother complained that her child did not respond to her—she did not smile, move, or vocalize. The mother interpreted the lack of feedback as a sign of her child's total defenselessness. The child would not be capable of protecting herself against the mother's possible wrongdoings. This made the mother feel dangerous, overpowering, and extremely anxious. The hypoactivity frequent in the premature infant is reminiscent of cases among animals, in which the mother will kill the offspring that show deviant behavior. Maternal behavior in humans might also depend on triggering stimuli stemming from the newborn.

Separation problems

The premature infant is quickly taken away from the mother in the moments following birth. Reactions to this separation are universal. The loss contributes to the process of anticipatory mourning described by Caplan and associates (1965).

Mothers experience a void, an amputation. They make remarks such as, "I never felt such a longing in my life." "It is as if they had taken out an organ." They express an intense wish to touch, to breastfeed the child. During this separation they imagine the worst possible outcome. They are positive that the truth is being kept from them and that the child is actually dying or is abnormal.

The anticipatory mourning can be so intense that the mothers refuse to contemplate their future relationship with the child. They avoid talking about the child with relatives. They rarely ask family members to visit the child. A typical remark is, "I don't want to think ahead until I'm sure." Only one mother sent birth announcements. None prepared a crib until the child made definite progress. There is a period of suspense, with an effort not to think about the child. This is in significant contrast to the total maternal preoccupation found in mothers with normal newborn infants.

The longer the waiting period persists the deeper will be the withdrawal of investment in the child. In some cases this withdrawal seems irreversible, with the possible results of deprivation syndromes (failure to thrive, battered child syndrome).

In favorable cases this break in the mother-child relationship begins to diminish at the first meeting between the mother and infant. It is only when the mother can handle her child, after he has made definite progress, that the relationship is revitalized and the mother allows herself to experience the gamut of maternal feelings.

In our study there was at least one case of totally irreversible rejection of a child. One of the mothers who had been most guarded in the first interview and refused to return for the follow-up had given birth to twins. The smaller of the two was kept in the premature unit for two months while the heavier one was taken home within the first month. When the smaller child finally went home, he developed a severe anorexia, which necessitated rehospitalization. After psychiatric consultation it was clear that the child who had been separated the longest from the mother had been totally rejected. Adoption by the grandmother was necessary.

Different sets of factors may be involved in explaining these defects in maternal functioning after separation. Maternal response needs to be stimulated by close mutual interaction between the mother and child from the onset. Also it is as if separation—during this sensitive period when mothering is established—may unleash aggressive impulses in the mother toward her child, which cause the mother to refuse closeness and avoid the child.

GENERAL CONSIDERATIONS ABOUT THE CRISIS OF PREMATURITY

The data of this study suggest that the birth of a premature infant produces a severe psychological crisis for the mother. Clearly more subjects would be needed, as well as control subjects of full-term infants, to qualify how characteristic these reactions are for prematurity. The present study has to be considered as a pilot one. Our data document that these mothers undergo particular anxieties that confront them with undue stress. This can interfere with the mother's psychological well-being and, most important, with the establishment of the mother-child relationship. This crisis is not, however, necessarily pathologic.

The establishment of mothering behavior is a fragile process. The premature birth, the unfinished pregnancy, the early separation between mother and infant, and the seemingly unresponsive infant all place the mothering response in jeopardy. The precrisis personality of the mother also plays a role in determining her response and the severity of the developing pathology in maternal behavior. We found Caplan's (1960) criteria of specific patterns of crisis behavior, as indicators of favorable or unfavorable outcomes, extremely helpful in understanding why certain mothers did better than others.

DIAGNOSTIC AND THERAPEUTIC CONSIDERATIONS

Caplan (1960) described three sets of coping patterns: (1) the mother's ability to master the situation by cognitive understanding, that is, the way she explains the prematurity and its surrounding circumstances; (2) the mother's ability to handle and relate her feelings, her emotional coping; and (3) the mother's ability to secure help from others.

Cognitive coping

Although these mothers were generally well educated, only a few were capable of asking for rational explanations of the prematurity. The characteristic attitude was a lack of active curiosity, which led to the persistence of irrational, guilt-ridden explanations. As it turned out, one of the most beneficial aspects of the interview was that it provided an opportunity to relay rational, medical information. One mother would not believe that her baby had not suffered from irreparable damage until she was shown the chest x-ray films.

Verbalization of feelings

Mothers who denied their feelings were characteristically unresponsive and "cold" during the interview. On the other hand, mothers who could verbalize their feelings, particularly their guilt feelings, benefited most from the interview and made good recoveries at the follow-up interview.

Securing help

The mothers were paralyzed. They could not seek advice and comfort from the nurses and physicians. However, this might also be a reflection of the hospital staff's attitudes. At the time of the study the premature unit was still partly closed to the mothers. The mothers were kept behind glass windows, strengthening their feelings that they were only an inconvenience, possibly dangerous, and intruding.

Aside from the therapeutic gain derived from the verbalization of feelings, the interview was responsible for other therapeutic advances. In several cases the existing situation was particularly anxiety provoking, reawakening previously experienced traumatic situations. In such cases the prematurity was massively invaded by anxieties and guilt stemming from the past. The interview was therapeutic, since it was able to help the mother with the present crisis by enabling discussion of the past situations that were causing much of the anxiety and by separating these from the present crisis.

As an example of this, one mother underwent massive mourning for her premature newborn. She was sure that he was going to die and thus preferred not to ask for any information about him. She was also under the impression that the doctors taking care of the baby were performing operations that would kill him. It turned out that when she was 5 years old, her 9-month-old sister suddenly became ill with an acute lung infection. The doctor was called. He took the sick sister away from home and returned with the child, dead, 2 hours later. The mother was sure that the doctor had killed her sister while performing an operation. She had never forgiven him, and now, as an adult, she was unable to trust doctors. At birth, when her newborn was taken from her, she immediately relived the scene when the doctor precipitously took her sister away from home, and she was convinced that her baby would also die.

This particular mother previously had another child, also born prematurely. When this infant reached the age of 9 months (age of sister's death) and developed a cold, she rushed him to the doctor, certain that he would die from a lung infection.

In the interview we discussed and emphasized the connections between the past events and the present. The mother was greatly relieved and was able to master her fear of the child's impending death. Her interest in her baby and her mothering resumed after the interview.

Another mother could not bring herself to visit her premature infant in the nursery until ten days after birth. She had recently lost her father after a long agony in the hospital, where he had been maintained by tubes for food and oxygen. The mother was afraid to see her child with tubes in the incubator, since it would reawaken the painful memories of her father's death and her fear that like the father, the child would die. After this connection was established, the mother was able to visit the infant and her mothering proceeded unhampered.

As other workers in this field have also noticed, we found that if a mother does not visit her child, this is a sign of pathology. The establishment of the mothering process is endangered and demands immediate attention.

The nurse's guidance in showing the mother how to hold, dress, and feed the infant was extremely important in helping her to overcome her mothering paralysis. It was as if the mother needed special reassurance and permission before she could go ahead with her mothering practices. Here it seems as if the nurse acted as the mother's own mother, teaching her the basic techniques of mothering.

In summary, preventive and therapeutic measures should be geared to optimal establishment of the mothering process. This work can be done on various levels:

1. At the level of hospital routine: The separation between mother and infant should be eradicated whenever possible. The premature unit should be run so that it promotes mother participation in infant care.

2. At the level of hospital staff: Nurses should take mothers under their wing, teaching and encouraging them when they first handle the child.

The communication of information should be encouraged, especially when mothers do not ask for explanations. The physician should establish a rapport with the mother to help her express feelings of low self-esteem and guilt. This does not necessarily require the extensive interview technique used in this study but can be done by a sensitive, psychologically alert pediatrician who knows how to listen to a mother's concerns.

Cases of frankly pathological deviations can be spotted whenever mothers show pronounced avoidance behavior (no visits), show marked denial when there are problems, evidence an absence of affective response, resort to constant accusation of the staff, or reveal consistent lack of maternal behavior. After discussion with such patients, if the maternal behavior fails to appear, the pediatrician should suggest psychiatric consultation.

Chapter 5

Caring for parents of an infant with a congenital malformation

Nancy A. Irvin, John H. Kennell, and Marshall H. Klaus

> The world breaks everyone and afterwards
> many are strong in the broken places.
>
> *Farewell to Arms*—Hemingway

The birth of a baby is the culmination of his parents' best efforts and embodies their hopes for the future. Thus it is not surprising that a newborn blighted with a malformation is a crushing blow to the parents and to everyone else who has shared in the event. However, human societies' responses to malformations are not uniform and may range from protection to exclusion.

Although United States society has elected to include most sickly or malformed infants through medical treatment, some societies have practiced euthanasia. For example, a tribe of African bushmen, the Zhun-twasi, practice infanticide with certain children. When a baby is born with a malformation such as agenesis of a limb, ear, or nose, with a malpresentation such as breech birth, or if he is one of a pair of twins, he is buried seconds after birth, even before he has breathed (Konner, 1972). This extreme, however, is rare and is often related to population or sex ratio control, not to the elimination of malformed infants.

In domestic animals a small or partially malformed kitten or puppy rarely survives. Often the littermates turn on the runt, or its mother abandons it. But this is not characteristic of the animal world. Reactions to a malformed animal are actually diverse, and many animals have been observed to sympathize with each other's distress or danger. Berkson (1974) noted that blind raccoons in the wild tend to do well, and Darwin (1871) described an old and completely blind but very fat pelican, who appeared to have been well fed by his companions.

167

Studies by Berkson (1974) of specifically damaged animals suggest that compensatory care for disabilities is found in animal groups with complex permanent societies in which individuals cooperate with one another to acquire food, rear young, and defend against predators. It appears that in these societies, aggression controls relationships but does not result in killing of animals. Berkson concludes: "In evolution there has been a development of social behaviors which maintain rather than exclude individuals from society."

The early recorded history of human society indicates that malformed infants have been treated in widely differing ways and have evoked a broad range of emotional reactions. The reactions parents experience today after the birth of a malformed baby are not novel. Warkany (1971) noted that when "a monstrosity was born, then man's emotions were aroused and he reacted to such misfortune with admiration, awe, or terror. His emotions toward reproductive anomalies often have led to extreme measures; he exterminated or adored the deformed of the species—and sometimes he did both."[*] After killing an infant with a disfiguring abnormality, he "often made an image in its likeness and set it up as an idol-god or demigod. Sculptures, carvings, and drawings of abnormal births by ancient peoples antedate the arts of reading and writing; they reflect early teratologic knowledge and interest in rare and unusual human beings. That such deviants were made gods or goddesses is understandable. During times when human deities were worshipped, it was the unusual human being who assumed divine status."[*]

Despite new scientific knowledge about the origins of congenital defects, ancient superstitions still plague modern parents. Because of the strong emotional reactions accompanying the birth, it is not surprising that the lore of the past surfaces to haunt parents of children with congenital malformations.

BASIC AND CLINICAL CONSIDERATIONS

The birth of an infant with a congenital malformation presents complex challenges to the physician who will care for the affected child and family. In the United States a major malformation occurs in two of every 100 births. Thus almost every nurse or physician will have a part in the care of these babies. Yet despite the relatively large number of infants with anomalies, understanding of the development of parental attachment to a malformed infant remains incomplete. A number of investigators agree that the child's birth often precipitates a major

[*]From Warkany, J.: Congenital malformations: notes and comments, Chicago, 1971, Year Book Medical Publishers, Inc.

family crisis, but relatively few have described the process by which the parents and family members adapt.

The objective of this chapter is to describe methods for helping parents from widely diverse backgrounds develop attachments to their malformed infants. This is difficult, since parental reactions are turbulent, and the usual pathways for the development of close parent-infant bonds are disrupted. The final absolute goal is best described by Bettelheim (1972): "Children can learn to live with a disability. But they cannot live well without the conviction that their parents find them utterably loveable. . . . If the parents, knowing about his [the child's] defect, love him now, he can believe that others will love him in the future. With this conviction, he can live well today and have faith about the years to come."

The strength and character of the original parent-infant attachment will influence the quality of the child's bonds with other individuals in the future. During this early period the design and weave of future interactions and attachments, which determine the personality structure, are set.

During the course of a normal pregnancy, the mother and father develop a mental picture of their baby. Although the degree of concreteness varies, each has an idea about the sex, complexion, coloring, and so forth. One of the early tasks of parenting is to resolve the discrepancy between this idealized image of the infant and the actual appearance of the real infant (Solnit and Stark, 1961). The dreamed-about baby is a composite of impressions and desires derived from the parents' own experience. Therefore, if the parents have different cultural backgrounds, the tasks of reconciling the image to the reality is more complicated. However, the discrepancy is much greater if the baby is born with a malformation, and the parents must struggle to make the necessary major adjustment.

The reactions of the parents and the degree of their future attachment difficulties depend largely on the properties of the malformation:

Is it completely correctable or is it noncorrectable?
Is it visible or nonvisible?
Does it affect the central nervous system?
Is it life threatening?
Will it have an effect on the future development of the child?
Does it affect the genitalia? The eyes?
Is it a single or multiple malformation?
Is it familial?
Are there other members of the family with a malformation?
Will there be a need for repeated hospitalizations?
Will repeated visits to physicians or agencies be needed?

COMMENT: Does the malformation have a specific meaning for the parents because of their occupation or their cultural background and expectations?   A. J. SOLNIT

The initial reactions of the parents largely depend on the answers to these questions, which will determine the long-term problems they will have to face.

Few studies have separated the different impacts of various malformations, but a number of investigators have noted that the more visible the defects are the more immediate will be the resulting concern and embarrassment. Even a minor abnormality of the head and neck results in greater anxiety about future development than an impairment of another part of the body (Johns, 1971). This is in agreement with the findings that disabled adults with visible impairments experience more disruption in their interpersonal relationships than do those with non-visible impairments (Zahn, 1973).

COMMENT: Recent studies have shown that even in nursery school, children tend to select as their friends their better looking peers. This trend remains through the life of the person, and everyone is naturally initially drawn to a handsome-, or strong-, or sweet-looking person and withdraws from a physically unappealing person. The homely or malformed child, and later, adult, will have to compensate for his unattractiveness by an unusual personality. Parents may react with the same initial negative feelings toward their visibly malformed child, but through increased contact the infant's own personality should facilitate the overcoming of these feelings.   N. JOSEFOWITZ

In several studies parents have reported that when they saw their infants for the first time, the malformations seemed less alarming than they had imagined. Seeing the children allayed some of their anxiety. In our own studies one parent reported, "We had been conjuring up all kinds of things—that there could be something wrong with every organ. But then what I saw was a relatively normal baby" (Drotar et al., 1975). Others (Daniels and Berg, 1968; Johns, 1971) report similar parental reactions—the information that something was wrong with the baby was often far more disturbing than the sight of the child. Mothers found that the time spent waiting to see the baby after being told about a congenital amputation was the most difficult to endure (Daniels and Berg, 1968). Both the mothers and the fathers were greatly relieved when they actually saw their children.

Some parents were reluctant to see their babies at first, expressing a need to temper the intensity of the experience. When these parents did see their babies, it seemed to mark a turning point, and caretaking feelings were elicited where previously there had been none. Roskies (1972) studied the mothers of children with phocomelia due to thalidomide. She describes four mothers who were debating whether or not to institutionalize their children. The issue was settled when they saw their infants and found aspects they could "cherish." "When one mother looked into her baby's eyes he seemed to plead not to be abandoned." In our studies the parents of children with visible anomalies had a shorter period of shock and disbelief than did the parents of a child with a hidden defect. The shock of producing a baby with a visible defect is stunning and overwhelming, but attachment can be facilitated by showing parents their newborn baby as soon as possible.

> COMMENT: "Possible" includes when the parents feel ready, since enabling parents to be active in the decisions and care that affect their child will enhance their capacity to cope with the challenge of having a child with a congenital malformation.   A. J. SOLNIT

When 194 mothers of babies with spina bifida were interviewed, two thirds of the mothers preferred to be told about the diagnosis as early as possible and were satisfied with the information they had received about the defects. Any delay tended to heighten their anxiety. They objected to being given an unnecessarily gloomy picture at first on one hand and on the other hand they objected to having the seriousness of the condition minimized at first and aggrandized later. For example, one mother of an infant with myelomeningocele was told that the baby had "just a small pimple on her back, but that was nothing for her to worry about." The parents attached great importance to the approach and general attitude of the medical and nursing staff. Most importantly, they often did not recall the words of the nurse, obstetrician, or pediatrician but did remember their general attitude. Mothers who were hurt by an apparent lack of sympathy tended to attribute the abruptness to a lack of feeling in the informant, rather than to the likely cause—the difficulty of imparting such painful information. Most mothers were impressed by the kindness and sympathy extended to them by the nursing and medical staff. Small acts of kindness were clearly remembered years after the event. D'Arcy (1968) concludes that "the initial counseling of the mothers of malformed infants makes a deep and lasting impression."

In our studies, despite the wide variations among the children's malformations and parental backgrounds, a number of surprisingly similar themes emerged from the parents' discussion of their reactions. Generally they could recall the events surrounding the birth and their reactions in great detail (Drotar et al., 1975). They went through identifiable stages of emotional reactions, as shown in Fig. 5-1, which is a generalization of the complex reactions of individual parents. Although the amount of time that a parent needed to deal with the issues of a specific stage varied, the sequence of stages reflected the natural course of most parents' reactions to their malformed infant.

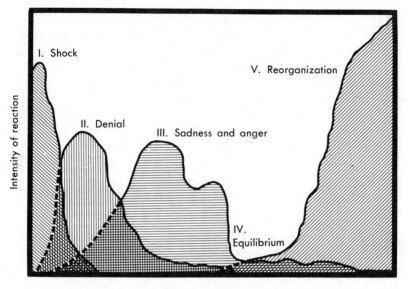

Fig. 5-1. Hypothetical model of the sequence of normal parental reactions to the birth of a child with congenital malformations. (From Drotar, D., Baskiewicz, A., Irvin, N., Kennell, J. H., and Klaus, M. H.: Pediatrics **56:**710-717, 1975.)

First stage: Shock

Most parents' initial response to the news of their child's anomaly was overwhelming shock. All but two of the parents reported reactions and sensations indicating an abrupt disruption of their usual states of feeling. One mother said, "It was a big blow which just shattered me." One of the fathers explained, "It was as if the world had come to an end." Many parents confided that this early period was a time of irrational behavior, characterized by much crying, feelings of helplessness, and occasionally an urge to flee.

Second stage: Disbelief (denial)

Many parents tried either to avoid admitting that their child had an anomaly or to cushion the tremendous blow. Each reported that he or she wished either to be free from the situation or deny its impact. One father graphically described his disbelief: "I found myself repeating 'It's not real' over and over again." Other parents mentioned that the news of the baby's birth did not make sense. One man admitted, "I just couldn't believe it was happening to me." Although every parent reported disbelief, the intensity of the denial varied considerably.

COMMENT: Between the second and third stage there is another stage that you mention later under doctor shopping (p. 177). It is kind of a bartering stage. There is often a return to religion or to giving to charities as if to say on a primitive, unconscious level: I have been bad, and I am punished, now if I promise to be good, my child will be made normal. One wishes to make "a deal" with God. It is also at this stage that there is the most danger of succumbing to quackery in the form of faith healers.

It is also my belief that anger precedes sadness or depression. The anger can be turned against God (who did not answer) and fate, but also against hospital staff, and as you mention, friends or relatives of the spouse. Doctors, nurses, and relatives can be warned that no matter how much one does for the mother or father, it is not enough, never right, and not appreciated. Of course the only help really wanted is to have the child made whole again, and nothing short of that will do.

N. JOSEFOWITZ

Third stage: Sadness, anger, and anxiety

Intense feelings of sadness and anger accompanied and followed the stage of disbelief. The most common emotional reaction was sadness. One mother reported, "I felt terrible. I couldn't stop crying. Even after a long while I cried about it." A smaller, but significant number of parents reported angry feelings. One father said, "I just wanted to kick someone." A mother reported that she was angry and "hated him (the baby) or hated myself. I was responsible." In most instances mothers feared for their babies' lives, despite strong reassurance. One mother said that she initially perceived her child as "nonhuman." "Holding him with that tube distressed me. Initially I held him only because it was the maternal thing to do." Almost all of the mothers were hesitant about becoming attached to their babies.

Fourth stage: Equilibrium

Parents reported a gradual lessening of both their anxiety and intense emotional reactions. As their feelings of emotional upset lessened, they noted increased comfort with their situation and confidence in their ability to care for the baby. Some parents reached equilibrium within a few weeks after the birth, whereas others took many months. Even at best, this adaptation continues to be incomplete. One parent reported, "Tears come even yet, years after the baby's birth."

Fifth stage: Reorganization

During this period parents deal with responsibility for their children's problems. Some mothers reported that they had to reassure themselves that "the baby's problems were nothing I had done." Positive long-term acceptance of the child involved the parents' mutual support throughout the time after birth. Many couples have reported that they relied heavily on one another during the early period. However, in some instances the crisis of the birth separated parents. In one case the parents blamed each other for the baby's birth. Another mother wanted to be isolated from her husband. "I don't want to see anybody. I just want to be by myself."

Despite the important similarities in parental reactions to various malformations, parents progressed through the various stages of reaction differently. Some parents did not report initial reactions of shock and emotional upset but tended instead to intellectualize the baby's problem and focus on the facts related to the baby's condition. Other parents were unable to cope successfully with their strong emotional reactions to the birth and, as a result, did not achieve an adequate adaptation; they were in a state of sorrow that lasted long after the birth.

A lack of opportunity to discuss the infant's diagnosis can create a situation in which the parents feel overwhelmed and unable to gauge the reality of their child's abnormality. If the mourning process becomes fixed as a sustained atmosphere of the family, the ghost of the desired, expected, healthy child sometimes continues to interfere with the family's adaptation to the defective child. These findings confirm the original creative work of Solnit and Stark (1961), which has become the foundation of most therapeutic approaches to the parents of the malformed infant. Their brilliant analysis consists of the following elements:

1. The infant is a complete distortion of the dreamed-of or planned-for infant.

2. The parents must mourn the loss of this infant—a process that may take several months—before they can become fully attached to the living defective infant.

3. Along with this process of mourning there is a large component of guilt that takes many forms (such as the "mother's dedication of herself unremittingly and exclusively" to the welfare of the child while excluding others in the family) and requires great patience of the individual helping the family, since the parents may repeat the same questions and problems many times.

4. There is resentment and anger, which nurses, pediatricians, and obstetricians must understand, since it is sometimes directed toward them.

5. The physician, nurse, and social worker should *not* interpret to the parents that the grief they are feeling is due to the loss of the expected perfect child, or should they attempt to compare this mourning response with any others the parents might have experienced, since it may rob the mother of the full strength and depth of her own grief by intellectualizing it.

6. The mother's attempts to withdraw her strong feelings from the

lost expected baby are disrupted by the demands of the living blighted child. The task of becoming attached to the malformed child and providing for his ongoing physical care can be overwhelming to parents at the time around birth, when they are physiologically and psychologically depleted.

7. The mourning cannot be as effective when the damaged child survives. The daily impact of this child on the mother is unrelenting and makes heavy demands on her time and energy. For example, based on interviews with ninety-six mothers after the birth of an anencephalic infant, D'Arcy (1968) observed that the mothers' sense of loss and grief was more acute than that of mothers of a surviving infant with a severe malformation. However, these mothers recovered sooner than mothers of infants with severe congenital defects who survived.

It is remarkable that families who must cope with the intense emotional experience engendered by the birth of an infant can assimilate the child into the family and begin responding to his needs as readily as they do.

As with other crises, successful mastery often strengthens people's ability to cope in other areas. The father of a boy with a congenital amputation described his confidence and pride in his management of the especially difficult time around his son's birth, his securing of treatment facilities, and his overall management of life. "I suppose you never know until you are all finished whether you have given your family what they need, but I try and I think I do a good job" (Daniels and Berg, 1968). Voysey (1972), in her analysis of the problems which parents and their disabled child face in encounters with those outside the family, notes that they develop special interactional skills. By dealing with occurrences that other people might find embarrassing and distressing in the course of daily life with their child, parents of the disabled learn how to treat these events routinely. These special qualities, which may be characterized as "understanding" and "self-sacrifice," provide a rationale for the "deep philosophy" that persons with a stigma are said to evolve (Goffman, 1968). The parents' identity, which was so compromised by the birth, may go through changes that result in a more positive self-image (Voysey, 1972). However, this kind of psychological maturity may appear slowly.

The struggle with the complex issues involves negotiating many tasks fraught with the potential for less than adequate resolutions. Several studies note outcomes in which parents, because of unresolved guilt and anger, develop an overprotective attitude toward the child, which can thwart his development. Managing disturbed feelings by denying painful facts about the malformation can also lead to less than adequate resolutions. Other members of the family may be neglected if parents ward off the grieving process by establishing a guilty attachment to the child (Solnit and Stark, 1961; Miller, 1968; Drotar et al., 1975). If the mourning process is protracted rather than diminishing or if it develops into self-reproachful depression, the parent will not be able actively to contribute to the family.

Responding to the circumstances surrounding the birth of an abnormal child in the best way is exceedingly difficult because of the ambiguities involved. For example, what is the difference between overprotectiveness and responding to special needs? Daniels and Berg (1968) quote one mother as saying, "It is hard, sometimes, to figure out what is being motherly and what is taking over. I want to help him as much as he wants and needs, but I don't want to hold onto him." Realistically, it is true that the physical care required by such children is much greater than that required by normal children. Recurring hospitalizations for some, and uncertain developmental predictions for others, intensify parental concern and often frustrate consistent planning so that it is difficult to determine when parents cross the boundary into overprotective behavior.

Another feature to consider is the notion of just what characteristics constitute optimal adaptation. If sorrow, depression, and anger are natural responses to the birth, and if the infant evoking these feelings continues to live, what is the right balance between mourning and acceptance? Olshansky (1962) coined the term *chronic sorrow* to describe some of the enduring aspects of parental reactions in adapting to a retarded child. Chronic sorrow at some level may be constantly present in parents, especially if the child will always be dependent on them, as in some cases of retardation. To expect the disappearance of the painful impact of this child on a family, under the guise that these feelings must be "resolved," can only force parents to deny their real feelings to professionals who may want to help. A useful stance for professionals might be to consider the rewards of shepherding a child with problems to a more successful level of functioning along with the need to come to grips with the malformation in the first place.

Many parents also struggle with these issues and search for some explanation of why this happened to them. Sometimes these struggles include much concern over the exact cause of the problem, which can be frustrating if a cause cannot be determined. When there is no acceptable medical explanation for the child's birth defect, the parents' genetic competence is called into question. They may try very hard to find a specific nongenetic cause for the anomaly in order to rid themselves of guilty feelings. Parents of children who develop mental retardation due to an illness, such as meningitis subsequent to birth, for example, seem to adjust much better than parents with a baby retarded from birth.

An analysis of the anguished reactions of parents assuming the new role of parent to a defective child helps to clarify some of the obstacles that physicians, nurses, and others, are likely to encounter. For example, the parents' search for causes, sometimes leading to doctor shopping, may not be due to dissatisfaction with the physician's diagnostic abilities as much as to the parents' need to alleviate their own guilt. Furthermore, the "active" search for services is often necessary because of the fragmentation of treatment facilities and can be one form of mastery in a crisis that parents are powerless to reverse.

It is disturbing for parents to encounter a discrepancy between their own intense emotional turmoil and what they believe is a lack of feeling on the part of professionals. The physician's objective professional manner may sometimes be mistaken for a lack of sympathy and may be met by generalized outrage on the part of the parents. Many physicians are able to compromise, maintaining their own standards of correct professional behavior and at the same time fulfilling some of the parents' needs for support. The baby can be presented to the parents in such a way that his attributes and normal features are highlighted. It is desirable to do this shortly after birth in the presence of both parents. This demonstrates to the parents that the hospital staff considers the baby an acceptable substitute for the wished-for baby and not a "piece of damaged goods" (Carr and Oppé, 1971).

> COMMENT: This focus can be helpful provided it is not used by physicians and nurses to "turn off" the fears, questions, and resentment that many parents need to express before they can see and here what the health personnel are presenting.   A. J. SOLNIT

Involving the parents in the care and planning for their infant allows them to enjoy satisfying feedback from him. It is also at this early stage that the groundwork is laid for an effective alliance of parents and professionals concerning treatment.

Nurses and physicians can facilitate the attachment of parents to their malformed infant in the neonatal period and as the child grows. Knowledge about the usual course of parental reactions helps the physician to take this into account in planning interventions. For example, a physician who knows about the disorganization which parents experience during the stages of shock and denial will realize that information about the child's condition and progress may have to be repeated many times.

> COMMENT: It is important to add that to talk with angry or depressed parents is not the natural inclination of the obstetrician, pediatrician, or nurse. The gratifications of these professions lie in either the delivery and care of the healthy infant or in the use of their medical knowledge to heal or remedy. With a congenitally malformed baby

they are often helpless and therefore feel useless. This of course is not so, and although at the time it is not evident that the extra visiting is doing any good, it is important to visit repeatedly and not to abandon the mother to her grief.   N. JOSEFOWITZ

In addition to their own emotional turmoil, parents must cope with the demands and expectations of those around them. With their ability to produce a normal child called into question and their emotional reserve at a low, they must face grandparents, friends, and neighbors. In this case society has few built-in supports such as those available in other crises such as the death of a relative or a community disaster. For example, friends and relatives send gifts and cards to the hospital after the birth of a normal baby but are confused about the proper procedure when the baby is abnormal, and they may find it easiest to forget to call or send anything. The parents are often reluctant to send out announcements of the birth or even to name the baby. As a result, they are likely to experience intense loneliness during the period immediately following the birth.

> COMMENT: There are no flowers in the rooms of these mothers. A maternity ward is supposed to be the happiest place in the hospital. A weeping mother disconfirms this, and one does not forgive her easily for disturbing the joyful atmosphere.   N. JOSEFOWITZ

The crisis of the baby's birth has the potential for bringing the parents closer as a result of the mutual support and the communication required for adaptation. On the other hand, in many of the families we have studied, the baby's birth estranged the parents. The ongoing demands of the baby's care increased the isolation between some parents, particularly if they did not share the responsibility. We have used the term *asynchronous* to describe parents who progress through the different stages of adaptation at different speeds (Fig. 5-1). These parents usually do not share their feelings with each other and seem to have particular difficulty in their relationships. Asynchrony often results in a temporary emotional separation of the parents and appears to be a significant factor in the high divorce rate after a major family crisis.

> COMMENT: Paradoxically, trauma such as the birth of a defective baby tends to magnify the weaknesses in a marriage more than it enhances the strengths of the relationship, and success, such as the easy birth of a normal baby will more often magnify or make more explicit the strengths of the marriage.   A. J. SOLNIT

The availability of the pediatrician throughout the child's early years puts him or her in a position to help with the family's adaptation. The pediatrician can be sensitive to the relationship between the parents, can determine which stage of adaptation each parent has reached, can check how aware each partner is of the other's progress, and may be alert to evidence of asynchrony. Parents have told of the importance of identifying the normal features of their child, which become increasingly evident as he grows. The pediatrician has an excellent opportunity to nurture this.

As a physician, nurse, or social worker follows the progress of the parents, each will be struck by the step-by-step nature of adjustment to a stressful situation such as this. There will be a tentative and perhaps ever-changing view of the child's potential. If reality indicates a less hopeful prognosis, the professional can present the news so that the parents can adapt to it in small amounts without losing confidence in themselves. Many parents describe that the most effective way they have found to deal with the challenge is to take things day by day. They try not to worry excessively about the uncertainties in the future or to dwell on the traumatic events of the past. Sometimes this can be mistaken for defensive denial. Unless the daily care and planning for the child is affected, however, this type of reaction seems to serve to protect parents from unbearable pain.

> COMMENT: It presents the problems in a "dosage" that both can be taken and that does not exceed the physician's capacity to predict what will happen.   A. J. SOLNIT

In one of our studies to assess each parent and to evaluate how he or she is managing, we have used the following interview. We have often been surprised by the unusual interpretations that parents have given about previous explanations of the defect. There are three points to consider in this interview:

Where each parent stands in her or his emotional reactions.
How the parent views the baby and the defect.
How each parent views the spouse and his or her emotional progress.

An outline of an interview that we use in our hospital is included on the following two pages.

INTERVIEW

Following is an interview with Mr. and Mrs. Cook,* the parents of Walter, their 6½-month-old son with Down's syndrome. This is their fifth child.

Mrs. Cook. Mongolism stuck out all over the place while I was pregnant. I read a lot of articles on mongolism, had seen a couple of television programs, and it seemed like it just stuck out. You know every time you're pregnant you're concerned about the baby, but you never say anything to your doctor because this is typical of every pregnant mother.

*The family's name has been changed.

OUTLINE OF FIRST COUNSELING SESSIONS

For parents of children with congenital anomalies

A. *Introduction and explanation of goals.* Early in the first session it would be useful to review with parents the purposes of the counseling with a statement such as the following:

Based on our experience with families who have infants with significant physical difficulties, the time after the child is born can be extremely trying for the parents and family. Thus it is usual for parents to feel upset and to have some difficulty handling this situation. It's a time when we have found that a great many families need extra support and help from people. In this regard many parents have expressed an interest in talking with their physician and other people about not only their child's physical problem but also about their reactions to the baby's birth. Such discussions seem to help the family cope more effectively with what is usually a very difficult situation.

As we related to you earlier, I'd like very much to meet with you both for _____ times to try to provide help to you during the baby's first year. Although we will be discussing many issues such as your own reactions to the situation, how you might handle the situation, and issues related to the baby and your other children, it is important that you feel free to use this time to discuss issues related to the situation that are important to you. From your acceptance you must have felt that such counseling might be useful to you. Have you thought any more about how it might be useful to you? (Both parents.)

The aim of this introductory communication is to structure the intervention, clarify some of the expectations we have of the parents, and state what they might expect of us. In addition, it is important to find out their perception of how we can help them and their notions about what they need most. The parents will have already been informed of their commitment in terms of time, and so on, and will have agreed to participate.

B. *Assessment of the parents' reactions.* One of the main objectives of the first hour, in addition to establishing rapport with the parents, is to assess how they have been coping with the situation both individually and as a family. From this assessment it would be possible to formulate goals regarding future sessions.

1. *Parental feelings.* The following questions might be useful in assessing the status of parental feelings:
   a. What was your initial reaction when you found out what was wrong with your child? How did you feel? *This is asked of each parent. The aim here is to help them recognize what their reactions are.*
   b. Can you recall your expectations of what the baby would be like? How you felt before the baby was born? *This question allows a beginning focus on the discrepancy be-*

tween the parents' hopes regarding the baby and their present feelings.
   c. What has been the most difficult thing about the situation?
2. *Parental perception of the child's difficulty*
   a. Can you describe what is wrong with your child?
   b. What have you been told about the baby's condition? By whom?
   c. What do you anticipate for the future?
   d. Is there information that would be useful to you that you don't have? *The parents' appraisal of the baby's problem is yet another focus of the later counseling sessions.*
3. *Parental reactions to the baby.* The aim here is to obtain an assessment of the parents' attitudes about and interactions with the baby.
   a. How do you feel about handling the baby? Do you feel close, etc.? Is the baby enjoyable?
   b. Does the baby present problems with feeding, etc.?
4. *Parental coping.* Given the parents' recognition of how they are feeling, it would be useful to assess how the parents are handling the situation.
   a. What do you do when you feel that way?
   b. Since the baby was born, have there been significant changes in areas such as mood, activities with friends, or physical complaints? *The objective here is to note the family's style of coping and eventually to have the parents relate their feelings to this, particularly if it is a maladaptive, defensive maneuver.*
5. *Parents' relationship to one another.* Throughout the session it will be important to note differences in parental response to similar issues; the focus here is on how the parents are communicating regarding the child and how they are handling the situation as a family unit.
   a. Have you been aware of each other's reactions?
   b. Have you discussed your reactions with each other?
   c. How are your reactions similar? Different?
   d. Has the baby's problem been discussed with the other members of the family? How have they reacted?
6. *Family's attitudes toward others.* The family's capacity to make productive use of other people, such as friends or family, during this period may be an important mental health support that should be assessed.
   a. Have you told your family or friends about the baby's problem? What have you said?
   b. What was your family's reaction to finding out your baby's problem? Your friends?
   c. How do you feel about their reactions?
   d. Have there been changes in your relationships to friends or family since the baby's birth?

Almost every mother interviewed in depth during pregnancy reports disturbing dreams or conscious fears about the well-being of the fetus she is carrying, suspecting that it is malformed, mentally retarded, or has a monstrous abnormality. When talking with parents who have actually produced a malformed baby, a report of this type of concern appears to be universal. When questioned months or years later, women who have had normal children occasionally report that they did not have this type of fear—but have they forgotten?

Mrs. Cook. But I did mention it to Dr. L., my obstetrician, three or four months before Walter was born, and he just said, "Oh, no, no way, no way could this ever be," and he just reassured me. Later I again approached him on it and he comforted me, "No way, no way."

It is important to emphasize that we are not sure what the obstetrician actually did say, but if the report is accurate, it is easy to see in retrospect that the obstetrician might have managed the situation differently. The apprehension of pregnant women over 35 or 40 years of age that their baby will have Down's syndrome is so common that it would have been appropriate for the obstetrician to suggest the possibility of an amniocentesis. It is usually wise to find out first just what the mother's concerns are and what she has already heard. It is also important to know if the mother would consider an abortion if she knew her fetus was definitely abnormal. Whatever her response, the procedure of amniocentesis and its advantages and disadvantages could be discussed. If the mother did not want an amniocentesis or if it was inadvisable because of the stage of pregnancy, the physician might comment in this vein: "Even though the risk of certain problems is increased at your age, it is far more probable that you will have a normal baby. The fact that you have already had four normal children certainly gives increased support for this. But, of course, we can't fully guarantee what the baby will be like until he or she is born."

Mrs. Cook. My pregnancy was different from the others I had had—I was tired throughout the whole pregnancy, just terribly, terribly tired. My legs swelled, which they had never done before, and I had a longer labor and Walter was transverse. So this was all different from the others.

Pediatrician. Was it these differences that made you worry about mongolism?

Mrs. Cook. No, not really. I don't know why I thought about it so much. I really don't. But then, of course, Walter was delivered.

Pediatrician. You had worried right up to the time of delivery?

Mrs. Cook. Um hmm. And then when he was delivered, still in the delivery room, I looked at him and I knew immediately he was. Just immediately. There was no question in my mind. I didn't say this to the doctor at the time. My doctor didn't deliver Walter; one of his associates did. And I said to him, "That baby isn't right." And he said, "Well, Mrs. Cook, I don't know you and I don't know your husband or your family. It's hard to tell." And I looked at him again, and I said he just isn't right. I just knew he wasn't. To me he was very typically mongoloid looking—the eyes, the tone, and a yellowish color. But then this may have all been in my mind because I had thought about this so much, you know. And all I knew was that I just couldn't talk anymore after I said that, just couldn't say another word. I was maybe dumbfounded or shocked, and woke up in the recovery room and Walter was at my side crying and crying and very tan, and I said, "Oh, just look at his face. He just isn't right." And he just kept crying and crying and I thought, "Just get him out of here, *just get him out of here*." And I didn't have the nerve to tell the nurses to get him out, but I thought, "God, just get him out of here." I didn't want him. All I wanted to do was run away. Get me out of this hospital, just get me out of here. And I said to Henry, "I want to go home." I was still in the recovery room and I wanted to go home. I just wanted to run away, run from the problem, and yet I knew I couldn't. And the nurse there was yacking a lot, and I thought, "Just be quiet, just be quiet." You know, I just couldn't stand her talking and then they took me upstairs on the maternity floor, and another nurse came by my bed and she kept yacking and yacking and I thought, "Be quiet, just shut up, in plain English, you know, don't talk to me." They put me in a private room, and I guess I just felt like this was the end of the world. I told Henry I just wanted to run away. And I couldn't believe it, I just couldn't believe it; it just couldn't happen to me.

This mother has described the characteristic early reactions to the birth of a baby with a malformation. First, she was so shocked that she could not talk. Second, she had a great urge to flee, to run away, to get out of the hospital. Third she reacted with disbelief. Even though she was absolutely certain that the baby had an abnormality, she could not believe that it was really happening to her.

Pediatrician. Up to this moment no one had confirmed your impression, is that right?

Mrs. Cook. Dr. M. who delivered the baby said it was questionable. He wasn't quite sure. Dr. L. came and he too said it was very questionable. They were both OBs too, and they couldn't see it, it was so questionable. They called in our pediatrician, and after checking him he confirmed that he had the signs of a mongoloid. But I knew it, I just knew it, maybe mother's intuition. I just knew it.

The two obstetricians were wise to be cautious. It may take a number of observations and some time to be sure about Down's syndrome in a newborn infant. Rather than rushing to a definite opinion one way or the other, they said that the diagnosis was questionable and called in the pediatrician. The same reactions that occur in the parents of a baby with an abnormality often occur in the nursing and medical staff, particularly the responsible physicians, in this case the obstetricians. They are performing under an unwritten promise to produce a normal infant and so may have the same difficulty as the parents in realizing that the pregnancy they have managed has resulted in the birth of a baby with an abnormality.

Mrs. Cook. I didn't have any motherly feelings towards Walter. They brought him in that same day and made me give him glucose, which you know they don't like anyway and I couldn't feed him. I didn't reject him, but he didn't want it and I couldn't be bothered with him. And Henry tried to feed him and he couldn't, and I said, "Oh, just put him back in the bassinet." Where, normally, you know, when you have a new baby you can't get enough of them. Every time they bring them to you, you just, oh, you just can't get enough of them. And I've had four, and every time it was the same. But I couldn't be bothered with him. He was different, that's all, I just didn't want to fuss with him. That was the first day. I never ever rejected him as far as telling the nurses I didn't want to see him or not have him brought to me. But I never had this warm feeling towards him, a motherly feeling toward him, until, I'd say, four or five days later did I really feel close and love him like I loved the other children. And then I did. And it comes, it really does. And yet I had all kinds of mixed emotions.

This mother is describing an interesting process which appears to be an exaggeration of that which occurs with normal births and is described in more detail in Chapter 3. Many a mother will report rather neutral reactions to her newborn baby in the first two or three days. Then suddenly the infant will become the most beautiful and marvelous baby in the whole world, and from that moment on she will report powerful feelings of love toward him.

We can speculate that a mother has an idealized image of her baby during pregnancy. When the baby is born, his appearance is almost always somewhat different from the mother's expectations. Not only may there be a discrepancy in sex, coloring, and size, but mothers in the United States are usually not prepared for the molding of the skull, forceps marks, vernix, and other characteristics of a newborn baby. It is important to question whether the process by which a mother readjusts the idealized image of her anticipated baby to fit with the real baby would proceed more smoothly and rapidly if the mother and baby were kept together constantly. Mothers in Horsholm, Denmark, who have kept their babies constantly in view at the side of their beds, tell about gazing at their new infants for hours to "take him in."

Pediatrician. You did a lot of crying during that time?
Mrs. Cook. Crying! I cried for two solid months every single day. I lost weight, didn't eat. Walter had jaundice, and I didn't care. I didn't care about him. They came to do the chromosome study test and they took a sample from his head and he has a lot of hair and they shaved his hair, and I saw the

stream of doctors in the nursery, I didn't care. It bothered Henry, but I didn't care. You know, it was like he really didn't belong to me, that I had no strong feelings for him. Dr. B., the pediatrician, came in one day and said, "Walter has yellow jaundice. Don't get upset, Mrs. Cook, if you see him under the light." And I thought, "Upset? I should get upset? I'm not upset." I didn't care. They told me that mongoloids have bad hearts, sometimes they don't live. I hoped he would die. I really did. Not because I hated him. I didn't ever hate Walter ever. I hated what he was and I hoped he would die because then we wouldn't have to make this decision on what to do with him. See it would be easy then; we wouldn't have to decide whether we were going to take him home or whether we were going to put him in a home. So if he died, he'd solve all our problems. And I didn't have feelings for him so I didn't care. And I was very open about it. I told all the doctors how "I don't care if he dies." But you see I don't feel that way now. When we came here this morning, we had an empty crib because we took Walter to my parents' house, and there was a void in our house. There really was.

Mrs. Cook has honestly described her wish for Walter's death. Many other parents of babies with abnormalities have described feeling this soon after the baby's birth, but this may be so unacceptable socially that probably many do not dare to express it. This is further evidence of the early desire to flee from the baby and escape the implications of his problem. The mother's reaction to a baby with an abnormality reminds us of a phenomenon associated with infanticide. This was a common event in Western Europe from 1750 to 1850, usually when the financial circumstances for families were so limited that it was inconceivable to mothers to feed another baby. It is of interest that infanticide almost always occurred within the first day or two after birth. Apparently, after the mothers had interacted with their babies for two days and developed an attachment, it was not possible for them to contemplate killing their babies.

Pediatrician. Mrs. Cook, you were talking about pregnancy and your worries about problems. Did you share them with your husband, did you two talk about them before you said you talked to the doctor? What kinds of feelings did the two of you have at that point during the pregnancy, and then once Walter was born?

Mrs. Cook. I don't think we ever really talked about it.

Mr. Cook. I remember one time that we did discuss it. I don't think we really talked about Down's syndrome or mongolism, and I don't think that particularly crossed my mind, but I think we both did have a feeling that we were going to have a different child. I don't know why it was there. I can remember one night when we were lying in bed that we did discuss the possibility. Gail had been so upset about her pregnancy and how she was feeling, she just didn't feel the baby was normal, and I said I've thought a lot about that too. So I think we both shared a feeling of being really concerned this time. We've always thought we'd been blessed with four normal, this is a tremendous percentage really, and grateful for the fact that we did have good healthy children. But we did have a funny feeling about this pregnancy.

Pediatrician. Did you prepare differently for this baby, had you thought of a name, and had you made other preparations?

Mrs. Cook. We thought of a name, and yet when it came time to name Walter, when they came for the birth certificate, I knew what I was going to name him but I couldn't. I couldn't. Maybe it was because I didn't want to put our name to something like that, I didn't want to associate our name with something that wasn't right. I know this sounds ridiculous, but this is how I felt and I said, "I don't know what I'm going to name him." This was the day after Walter was born. And every day the nurses would come in and say, "Well, have you named Walter (not Walter, but him) yet?" And I said "No," and I knew what his name was, but I said, "No, I haven't," and then it really perturbed me because they kept after me and I said, "Darn you, you're always asking me what we're going to name him." I was in the hospital for ten days and you know I called downstairs to wherever they file the birth certificates and gave them his name, the last day. And I remember when they would bring Walter in, they'd always check the name band with the beads around his neck and after a while they just didn't do this any more, the older nurses, because they knew who Walter was, 'cause we had been there so long. But they had some student nurses on one day, and this one student had been on for a couple of days and had gotten to know me and yet when she came in, she said, "C-O-O-K" and checked my name, and I said, "Why are you checking our names? You ought to know that there's only one in there like that, in that nursery." And then I apologized after, but I thought, "You dumb nurse, you ought to know there's only one baby like that." But these were my feelings, you see.

Questions about the baby's name are often revealing about parental attachment to a baby. There is often a long delay in assigning a name when the baby has an abnormality or is premature. Here the difficulty a mother faces in detaching from her expected ideal baby and attaching her affections to the new baby with an abnormality may become apparent in the hesitancy of a family to use a treasured name they had planned for their perfect baby.

Mrs. Cook is beginning to show more and more evidence of anger, another early reaction. Here she is upset over a hospital routine. From an objective point of view, hospital routines that have been set up to help parents are often inappropriate for parents with a sick or abnormal baby. However, there is going to be considerable anger after the birth of a baby with an abnormality, and it is better for this to be directed against the hospital staff and hospital routines than against the mother herself or other members of the family.

Pediatrician. Did you get angry?

Mrs. Cook. Yes, yes.

Pediatrician. At other people?

Mrs. Cook. Yes, I'm not that type either. I never get angry with somebody unless they get very angry with me. I don't jump on people as a rule. You know, when they were always asking me if I had named him. I didn't want anybody to know about Walter. We didn't call anybody. Henry didn't call any of our friends, as a matter of fact even our relatives. I wasn't on speaking terms with my mother at the time, and I had Walter on a Saturday, and my family never knew until Thursday that I had had the baby. And that was only because my sister-in-law had called our house and talked to the children and then called me at the hospital and then I told her. She was very upset and told my parents, but prior to that we didn't let anybody know, none of our friends or anybody. Normally when you have a child, it's a happy time and you pass out cigars and candy and you call all your friends and you're elated. But when you have a baby with a problem, you suppress all this and you don't do any of this and you're not happy. It's a different time.

This mother describes dramatically the contrast between the rewards given to parents after the birth of a normal baby and the attenuated and distorted reactions after the birth of a baby with an abnormality. Many customs and traditions usually reward a mother for the production of a normal healthy baby and produce an atmosphere that probably enhances the mother-infant relationship. The parents' efforts to keep the information secret contrasts strikingly with the usual wish to broadcast the exciting news from the housetops, with telephone and written messages going to friends and relatives so that all can share in the joyful occasion and give their congratulations to the mother. Mr. and Mrs. Cook, like most parents of a baby with an abnormality, are concerned, from the instant of birth, about how their family and society will react to the baby and to them as his parents. During the period right after birth the parents watch everyone within the hospital setting closely for their response to the baby. As the dust begins to settle after their first shock, they begin to worry about what individuals outside the hospital will say and do.

Mrs. Cook's comments remind us that society has no customs, traditions, or rites to support parents when they need it the most—that is, when they have a baby who is abnormal. It is still the custom in some societies to dispose of any baby born with an abnormality. In the last few years there has been considerable discussion about what interventions physicians should make if a baby such as Walter has an abnormality that would normally be treated with surgery. These discussions have usually led to stormy debates between those of differing opinions. It is the wide range of reactions that makes the future of parents so difficult.

They do not know who will be upset that they have produced an abnormal baby and who will be understanding and supportive. Perhaps the relatively recent development of services for handicapped children and supportive programs for parents represents society's long-delayed response to their needs.

Pediatrician. Can you remember what you told your family and friends?

Mrs. Cook. I don't know, Henry did the calling.

Pediatrician. Did you mention that there was a problem?

Mrs. Cook. Oh yes, right away, we told them. When my sister-in-law called the hospital, I told her that when I had the baby and we didn't let them know, it was because it was mongoloid.

Mr. Cook. I think the hardest part was telling our children and that she delivered . . .

Mrs. Cook. Had it Saturday morning, almost at 10:00 in the morning.

Mr. Cook. It was very late in the afternoon when I called home, and of course our oldest daughter answered the phone and was real happy to hear that we had a boy. I didn't want to tell her over the phone that there was a problem, but she wanted to know how things were and everything, and I broke up and . . .

Mrs. Cook. I think she wanted to know what color the baby's eyes were.

Mr. and Mrs. Cook. Because we have three brown-eyed children, and boy . . .

Mr. Cook. And that really [*Mrs. Cook.* Did it!] hurt. I told her that there was a problem that I didn't just want to talk about at the time, and I said that I'd tell them when I got home. It was a real difficult time.

Pediatrician. Were you still down in the delivery room, Mr. Cook?

Mr. Cook. Not in the delivery room. I was called upstairs in the recovery room when Gail and the baby were there. I had a real strong feeling that something was ·wrong, because I didn't expect the delivery to take so long. We went in Friday night about midnight, and I was there until, gosh, I think it was almost 11:00 in the morning when they called me upstairs, and actually I had a strong feeling about it. I said a little prayer when I went up in the elevator, and I said if something's wrong, I hope Gail is all right and she was, except for the emotional shock. But as soon as I looked at Walter, it was obvious to me, too, that he wasn't normal, and I couldn't believe it either. It was a hard thing to accept. I tried to console Gail, but all Gail was concerned about was getting out of the recovery room and getting away from the baby, and they finally did take the baby. And we, Gail and I, spent quite a bit of time together in this private room, and I guess our first thoughts were how do we get out of this? We just can't take this baby home, and even that evening I tried to make some contacts with people to find out what homes were available, and to talk to some doctors and friends, and some organizations I'm affiliated with. I guess we were just trying to find some way to avoid the situation. This was a very difficult period.

Mr. Cook shows a similar urge to get away from the baby and to escape the problem he presents. This reaction has been reported almost universally by parents who have been through this experience. During this period decisions are made and action taken that in retrospect may be unfavorable for the long-term well-being of the parents and family. Families who have exceptional political connections or financial resources have often been able to move ahead rapidly with plans for institutionalization of their baby with Down's syndrome. Repeatedly it has been observed that those parents who at first have been pleased decide in a few months or years that this was a poor decision, and then they have to face the difficult task of attempting to establish some kind of relationship with their baby who is now a stranger.

The evidence that it is important for the mother and father of a normal newborn baby to be with their infant leads one to recommend and encourage parents to remain in close contact with their abnormal newborn baby as much as possible. There is only limited scientific information to guide medical and nursing staff in the early care of a mother with an abnormal infant, but many clinical experiences suggest the beneficial effects of keeping mother and baby together after birth as much as possible. In the case of Mrs. Cook it was probably wise to move with the mother—to take the baby away from her for a short period and then to encourage a reunion after she had time to recuperate. She needs time to "take in" the baby, but probably she cannot do this until she has recovered from some of her early shock reactions.

It is important to point out that this hospital allowed the father to visit at all hours and that Mrs. Cook had a private room.

Mrs. Cook. You might say that Dr. S. is a psychologist, which I needed desperately at times, who helped me over quite a bit of the hump. But everybody was so gracious, and then I couldn't have asked for better personnel on the floor, they were just marvelous, and all the floor nurses, my doctor and Dr. M., the one who delivered Walter, Dr. B., the pediatrician, and also my old pediatrician whom I dearly loved and had had for the other four children. But he is a half hour from where we live, and Dr. B. is only 10 minutes away, so I decided we would have him. But he came in to see me three times and consoled me, and I just couldn't have asked for better treatment, everybody was so gracious, so kind and understanding. And the nurses said that whenever you feel like you want to talk, just call any of us, and they did. I didn't even have to call them, but they'd come and when I started talking, which I did a lot, they'd listen. And they sat with me a couple of times. And the maternity surgery nurse that helped deliver Walter came down the next day after I'd had Walter and stayed with me for the morning and tried to pull me together, and then she came down on another night to see me. I thought this was fantastic, you know, just a stranger who felt that maybe she was doing me some good or maybe thought there was a personal thing because she's really a wonderful person. And everybody was just so gracious. And that helped an awful lot. If I were alone in the hospital without anybody caring, let's say, it would have been a lot worse. And yet it was so bad. I was on tranquilizers and sleeping pills and still couldn't sleep. It was something you just couldn't believe had happened to you. I didn't want to take Walter home, and yet I couldn't give him up. So I was really torn between the two. And I really got to love him. And at that hospital they have that thing where they have the babies in your room if you want it, and of course me having four children I don't think I needed that. But Dr. S. thought it was wise if I got to know Walter and adjusted to him in the hospital before I took him home. And I had him a couple of days in the room and this was good too. And the tenth day when we left, I loved that baby dearly. I knew that I couldn't give him up. But it was ironic because at the very beginning I wanted to run away. And then when I stayed, Dr. L. (obstetrician) said I could go home on that Friday, which wasn't quite a week. I didn't want to go home then. You see I didn't want to face the reality at home then. And I said, "Oh, couldn't I just stay for a couple more days?" And he said, "Oh, sure, fine." And those couple of days did it. Because then I was ready to go home. But it was ironic because at the beginning I couldn't wait to get out of that hospital—I wanted to just blast out of there, you know? And then when I could, I didn't want to.

Everyone at this hospital should be congratulated for their remarkable degree of flexibility, understanding, and support.

> COMMENT: The "therapeutic environment" in this hospital suggests that the physicians, nurses, and other personnel work daily at having a warm, receptive, flexible environment that is people centered rather than technique centered. Such a human environment requires that the medical, nursing, and administrative directors have indicated to all that the highest priority is to please and take excellent care of each individual according to his or her weaknesses and strengths while maintaining the highest scientific and technical standards. These leaders must have demonstrated in their own behavior that humanitarian and technological considerations are harmonious and not in conflict. A. J. SOLNIT

The obstetrician's flexibility turned a possibly disastrous discharge into a welcomed and successful one. As we have mentioned before, it is generally wise to follow the lead or the readiness of parents in making recommendations in a situation like this, where so many complicated factors are interacting. Then, in addition to the desirability of keeping the mother and baby together as much as possible, it was also important to provide as much realistic support and encouragement as possible to the parents during this early difficult period. When Mrs. Cook says, "If I were alone in the hospital without anybody caring, let's say, it would have been a lot worse," she reminds us of the situation of many other mothers that results from the pressure of patient care, inflexible rules, lack of staff understanding of what the family is going through, and reactions of staff members who are so upset themselves that they are unable to provide interest or support to the family.

Pediatrician. How did you adjust to the reality at home?

Mrs. Cook. I don't really think there was any adjustment. As far as the family goes, the children just adjusted beautifully. They accepted him. We told the two older ones, and we didn't tell the two young ones because we didn't feel that they really understood. And yet, I said to Henry that it wasn't fair. How could we let these two little fellas live in a world, well, make-believe world you might want to say? They're a part of our family; they have to know what's going on. And why cover it up? And I just couldn't believe it. And the only reason we didn't was because we had talked to a few doctors who said, "You don't have to tell the young ones. You can tell them that he's a little bit different, but you don't have to tell them unless they notice it." But I didn't feel that was right. So we went along for one month like that. And I said to Henry, "I feel that we just have to tell them, we just have to. Why should they feel that Walter is normal when he's not? And why not tell them now instead of maybe their finding out from somebody else or finding out later?" I just didn't feel it was fair. And Henry told them.

Mrs. Cook has demonstrated how important it is to avoid secrets within a family and the great advantage of opening lines of communication even if young recipients do not fully understand what is being expressed. When a baby with an abnormality is born, it is not unusual for important medical information to be given as a secret to either the father or the mother, who is then inhibited from communicating normally with his or her spouse and other members of the family. For this reason it is extremely important to talk to the parents together about any neonatal problem. Even better would be to talk to the entire family together. This is sometimes possible with a family like the Cook family. Visits by siblings are still restricted in most hospitals, but several are now experimenting with this. (Dr. Peter De Chateau [1974] reports that experience with free visiting by children to his maternity unit in Umea, Sweden, has resulted in no increase in infections.) If this were the policy in more maternity hospitals, it would then be feasible for the physician to explain the problem to everyone in the family at the same time. The difficulty that Mr. and Mrs. Cook encountered in telling their older children about Walter's problem is not unusual. Many parents are so reluctant to tell an older child that they may keep a baby's problem a secret from all the children and in this way disrupt the family cohesiveness.

Mr. Cook. We told them as simply as possible what the problem was and didn't go into any detail with them, and they asked questions and we answered them. We felt better about it when we knew that everybody knew, you know.

Mrs. Cook. You can't hide something like that.

Mr. Cook. No.

Mrs. Cook. You don't do that. And then they didn't accept it graciously because they knew that there was something there. There was a sadness thing with Walter, and our little 7-year-old said, "I think I'm going to cry." And what's so beautiful, I think, with children is that the 7-year-old said to me one day, "When I get married and I have a baby like Walter, I would just love him and keep him."

Pediatrician. You mentioned that you cried every day the first two months— did the children notice this and wonder?

Mrs. Cook. They did. They looked and they wondered. And it bothered me, what they were thinking, and I moped around, you know, and yet they didn't ask questions.

Pediatrician. It must have been difficult to tell your children about mongolism or Down's syndrome because you didn't know much about it, did you?

Mrs. Cook. No, and I don't think they really asked. All we said was that he was going to be retarded, and they understood what retarded children were.

Mr. Cook. They'd seen slow learners before.

Mrs. Cook. We told them that he would never get married when they asked us, and that he'd never be a father, and that he wouldn't go to their school. And they accepted that just as it was. We didn't have to say anything more. They know he's different, but that doesn't make any difference to them. He's a joy, and he laughs and coos and he does everything that a normal baby does. He's no different to them. They love him.

Pediatrician. Is there anything you want to say about how everything went after you got home?

Mrs. Cook. All I wanted was for Henry to give me the compassion and the understanding and the warmth that I needed at this time. Prior to this Henry and I hadn't been getting along as well as we should have been, and we had our ups ond downs, and I guess a lot of it was me. I didn't treat him like I should have treated him. I wasn't compassionate and I wasn't kind and understanding. I think this happens sometimes when you have a large family and you're going off in so many different directions and you don't have as much time with each individual as you would like to, and I wasn't the wife I should have been to him. And so we really did have our ups and downs. And when I did get pregnant, I had thought of abortion but after thinking it over I just couldn't do such a thing, I just couldn't. I knew I couldn't live with myself anyway. I thought we had been getting along well before Walter came, like a couple of months or so before Walter. And Henry was great to me in the hospital. He came every day and held my hand and consoled me. And the personnel were so wonderful to him because they let him come at any time of the day and stay with me all day, which is unheard of. Visiting hours are from 6:30 to 8:00, and Henry came at 12:00 or 1:00 and stayed all day. And they really gave us a lot of privileges that they wouldn't have given us under normal circumstances. But he was compassionate and warm.

Henry brought me flowers the very next day after I had Walter, and I said, "What did you do that for? I don't want the flowers. Why waste your money on such a thing?" You know, I didn't want any gaiety. You know, no cards, no flowers, I didn't want any of that. But Henry is a very wonderful person, and I was telling all the nurses I wouldn't have gotten this far in the hospital without such a wonderful husband. And I bragged and boasted about him. And he is. I couldn't ask for a better husband. Nobody could. He's a wonderful father and a wonderful husband and I'm very lucky, really. And I just bragged and bragged about him. But you see I never told him. And I told Dr. L. (obstetrician) that I don't know what I would have done without Henry, and I told Dr. S. (psychologist) that I know now that I need him more than anything else in the world and I'm so lucky to have him and I don't know what I'd do without him. But I didn't tell him. And when we came home, I guess all I wanted for him to do was to sit with me, and to give me comfort which I never needed before, and he was very busy and taking care of the house and taking care of the four children, which needed to be done anyway. And he wanted me to rest a lot, and I'd say, "Oh, Henry, just come and sit with me." He said, "I can't. I've got this and that to do and I've got to fix dinner and I've got to go grocery shopping and I've got to do so many things, you know." Well, I didn't care about that. All I wanted was comfort and understanding and for him to tell me, "We can lick this together." And he didn't. That bothered me. And we went to Dr. S. two weeks after Walter was born because he was going to try to help us together over this hump. And we came that evening. Oh—prior to this Henry felt that I was picking on him for little things that he was doing in the house, like I said, "Don't put so much formula in the bottle because Walter isn't taking it and you're just wasting it," or "Do this," or "Do that," and I did pick. But he kept thinking I was picking on him, and he said, "Gail, quit picking on me. I'm doing the best I can." And I said, "I know that." And he said, "Well, just quit picking on me." And I wasn't. So we had gone to Dr. S. that night, which was two weeks after Walter was born, and we came home and there was a baby scale on the floor and the baby's dresser next to the scale, and Henry pulled out this drawer and I bumped the scale and I said, "My gosh, you're always ruining things." And then I was feeding Walter and I said, "I told you not to put so much formula in the bottle because you only waste it." And he said, "You're always picking, always picking." He said, "You have to have everything just so." And he said, "You'll never change. God Almighty isn't even going to change you." He said, "You have to have everything just so. And now you've got something that isn't just so." Henry didn't mean it like that, but those words stuck. To have your husband tell you or throw it in your face that you have something that isn't just so. But he helped make it, you see? And this killed me because I had a broken heart right then and there anyway. I was dying inside. I had such a broken heart, and then he threw it in my face again. See, I was really down.

There is so much in what Mrs. Cook is saying that we will interrupt briefly. The stress resulting from the birth of a defective baby produces such guilt and anger that small differences between parents may be magnified into major disruptions. Separations and divorce are frequent consequences. It was clear that these words hurt Mrs. Cook, who already had suffered a major blow to her self-esteem because of the birth of a defective child. As a result, she has remembered every single word. Several years later she still remembers these words and still does not forgive her husband for uttering them.

Mrs. Cook. And another thing I'd like to add to show how mixed up I was—Henry's company sent me a plant, and it was a monster. I don't like plants anyway, I love flowers. And this thing was so huge and was beginning to die, and it was a very depressing thing to look at this plant dying in front of me. And this upset me terribly, and I mentioned it a couple of times to Henry. I said, "That plant is so ugly. I hate it." And this wasn't new, you see. So I kept complaining about the plant, so one day he got it and he hid it behind the chair in the room because it was so ugly and it really wasn't ugly. It was just that it was dying. The next day or maybe even that same day he called me from the office. I said to him, "I don't want that plant." I said, "You tell the florist to come and get that plant. It's ugly and it's dying," and I said, "I'm dying inside as it is, and I don't need to see something else dying in front of me." So they reordered, and I got a dozen gorgeous yellow roses which were beautiful. But you see just a plant upset me. But this plant was dying and I was dying inside. And I didn't want any part of this plant. It was dying and it was ugly and I hated that plant and we brought it home and I still hated it. And I got rid of it. You know, it's dumb. But that's how I felt. You have so many mixed-up feelings, terrible feelings, that when you're rational you would never ever have. But anyway, back to my feelings, it was Henry and I. I thought that he was going away from me. And when he went back to work, it seemed like every night he'd come and he had to be busy doing something. It was close to Easter then, and he said, "Well, I've got to go out and buy the boys pants, and I've got to go out and get them shoes. I've gotta do this, I've gotta do that." Every night it seemed like he wanted to get out after dinner and do something. And it made me feel kinda funny. Well, I don't know, he has to tell you the rest because that's his situation.

It is fascinating to observe that in the depths of her reaction to this depressing situation, Mrs. Cook identified herself with this ugly and dying plant. It is probable that she is using this means to describe the psychological wound which she feels deep within herself and which is presumably present in most parents who have a defective baby.

Mr. Cook. Well, then, I guess to make it as brief as possible, I guess my way of not accepting a situation was to turn completely away from it and to stay busy and, as Gail's mentioned, never have time for her or for Walter. And turning away from it even further, turning to someone else, having an affair, and feeling that this was real, that it was a real thing, that I get away from Gail, and that we haven't been getting along for years. And this other party was so available that it happened very quickly. And before you knew it I was deciding that I no longer loved Gail. I loved the children and accepted Walter, but I had to get away. And finally I packed my bags and left and even thought deeply about divorce and remarriage and everything else. It took almost a month before I came to the realization of what I was doing, and did finally come back home to stay. But I think it was through viewing some films down here that it really hit me what I had done. I didn't realize I was running away from Walter. And that's exactly what I was doing. I couldn't accept him. And yet today, boy, you couldn't take him away from me. He's just great.

Mr. Cook's behavior is not unique after the tremendously shocking and demoralizing blow that follows producing a baby who is abnormal. What is unusual is, first, his willingness to tell about this so openly and so early and, second, the combination of events that enabled him to understand why he was behaving in this manner. The physician often does not learn about such behavior until months or years later. Even when he is aware of a major change in behavior, for example, alcoholism, it is often difficult to help a parent to understand the association between this and the birth of a defective baby.

Mrs. Cook. What was so funny, Henry just said, "You know I loved all the children," but he said, "I have never loved any of them in six months as much as I love Walter." And it's so true. He's normal to us. He really is. He's beautiful.

Mr. Cook. We are trying to definitely keep our feet on the ground and realize that although he is doing a lot of things that normal children would do at this time, he may not always be able to reach a normal level, and maybe we won't be really prepared for that. But we think we're trying to prepare ourselves for that. If we could go back just to the situation in the hospital either one or two days after Walter was born. I was so anxious to see if we couldn't find a home for him. We wanted not to accept him and wanted to find some place where we could ease our guilt and our conscience by putting him into a good home. The people in hospitals really don't make it easy for you. They don't tell you that you have this option. I think that's a good thing. I don't think they should encourage people to make contacts and to put their children into a home unless they're really severe cases. I think they should be given this period of adjustment to accept their children. If they made it easy for you to just leave the hospital and just leave the child behind, I think that this would be very damaging, not only to the parents but certainly to the child.

Mr. and Mrs. Cook are trying to teach us several important lessons. Mr. Cook apparently recognizes that the child who is left behind in the hospital will not only be deprived of the stimulation and care of his parents but that the parents themselves will suffer. In the past it has not been unusual for physicians to encourage the parents to go home for a period to adjust themselves for the baby's return home. Mr. Cook's advice agrees with several studies suggesting it would be better to keep the parents and baby together and allow the mother and baby to go home at the same time. Many babies with Down's syndrome have cardiac or other abnormalities that require prolonged hospitalization, but it would appear to be desirable to keep the mother and baby in the hospital together for the entire period or as long as is feasible.

Mrs. Cook. I was appalled at the fact that an older nurse came in one day and she said, "Mrs. Cook, are you going to take Walter home?" And I said, "Well, of course." This was two or three days after Walter was born. And I didn't even think that I could leave him there, you know. But I said to Henry, "How can we take him home and then pack him up and then take him some place?" I couldn't do that. I just couldn't. It would eat me up inside. You know, I was thinking this morning that Walter wasn't there for the first time since he was born, and I thought, "Now how could I adjust to Walter not being here?" And it didn't bother me too much because I kept thinking in the back of my mind that he's coming back home. But I thought again this morning, "Would it bother me?" Yes, it would. It would eat me up inside, not knowing—is he being fed now? Is he having his bath now? Is he clean? And I'd say over and over again to him, "Who would love you? Who would keep you happy? Who would give you a bath and give you all these kisses and everything?" You know they wouldn't. And he thrives on it. He just does.

Pediatrician. You've spoken very nicely about your feelings and your children's feelings. What about grandparents and cousins? What has it meant to them?

Mrs. Cook. No difference whatsoever. Now. But I think at the time when we were thinking of putting Walter in a home, Henry's dad was upset but he didn't say anything. He's a very close-mouthed person, and he keeps everything inside of him. But we could see that he was upset.

Mr. Cook. . . .

Mrs. Cook. Yes, Henry's mother passed away, and yet he came to the hospital every single day to see me and couldn't wait to get to that nursery when it was time and behave like a proud grandparent. He didn't think that Walter was any different. He was proud. He'd say, "Isn't he beautiful? Just look at him." And he was. Believe it or not he was one of the most beautiful ones in that nursery. He wasn't ashamed to go to that nursery and show them that card and have that baby brought up to him. He was proud. Really proud. And you see he came right from the beginning because he knew. But my parents, they came twice to the hospital because, see, they didn't know until the very end, and my mother was very upset with me because of my thinking of putting Walter in a home. She said, "Oh, how can you do that?" She said, "You know if I were younger, I would take that baby and raise him." And my mother isn't old, she's 58. But she said, "I would take him and raise him." And she was very, very upset with me. And yet, they too, when they went to the window, they beamed. But I would go with Henry to see Walter every night, but the first night that my mother came she came with my sister-in-law and we went to the window. Of course there was this whole crowd of people there seeing the babies, and I just broke up hysterically out in front of everybody and had to leave and go back to my room. Believe it or not, as I said, Walter was very, very beautiful and he still is a very good-looking baby, and yet at the time I was maybe not embarrassed but hurt, hurt because he looked different. There were thirty-five babies in there, and there was only one like Walter. But then that same week there was another one born. And then I felt very, very lucky because this baby was much worse than Walter. My parents miss Walter when they don't see him. They love that baby dearly. And you do. There's something special. There's a feeling that you can't describe. It's only inside. Your heart knows it. Really. I hold Walter close to me, and my heart knows that he's just beautiful and special.

Pediatrician. Do you really see any differences between him and the others at this point?

Mrs. Cook. None whatsoever. I'm sure there's going to be, but right now there isn't.

Mr. Cook. He may be a little happier, I think, than some of the others were. I think our other children cried more; they'd let you know that they were hungry. They wanted to be changed and they wanted to eat right away. He doesn't. He wakes up and he'll give you a smile and be real happy and content and wait until you feed him.

Mrs. Cook. He's just love.

Mr. Cook. He's special that way.

Mrs. Cook. I think it's because he's contented because he knows he's loved and he's in a house where he gets so much love and affection. He's fed, and he's dry, and he's full, and he's happy, and what more could you want.

Pediatrician. Can I ask where you are with your feelings now that you've gone six and one-half months. Are you low, or do you feel you are rising up to where you would have been with your other children at this point?

Mrs. Cook. Let's say we rise and fall.

Mr. Cook. There are good days and bad.

Mrs. Cook. There are more good days than bad days, though I'm sure that with the months it's going to get better. I look at Walter sometimes and especially when he's sleeping in bed, he's beautiful, oh, he's just beautiful. And you just don't think that he's ever going to be anything but beautiful. And then there are other times when I look at him and he's so happy and I think if only somebody could change him. And I said to him just the other day, you know I talk to him so goofy anyway, I say, "Oh, Walter, I would give anything, just anything to change you." We have a very lovely, quite expensive house and I thought I'd give it all up with all this gorgeous furniture and everything and I'd live in something that wasn't up to our standards if we could change him. I'd do anything because I want him to have a chance, and I think he doesn't have a chance to live a normal life, but then who am I to say. But I would give anything if he could.

This sounds like the bargaining of a patient with a fatal illness.

Pediatrician. Have you been hearing about what has been done with other children with Down's syndrome or about possible treatments for children with this condition?

Mrs. Cook. I don't want to have Walter be a guinea pig per se, I mean with vitamins and shots and this kind of thing. But as far as research or testing, I'm all for that and I'd be willing to help anybody that has a problem like Walter's. If Walter can help by research or any of this, I'm all for it. I just hope that some day they can find the cause of this so that we don't have other children like this because it's just . . . it's a traumatic experience for parents as well as children in the family, and for the individual because it's not fair, it isn't fair to him. They should have a normal life like we do.

Pediatrician. Are there suggestions you have for nurses or doctors about anything else that they could do to help parents go through this—the first few days in the hospital or the next days at home?

Mrs. Cook. I think the biggest thing, the biggest thing doctors and nurses could give to a parent is compassion. That is what you need. Because I was just elated with all the compassion that I had from doctors and nurses. You have to tread lightly when you speak to parents because this is a blow. You have to be warm and kind and understanding because this means so much. It really does. You can't push your way in, and say, "OK, you have a baby with Down's syndrome and it's your problem." You can't do that. You have to tread lightly. Give them compassion, warmth, understanding, because you need this. I know, because I had it. And if I hadn't, I wouldn't have been able to get over that hump in the hospital.

Mr. and Mrs. Cook again remind us of the remarkable care provided for them in the hospital. Mrs. Cook may be correct when she says she might not have been able to get over that hump without this assistance.

Pediatrician. You said people came to let you talk. Were the nurses available to sit down by the bedside and talk and stay with you as you felt you wanted to talk?

Mrs. Cook (nodding agreement). Well, I never called them, but you know they would come in for different things. And when I started talking they were never in any hurry to leave. And of course, they pampered Walter in the nursery, and that made me feel good too. You know, Walter had a lot of hair, they would put a curl in his hair with Vaseline. It just made me feel good to think that they had a warm feeling, that he wasn't just something that wasn't right, you know, if they had put him in a corner because he wasn't like the other thirty-four or thirty-five. But they made more of a thing of Walter. And I think that this goes over. It really does. Because when you know that somebody else cares and somebody else is making a fuss over your child that isn't right, then I think this means a lot to you too.

The concerns that Mr. and Mrs. Cook had about the hospital personnel as representatives of all of society were refuted by the warm concern of the staff in the hospital. Probably this had a major effect on their feelings about Walter. What is done to a baby with an abnormality is probably more important than what the hospital staff say. Parents keep looking for objective evidence of how the staff members feel about their child; they watch to see whether as much attention is given to their baby as to others, whether the baby is placed out in the open or in a corner of the room. This fits with the observations made by Roskies (1972) in her studies of the mothers of children born with phocomelia due to thalidomide. On the basis of her research she believes that the reactions of society were the most important factor in the parents' attachment and adjustment to their child with a handicap. She proposed that governments should provide extra money and other supportive services to make up for the extra problems encountered with a baby with an abnormality.

> COMMENT: I would disagree and say that the reactions of society were *among the many* important factors in the parents' attachment and adjustment to their child with a handicap.   A. J. SOLNIT

Pediatrician. Mr. Cook, is there any suggestion that you have for anyone who is in a position to help a father or family during the first days, weeks, or months after the birth of a baby with mongolism?

Mr. Cook. I can't think of anything that particularly helped me at the time perhaps because even at that time I was shutting the thing off a little bit. I think I was more concerned for Gail, and I do remember one thing that Gail didn't mention. One of the nurses came down to talk to both of us, and she had a sister who had Down's syndrome. The fact that she came down and talked to us about it and told us about her sister, who I think at this time might be 19 years old, was kind of a relief. I guess you do need some consolation that you're not alone. I haven't seen diseases or ailments, but if you find that you're in a situation, there are usually so many others who are too. We're beginning to find out there are a lot of children like this.

One of the major concerns of parents of children with Down's syndrome and other handicaps is their lack of knowledge about how frequently the problem occurs. It always appears to be reassuring for parents to know that there are many other children with the same problem and many other parents going through the same reactions and experiences. It is fortunate that this information could be supplied to these parents from a source that they could trust most easily. This is another evidence of the thoughtfulness of the nurses in this institution.

Mr. Cook. And I think the one consolation is that there apparently is going to be more help for children like this and better education, and they know more about it. Like Gail, I feel that if we helped a little bit through telling you today, I am sure that there is going to be more help for other people in the future.

The spirit of hope provided at the present time by the improved programs and educational facilities for children with Down's syndrome is encouraging for parents and may enhance their attachment to their infant during the early weeks.

Mrs. Cook. I'd like to inject one more thing about all this compassion I had in the hospital which was so wonderful I thought. The evening after I had Walter, Henry's dad and his future wife and our oldest daughter who was going on 16 years came to the hospital, and they went down to see Henry in the nursery, and the nurse in charge of the nursery that evening came down to me and said, "Mrs. Cook, do you think your daughter would like to come in the nursery and hold Walter?" And I said, "Oh that would be great." And so they lined up three chairs in the nursery, they all put on gowns, Walter was only 1 day old, and they all got to hold him. And you know it was fantastic. It really was. You see they did things that were just a little bit different than the norm. And this means a lot. This really does because people cared. They really did. And because they let Henry come any time of the day and let him stay with me, they cared because they knew that meant a lot to me. You don't realize how much compassion means at a time like this because that's all you can give somebody who has a baby with a problem. Just compassion, that's all. You can't give them anything else.

> COMMENT: Attention to matters of *identity* is a critical element in the management of the birth of an infant with a congenital malformation. With such a birth the parents' previously formed notion of what their baby would be like—the infant's anticipated identity—abruptly is either modified strikingly or lost almost completely, depending on the extent and character of the malformation. The baby the parents now confront is certainly not the one anticipated and desired. Not only is the baby different from what might have been but almost everything else, including themselves, seems no longer the way it was—a *lifequake,* as it were.
>
> Unlike other anticipated bundles that are delivered by a department store in the wrong model or damaged, one cannot return or exchange a malformed baby. The baby, a product crafted by the parents, cannot be returned, exchanged, or put in the closet. Rather, he requires intensive parental care. That the baby's identity is unclear is evidenced by the parents' described reluctance to name the baby or to send out birth announcements, as if by these delays the strange interloper will go away.
>
> Physicians and nurses have a privileged opportunity to help parents, siblings, relatives, friends, and other hospital personnel who relate to the family form as realistic and positive identity as possible for the baby. Not only does this healing process take time in mourning what was lost and the way things were and in forming a new identity, but it must go on while the parents themselves are in a state of anomie. It is almost an unreal experience in which the sweetness of nostalgia is interrupted by the bitterness of disappointment. It is, indeed, a bittersweet time.

What are some of the ways in which this process can be facilitated?

1. Permit the parents to see the baby. As noted in this chapter, a shorter period of shock and disbelief seems to be associated with physical anomalies. I would strongly advise that wherever possible the physician examine the baby in front of the parents, emphasizing normality while delineating deviations from the normal. This shared examination permits the parents to understand better the nature of their baby's difficulties, encourages them to ask more questions than they otherwise would, and gives the physician an opportunity to convey something of the baby's personality, the way in which the baby will respond to the parents. This identification of the baby's responsiveness, the physician's regard for the infant as a person rather than as a malformation, importantly promotes the parents' acceptance of the *baby* as well as the reality of the *malformation*. Then, too, this open examination subtly facilitates communication between the parents while they are both focused on the baby. If multiple separate anomalies are present, for example, a cleft lip, myelomeningocele, and clubfeet, the examination is best segmented and only one major area is covered at one time.

2. Explain repeatedly the identity of the baby. While seeing the child and family over a period of time, the clinician helps the parents to clarify the baby's identity, with a special emphasis on normality.

3. As suggested by Roskies (1972), the identity of the baby and his or her acceptance by the parents may be influenced to some extent by the way in which the baby is identified and accepted by society. Understanding, kindness, and nonsegregation of the baby in the nursery are ways in which the hospital society can convey a positive identity. This attitude has been especially enhanced in settings such as the Parent Care Pavilion at the James Whitcomb Riley Hospital in Indianapolis, Indiana. Such arrangements for care help to create a special feeling of inclusion among families who have children with malformations.

4. Encourage the parents to explain the situation to friends and relatives so that they in turn have some clear identity to which they can respond by calling, visiting, or writing.

Not only does the baby's identity change but also that of the parents, both their self-identity and how they perceive their spouse. Initially, the parents' identity may be severely stressed, distorted, or even shattered. It is a time that I would term a *social* or *crisis delirium*. Physicians and nurses have a role in the constructive reconstitution of the individual and joint parental identities.

It is, of course, true that some persons can grasp the essence or identity of a situation or of a person more quickly, more comprehensively, or more accurately than can others. This truism obviously applies also to the identity of a baby with a handicap. The time required and the extent and accuracy of the perception achieved depend on many factors, including intelligence, experience, level of anxiety, and degree of denial of the parents. Beyond the identity, the extent to which this is accepted by the parents is also determined by many personal factors, both historical and contemporary, including importantly the baby's responsiveness to the parents. Although the extent to which such acceptance can be facilitated and promoted by kindness and compassion in the hospital is unknown, there would seem to be little doubt that the way in which the parents see the identity of the child, themselves, and the response of society helps to determine parental behaviors for better or for worse.

Identity and time are closely intertwined in the relationship between the baby and his parents and between the parents and health professionals. The advice given in this chapter to segment care in short periods that can be encompassed and mastered by the parents is a wise counsel. Time is required for identities to be formed and reformed and for achieving care that attends to the parents' mind and heart—caring for them as persons, promoting their sense of comfort, supporting them through periods of discouragement, and helping to strengthen their parenting capacities.

In placing this brief discussion in a much larger context, the care of the baby with a malformation may be viewed against the background represented by Fig. 5-2. This attempt to depict the scope of child health

Components of child health	Child health constituencies		
	Child	Family	Community
Strengths	A	E	I
Resources	B	F	J
Vulnerabilities	C	G	K
Illness and problems	D	H	L

Fig. 5-2. The scope of child health services.

services includes both the constituencies of the child health professionals—the child, the family, and the community—as well as the components of such care—illness, vulnerabilities, strengths, and resources. Child health professionals need also to attend to the strengths, resources, vulnerabilities, and weaknesses of the physicians and nurses as they care for the infant born with a congenital malformation.   M. GREEN

RECOMMENDATIONS FOR CARE

1. *Initial contact.* We consider it of high priority to bring a baby to the mother as soon as possible so that both parents can see him and observe his normal features as well as his abnormality. Any period of delay during which the parents suspect or know that their baby may have a problem but are unable to see him heightens their anxiety tremendously and allows their imaginations to run wild. They may jump to the conclusion that the baby is dead or dying while he is actually doing well and the problem is a cleft lip. The longer the period before they see the baby the more distorted and fixed their concept of the baby's condition may become. The parents' mental images of their infant's anomaly are almost invariably much more grotesque than the actual problem. Whatever is said to the parents initially is usually indelibly imprinted on their minds. This places a sobering responsibility on the shoulders of everyone caring for the mother and baby because the words used in discussing the baby with her may affect her initial attachment process.

> COMMENT: I agree with the principle but not with the paramount importance given to what is initially said to the parents or to the tendency to view the first words used in discussing the baby as having a permanent effect on the attachment process. Granted that what is said and when is highly important, it may not be possible to know how to put it to the parents until they have expressed some of what they fear and feel. The process of explaining and listening is where the emphasis belongs, as is illustrated in the case of Walter's parents.   A. J. SOLNIT

2. *Positive emphasis.* When first showing the infant with a visible problem, it is important to show all the normal parts as well and to emphasize positive features such as his strength, activity, and alertness. It is sometimes surprising that malformations that appear obvious, striking, and bizarre to the physician sometimes do not seem to the parents as frightening or disfiguring.

3. *Avoiding tranquilizers.* We have strong reservations about the use of tranquilizing drugs for the parents of a baby with a congenital malformation. Tranquilizers tend to blunt their responses and slow their adaptation to the problem. However, a small dose of a short-acting barbiturate at bedtime for sleeping is often helpful.

4. *Special caretaking.* Most maternity units are designed for the care of normal mothers and babies. Therefore, when a baby is born with a problem such as a congenital malformation, the mother's mood and needs are out of step with the routines of the floor. Usually there is no special provision to meet the needs of the small group of parents with babies with malformations, who suffer from the assembly-line routines set up to provide care for the large volume of parents with husky and fully intact neonates. Physicians and nurses may cheerfully burst into the room and ask how the baby is doing, forgetting that he has been kept in the nursery because of the problem or has been transferred to another hospital or division. We find that it is usually best to assign a specific nurse to the mother of a baby with a congenital anomaly. This nurse should have the ability to sit for long periods with the mother and just listen to her cry and tell about the powerful reactions, which are often disturbingly critical and negative. Not everyone on a unit will find this an easy task, so it should be given to a physician or nurse who is willing to listen and who feels prepared to assist the parents of an infant with an anomaly. This task is draining and may seem unrewarding to someone who has not had follow-up experience with families.

5. *Prolonged contact.* We believe that it is best to leave an infant with his mother for the first few days so that she can become used to him rather than rushing him to another division or hospital where the special surgery will eventually be done. Obviously, if surgery is required immediately, such as for an omphalocele or diaphragmatic hernia, this must be done without delay, but even in these cases it is desirable and usually safe to bring the baby to his mother and show her how normal he is in all other respects and to let her touch and handle him if at all possible. The father should be included in all discussions and in all periods with the baby. We try to arrange for the mother and father to have extended periods with their infant to become acquainted with all his features, both positive and negative. The mother of a normal infant goes through a period of one to three days in which she gradually realigns the image in her mind of the baby she expected with the image of the actual baby she delivered. When the baby has a malformation, the task of realigning the images is more difficult, and the result is a greater need for prolonged mother-infant contact.

> COMMENT: Where the mother asks for interruptions in the closeness of the infant and herself, her tolerances, as well as those of the father, should be given appropriate weight in the arrangements. A. J. SOLNIT

6. *Visiting.* It is wise to extend the visiting hours in the maternity unit to allow the father to spend prolonged periods with his wife so that they can share their feelings and start working through their sequence of reactions as synchronously as possible.

7. *Questions.* It has been our clinical impression that parents who are making a reasonably good adaptation often ask many questions and at times appear overinvolved in the details of clinical care. Although these parents may be bothersome at times, we are usually pleased when we see this behavior. We are more concerned about parents who ask only a few questions and who appear stunned and overwhelmed by the infant's problem.

8. *Adaptation.* The process of adaptation to a malformation requires a long period of time before the parents are able to take care of the infant easily. During the early phases, when they are mourning the loss of the perfect baby they had anticipated, they are often unable to manage rather simple procedures. For example, tube feedings that can be managed easily at two to three months sometimes cannot be handled by fairly adept parents in the first few days or weeks.

9. *Explaining findings.* Many anomalies are highly frustrating, not only to the parents but to the physicians and nurses. When things are not going well, the physicians and nurses may go through some of the same reactions—feeling defeat, sadness, anger, and anticipatory grief—as the parents. It is important for the medical staff to be aware of their own feelings and to guard against withdrawing from the parents or the infant. The many questions asked by a parent who is trying to cope with the problem and understand it often tend to be very frustrating for the physician, especially if the parent asks the same questions over and over again during the first three to four months. It is important that the physician be available during this period. It often seems as if the parent has lost his or her ability to remember and may appear quite stupid. We have been surprised how frequently parents forget that they have ever been told about a problem. The psychological reaction of denial is sometimes so strong that they may insist they have never heard about the kidney problem, or the mental retardation, or the possibility that the anomaly might be genetic, even though these may have been discussed on several occasions for periods of at least an hour.

> COMMENT: For the physician or nurse these repeated questions may be experienced as an irritating reminder that they are associated with a defect, handicap, and failure in producing a healthy child. A. J. SOLNIT

10. *Possible retardation.* We strongly believe that if there is a chance of the infant being retarded, we should not discuss it with the parent unless we know with almost absolute certainty that the infant is damaged. This controversial recommendation stems from the many cases in which excellent physicians expressed this suspicion, but later found that this was incorrect and then discovered that they could not convince the parents that the child was normal even years later. Many of these youngsters have subsequently experienced major developmental disturbances be-

cause their parents continued to manage them as if they were retarded. It is also extremely difficult to make predictions about such babies in the first few weeks of life. In our own high-risk nursery we found that expert neonatologists and neurologists, using all the common medical procedures, made correct predictions of normality or abnormality in complicated high-risk infants only 50% of the time (Miranda et al., 1974).

11. *Progressing at parents' pace.* It is generally difficult for parents to absorb information about several major problems in their baby all at the same time. We try to move at the parents' pace and show them one problem at a time (or wait until several can be put together in a package, such as a definite syndrome). We inquire each time how the infant seems to them and what they understand now about his health and progress. For example, "Maybe you could tell me how you see the infant today. What do you see as the baby's problems in the future that we will work on together?" If one moves too rapidly, the parents tend to flee and usually are unable to take in all the medical material.

Before speaking with a parent about a malformation, it is good to understand just what is known about the baby's problem and to be aware of the type of complications that might arise. This often requires a period of time to read about the problem so that the nurse or physician is more relaxed in talking with the parents.

12. *Discussions with parents.* The series of reactions to the birth of a baby with a malformation are such that each parent may move through the stages of shock, denial, anger, guilt, sadness, adaptation, and reorganization at a different pace. If they are unable to talk with each other about their reactions and feelings concerning the baby, a severe disruption in their own relationship may develop. Therefore we often have several private meetings with both parents, using the theory and techniques of crisis intervention. We ask the mother how she is doing, how she feels her husband is managing, and how he feels about the infant. In his presence we then reverse the questions and ask the father how he is coping and how he thinks his wife is managing. Thus they start to think not only about each other but about their own adaptation. Often communication between the parents improves after one or two of these sessions.

13. *Communication between parents.* If the parents are communicating reasonably well, we often tell them to spend some time alone together after supper and go over how they have really felt hour by hour from the time of the baby's birth, to talk about their own feelings and impressions no matter how wild they may be. A cocktail or sherry may make it easier for them to talk. One parent is sometimes amazed by the revelations of the other, and often each one does not fully appreciate until this time

that the other had some of the same thoughts but was afraid to mention them.

14. *Staff meetings.* It often appears to the physician and nurse caring for an infant with a malformation that they are impotent because they are unable to change anything important in the infant and therefore that they have no specific role. But this is not the case. As a matter of fact, they have an important job and in the end can look forward to greater rewards than with other patients and parents. The personnel caring for malformed infants need to discuss these issues frequently. We have found it helpful to have a meeting with the nurses in our nursery to discuss the difficult problems. We ask them to select the issues for discussion. In addition to this the physicians should also have some place to talk about their own problems and concerns and to discuss how difficult they find it to share their reactions and worries. This is especially true with young house officers. In the past we avoided these difficult topics, but it has become increasingly apparent that this was a serious oversight because of the powerful and potentially damaging reactions of both parents and caregivers. It might have been anticipated that intensive care units would put such a strain on nurses and physicians as to necessitate some means of helping them with their intense reactions.

15. *Keeping family together.* One of the major goals of the interviews is to keep the family together both during this early period and in subsequent years. This is best done by working hard to bring out the issues early and by encouraging the parents to talk about their difficult thoughts and feelings as they arise. It is best for them to share their problems with each other. Some couples who do not seem to be close previously may move closer together as they work through the process of adaptation. As with any painful experience, the parents may be much stonger after they have gone through these reactions together. We would recommend that young medical students and house officers sit in on the interviews and observe older faculty members talk to parents in a series of visits over a long period so that they may see not only the initial reaction but also the eventual adaptation achieved by the parents. Interviews with the parents of a malformed infant are usually frightening and upsetting to young physicians. The initial challenging reactions can be placed in better perspective if they follow parents over a period of time with an older experienced physician. We have included an interview to give the reader an idea of how we handle them.

16. *Adaptation to stress.* Each parent's adaptation depends on his or her background and adaptations in the past. For many young people this is the most difficult problem that they have ever had to deal with in their own lives. However, their own past behavior and family experiences often give us a clue as to how they will react and what their indi-

vidual process of adaptation will be. Some parents have had turbulent earlier periods in their lives with their own mother and father. Under stress they may return to the behavior and problems of that period. In others, if the malformation resembles a malformation in a relative or in himself or herself, one parent may believe he or she is the cause of the malformation and so feel tremendously guilty. In most cases this can be discussed and clarified. It may be helpful to ask parents how they have reacted under stress in the past.

Chapter 6

Caring for parents of an infant who dies

JOHN H. KENNELL and MARSHALL H. KLAUS

> Give sorrow words; the grief that does not speak
> Whispers the o'er-fraught heart and bids it break.
>
> *Macbeth*—SHAKESPEARE (act IV, scene 3)

In the modern industrial society the death of an infant is an uncommon event in the life history of a family. In past centuries (and even today in many religions and cultures) there was a ritualized pattern of mourning behavior to be followed after the death of a close family member. However, over the past fifty years in the Western world, death has been moved from the home to the hospital. The sequence of grieving practices for the family has broken down. As a result, the traditions that have been developed over the past hundreds of years to ensure that the mourning reaction in the survivors follows its biological course have been in part lost.

In the last decade the care of sick, severely ill, and dying infants has been concentrated in high-risk neonatal centers, where the emphasis has been mainly on the infant and mother before the death of the infant. Recent long-term studies have shown that the mother suffers a tragic outcome in one third of the perinatal deaths. Culberg (1972) found that nineteen of fifty-six mothers studied one to two years after the deaths of their neonates had developed severe psychiatric disorders (psychosis, anxiety attacks, phobias, obsessive thoughts, and deep depressions). Because of this, it is necessary to examine in detail how to care for the family after a neonatal death.

This chapter will review the normal behavioral changes following the loss of a neonate, explore the physician's and nurse's reactions, and offer suggestions for the management of the family.

BASIC CONSIDERATIONS

Adults experience intense mourning and grieving (usually lasting around six to nine months) only when there is an intimate affectional bond with the deceased, as with close relatives or friends. Some investigators have suggested that the length and intensity of mourning are proportionate to the closeness of the relationship prior to the death. It is important for health care workers to realize that in some women affectional ties to their babies will begin or accelerate with the development of quickening and fetal movement. By the end of the second trimester, the majority of women who initially rejected pregnancy have accepted it. After she feels some quickening, a woman usually begins to have dreams about what her baby will be like and will attribute some human personality characteristics to him or her. One mother commented, "If I had to lose any of my children, it would be better to lose one I hadn't become attached to. If anything was to have happened to her, I would have preferred it then in the first three months. After that, well, especially after you feel life, then it becomes more personal—more of a personal feeling. After that time you start feeling better physically, mentally, and everything else. When you feel life, it is a person in your mind and you start picturing in your mind what it's going to look like when it's born—is it going to be different from the others? After that fourth month, you'd like to have the chance to take most anything, regardless of what it is."

At this time there is a further acceptance of the pregnancy. Sometimes significant changes in attitude toward the fetus are observed; unplanned and unwanted infants may now seem more acceptable. Mrs. R. said, "I think that anyone who finds out she is pregnant doesn't exactly jump with joy, but after a few months I was glad. It was about four months before I could really accept the fact of the baby." Objectively, the health worker finds evidence of this in the mother's preparation for the infant—the purchase of clothes, a crib, the selection of a name, and so on. Thus affectional ties are forming before the birth of the infant.

Observers have noted intense mourning reactions after a neonatal death, lasting for periods of four to six months, similar to those seen after the loss of an older close family member. Some observers have suggested that the intensity of the mourning and grieving after the early loss of an infant is strong evidence for the presence of a close affectional bond. However, Deutsch (1945) suggests that grief after a stillbirth or neonatal death is not the same as that after the loss of a beloved adult relative, but it is rather the nonfulfillment of a wish-fantasy. In any case the sequence of events is the same as that in the classical descriptions of Lindemann (1944) and Parkes (1972).

Lindemann observed that the clinical signs of acute grief in adults are remarkably uniform. Common are sensations of somatic distress occurring in waves and lasting from 20 to 60 minutes; a feeling of tightness in the throat, choking, and shortness of breath; the need for sighing; complaints about a lack of strength and exhaustion; an empty or lonely feeling; a slight sense of unreality; and a feeling of increased emotional distance from other people. One mother commented, "It seemed like I got weak all over, and I had to sit down because I would feel like I was going to faint." A father complained about his wife, "She's so cruel all at once that she doesn't see anything around her—it's like she was closed in a tube or something, rejecting everything on the outside."

A feeling of guilt often torments the mother. The bereaved woman reviews the period before the death for evidence of her failure to "do right" by the deceased. Mrs. G. says, "It's still so hard to believe. I can't think of anything I might have done. I've searched and searched to see if I had done anything during my pregnancy which might have harmed the baby. . . ." She accused herself of negligence: "I felt if I had put on weight, he could have been a full-grown baby, full term. Maybe if I had eaten more, the baby could have weighed more."

In addition, there is often a disconcerting loss of warmth in relationships with other people because of a tendency to respond with irritability and anger. Even though friends and relatives make a special effort to maintain a friendly relationship, parents often wish not to be bothered. Mr. G. remarked, "The biggest problem was talking with friends about it after you sent out notices to everybody, you know, and everybody calling you up, and opening letters—'Sorry to hear about it'—and all this. Then it all comes back."

Activity through the day shows remarkable changes. "I had a feeling for a while that there was an awful lot of confusion. . . . I wanted to close the doors and be by myself a lot." At the same time the capacity to initiate and maintain organized patterns of activity is lost. The bereaved parent clings to the daily routines, but these do not proceed in an automatic, self-sustaining fashion. "I just don't care. Let me put it that way. It just is too much effort. If my husband forces me or pushes me to do something I do it."

Five reactions can be summarized as pathognomonic of grief:
1. Somatic distress
2. Preoccupation with the image of the deceased
3. Guilt
4. Hostile reaction
5. Loss of the usual patterns of conduct

In a detailed study of twenty-four mothers who lost infants in the first twenty-two days after birth, common symptoms were sadness, loss of appetite, insomnia, preoccupation with thoughts of the infant, irritability, and loss of normal behavior patterns (Kennell et al., 1970). As described by Parkes (1965a), "At first the full reaction may be delayed or there may be a period of numbness or blunting in which the bereaved person acts as if nothing had happened for a few hours or days or up to two weeks." Thereafter, attacks of yearning and distress occur, with all the reactions described by Lindemann (1944). Parkes adds, "A dead person is commonly thought to be present, and there is a tendency to think of him as if he was still alive and to idealize his memory." One mother, disturbed by dreams of her baby, says, "I'd wake up and I wouldn't know where the baby was, but I'd want to hold her. . . ." Parkes continues, "The intensity of these features begins to decline after 1-6 weeks and is minimal by six months, although for several years occasional brief periods of yearning and depression may be precipitated by reminders of the loss."

Lindemann, Parkes, and others who have studied mourning extensively have strongly emphasized that full expression of emotional reactions in a grieving person is necessary for the optimal resolution of the mourning reaction. Yet many hospital practices and efforts by hospital personnel and relatives tend to discourage or "bottle up" these reactions. One mother complained, "When I started to cry in the hospital, they wanted to give me a tranquilizer. I would say, 'Gee, if I could just cry, maybe I would get it out of my system.' " If mourning is impeded and not allowed to run its course, pathological grief can result.

RECENT CLINICAL OBSERVATIONS

When a newborn dies in the hospital, all evidence of his existence is usually removed with amazing rapidity, and nothing is left to confirm the reality of his death. "Everything just happened so fast . . . my mind kept going around in circles. I didn't really understand," said one mother. "Just last Sunday I was thinking about her, thinking that my husband and I were the only ones who saw her—it's like there is not proof there ever was a baby. We were the only ones who ever saw her, and it was just for a couple of days. When a baby dies that small, there's no funeral, no masses. It seems like sort of a shame that there isn't something more. . . . I felt I was on an island by myself . . . lost. . . ."

Often no special arrangements are made for the parents. They may not have any privacy or a comforting individual who allows them to express their grief freely. There are usually no planned follow-up contacts with the family to see how the mourning process is proceeding, and information about the results of the postmortem examination is sometimes delivered in a letter.

A recent study (Kennell et al., 1970) focused on the emotional well-being of a mother after touching her baby before his death. There were no pathological reactions in mothers who had touched their infants prior to death, except for one mother who also had a pathological reaction after the death of a previous infant whom she had not touched. The mothers described how painful it was to be located on the maternity division, in the same room as a mother who had a healthy baby, and where the cries of healthy babies could be heard. Most of the mothers stressed the desirability of being in a room on a different division, away from the maternity staff who often caused distress. As one mother mentioned, "They would keep my mother downstairs about half an hour, telling her I was feeding the baby and I didn't have a baby to feed. . . ."

The mothers complained about hospital practices that dampened mourning responses, and they commented on the desirability of allowing a mother to decide for herself whether she wished to see and touch her baby, living or dead. Many mothers had comments about touching their babies. "I didn't get a chance to really touch him, to hold him like a mother. This is something a mother wants to do so much, to touch the baby. Even though she knows she can't pick it up, she wants to touch it. I love to touch it. Sometimes I dream about him, and I can see him, and I wake up. I didn't really pick him up. But the dreams go that I'm picking him up and holding him, and I know I didn't do it. So I wake up because I wanted to so bad." Another mother said, "They told me I could touch my baby, but I didn't want to. She was so small and she looked so fragile I was afraid to touch her. I was afraid that just the fact that I touched her would give me a little more hope and would make it harder for me if she didn't. . . . I didn't want to make anything more difficult." Another mother believes that touching the baby is a form of communication: "You're not just looking at it, you're trying to get something across to this child through touching it. And you have a feeling maybe they know, maybe they can sense this." Mrs. G. concluded, "We had a lot of anticipation. In fact, right now, since I never held the baby or anything, it's all more or less anticipation and not reality."

In interviews many months after the death of an infant, several observers have noted that parents had been greatly comforted by the nurse or physician who expressed sadness or empathy with the parents' plight. The parents expressed at the same time great anger toward health personnel who had been overly cheerful or abrupt or who dealt rapidly with the process of explaining the loss so that they could proceed with obtaining autopsy permission.

Many parents were surprised by the intensity of their feelings of grief and believed that they were psychiatrically disturbed or had developed a severe illness and needed help. This is important for the physician to remember.

Parents commonly reported that their close friends and their relatives were not always supportive, failing to realize that the loss of a newborn infant is a tragedy and normally results in a strong mourning response. Mrs. M. said, "After you've lost a baby, you always think about it most of the time because people want to know how it was to have a baby and lose it, and you have to keep going over it for them." Traditional supportive behavior patterns that existed over centuries are no longer available or acceptable in situations such as the death of an infant. In addition, new cultural patterns tend to deny the reality of death. It appears that in the modern world, new behavior patterns are not seasoned to the needs of the parents. Their mourning reactions may actually be affected in adverse ways.

PHYSICIANS' REACTIONS

In Sweden, Culberg (1972) observed that stillbirth and neonatal death evoke a sense of guilt in the staff on a maternity ward. He observed three different ways that staff members handle the anxiety associated with a death: (1) avoidance of the situation, (2) projection of personal feelings onto the patient in the form of aggressive or accusing behavior, and (3) denial and "magical repair" (". . . forget it . . . get a new child . . . give heavy doses of sedatives"). In another study, in Australia, Giles (1970) noted that physicians managed bereaved mothers by treating physical symptoms only and by prescribing sedatives liberally. They avoided discussing the baby's death in about one half of the cases. In the same study many mothers complained that junior physicians had not answered their questions but left them to be answered by senior physicians, who in fact never visited them. Of forty mothers, twelve believed that they were mainly helped by visitors, ten by talking to a physician, and another ten by talking to members of the nursing staff.

These reactions on the part of the physicians can be easily understood if one analyzes what is happening to them.

A number of strong emotional responses well up in the physician at the time of an infant's death. From past training the physician knows that the patient's total care will be reviewed for the autopsy and the perinatal pathology conference. With the myriad treatments and combinations now available, the physician wonders whether other combinations would have been successful. Young house officers and older physicians alike often raise this question: "What would the results have been if we had moved in another way—if we had raised the oxygen or given a transfusion earlier?" Thus, like the parents, the physician, often partly attached to the infant, is plagued by a feeling of guilt when an infant dies. On top of this the physician also has several difficult tasks, one of which is to face the family with terrible news, realizing that this will result in tears and great sadness as well as hostile feelings. To add to the problem the intensive struggle for life now practiced in most neonatal units has some of the spirit of the sports arena, where a "loss" is almost unacceptable. In some units house officers have mentioned, with a hint of irritation, that one does not expect a baby to die these days, especially if the right things are done. Young physicians often believe they are a failure at their job and that there is little they can do now: they have no tools, no instruments, no medications. In addition, during discussions with the parents, the physician is held back by a sensitivity to their reactions—both by tears and by the nonverbal messages of anger that are present and normally accompany true mourning and grief. However, in contrast to feelings of uselessness, the caretaker has a singular opportunity to make an important contribution to the health of the parents and to the integrity of the whole family. To do this the caretaker must assist the parents in getting under way with the expression of their grief reactions, must encourage the mother and father to communicate their feelings to each other, and then must help them to help the children at home. Obviously future children will be affected by this loss if the parents are unable to get through their grief reactions.

It is important for the physician to realize that these beliefs are also held by all the personnel in the unit, from the secretary to the staff nurse. The physician will often pick up feelings of anger and disappointment from a nurse, since his or her directions led to failure. This is especially true when the nurses are as intimately involved as they are in the present intensive care units. For example, the nursing or bagging* of a tiny infant puts that life into their hands and leads to a strong attachment. We have found that it is difficult for the nurses to function easily unless they discuss these feelings, and we have a meeting every two weeks at which these and other problems are aired.

TASKS FOR THE PHYSICIAN AND NURSE

The caretaker has three major tasks: (1) to help the parents digest the loss and make it real, (2) to ensure that normal grief reactions will begin and that both parents will go through the entire process, and (3) to meet the individual needs of specific parents.

The work of Culberg, Kennell, and others has shown that there are several factors that help to make death real. First, it is important to permit the parents to visit a sick infant, even if the infant is on a respirator and appears quite ill. (It should also be noted here that the parents should only visit when they want to and should never be forced.) Second, we have found it beneficial for the parents to be permitted, if they desire, to view or touch their dead infant (often a harrowing experience for the physician and nurse). The infant usually does not look as he did when he was alive, but this experience helps to make the death a reality. Third, we suggest that simple or private funerals be arranged—traditional rituals which promote grieving—where again the death is made real. In many hospitals it has been the custom for the hospital to dispose of small infants

*Method of assisted ventilation.

as a service to the parents. However, this practice removes all evidence of the infant extremely rapidly so that the infant may become like a dream to the parents, which may retard their grieving. As Mrs. D. said, "I think that all mothers this happens to should go to the burial. My doctor was against it. Some of the family was against it. Some of the family was against having anything at all. I don't believe in that. I couldn't see lying in a hospital bed or going home while my son was being buried. I had to be there."

We have found several steps to be helpful when assisting parents through the normal mourning process. We meet with the parents three times. The *first* time is right after the death. At this moment they are so overwhelmed by the news of the infant's death that they are unable to hear anything else. However, we do describe the details of the mourning process in simple terms. We explain that they may have pains in their chest and have waves of sadness come upon them intensely for the first two weeks and then gradually diminish, tapering off until they cease at about six months. At times they may imagine that they see the baby alive. "The first night . . . when I first came home from the hospital, I wanted the baby and I didn't know where she was." Parents will often find themselves angry with each other and their friends and feel guilty about the death of the infant, believing that actions they could have taken would have saved the infant or prevented his illness in the first place. They may believe that they are going crazy.

We meet with the parents for the *second* time in the next two or three days. At this time it is much easier to review the grieving process. It is important that they understand what the usual reactions are so that they will not think that they are ill. We emphasize again that grieving is a normal and natural process. We point out that many people, including friends and relatives, will not understand the extent of the loss and will say things that will greatly disturb them, such as, "You can always have another baby," "The baby was probably better dead," "You must pull out of this." Often people will try to get them to go out, to become involved in activities. We find it best for them to attempt to do what they think they feel like doing, but not to try to force themselves to pull themselves together or to go out. We especially stress that the parents move together and keep up their rapport and communication. If the father has been sad during the day, he should come home and tell his wife about his sadness rather than hiding it. "He felt terrible. He'd go upstairs and cry alone. If you can cry with somebody you're better, but he cried alone." "He doesn't think about it as much as I do. And when I do, he tells me, 'Maybe it was for the best.' He just mopes around. . . ." "All we did was talk. Stayed up until 2:00, 3:00, 4:00 in the morning just talking about anything and everything. We would always fall back on the baby. It seemed to start out with the baby and end up with the baby. I think it does good to talk." Often we have seen parents move farther and farther apart—the father not wanting to share his sadness with his wife. "I kept busy working . . . that and a guilt feeling. I felt maybe I had done something wrong. We picked on each other . . . about two months. About Christmas time we had a big argument, and I realized I had to face the baby's death. After that we seemed to get closer." "We couldn't discuss things with each other. Maybe that's where I got the feeling of guilt. She would start talking about the baby, and I would say. 'Forget it, the baby's dead.' I guess I was at fault. She wanted to talk it out, but I would say, 'Drop it.' " "Whenever it would come up, I would usually kind of change the subject. You know, you don't want to dwell on it too much. . . ." We suggest that it is important for the husband to tell his wife about his sadness and to let her tell about her own so that they may cry together. "I tried to comfort him and he tried to comfort me and we both ended up crying." It has been particularly striking for us to see how American fathers act after a loss. They often become extremely active, frequently taking on extra jobs or duties outside the home. As well as providing an outlet for their own feelings, these extra jobs may interfere with the husband's support of and communication with his wife. At this second interview it is important to keep lines of communication open and to make plans for another conference in three to six months. It is essential that the physician does not just talk but spends a great deal of time just listening. Obviously every patient's needs will be individualized. One must not be afraid of tears—there will often be a great deal of crying, and physicians should not be afraid of this, for themselves or for the parents. Many parents have mentioned that they appreciated the physician's empathy.

The *third* meeting with the parents occurs three to six months after the death. We meet with them to ensure that their grieving is progressing normally and that there is not a persistently high level of mourning or any other sign of pathological grief. As described by Lindemann (1944), these abnormal reactions often involve the same mechanisms as seen in normal mourning but are manifested in a distorted fashion. They include the following: overactivity without a sense of loss, acquisition of symptoms associated with the baby's illness; psychosomatic symptoms such as colitis, asthma, or rheumatoid arthritis; alterations in relationships with friends and relatives; furious hostility toward specific persons; repression of hostility, leading to a wooden manner resembling that in schizophrenic reactions; and lasting loss of patterns of social interaction and activities detrimental to one's own social and economic existence. If these symptoms are noted during this interview, a referral should be made to a psychiatrist.

Helping parents through these experiences is an extremely difficult assignment, but we have been rewarded by the thanks and expressions of appreciation parents have relayed to us later.

INTERVIEW

The following interview with Mr. and Mrs. Day* took place three weeks after their infant's death. Only portions are included, since this was a long interview.

Pediatrician. It is now three weeks since your baby died. Can you tell me how things have gone since the baby passed away? The feelings you both have had?

Mrs. Day. I can't sleep. I toss and turn. I wasn't thinking about it, but as soon as I saw an article in the paper with a baby in an incubator, it all came back to me. I usually see her in the incubator with them pumping oxygen into her lungs, and she's kicking. I close my eyes and I see her. My husband . . . it doesn't bother him too much . . . it's me.

Mr. Day. It's something you have to go through. These things are bound to happen. It's one of those things you have to learn to live with. It's hard to explain what happens to you. It's very, very hard to explain. I would rather not say to anybody . . .

Pediatrician. You just hold it in?

Mr. Day. Yes, hold it in . . . this is something you cannot describe. I try to live as best as I possibly can. My wife is doing a great job. It's been a tremendous strain upon her, and she has come through victorious. I want to commend the doctors and the staff of people who worked so hard on the child. They did a wonderful job.

This is an unusual interview because the father has told about holding back his reactions very early. It would probably have been appropriate at this point to indicate to the father and the mother that it is natural for parents to feel distressed as they recall this sad experience and that it is all right to cry. Such favorable comments about the doctors and staff at this stage tend to make us a bit wary that criticisms will be forthcoming. It is worth noting that neither parent refers to the baby by name. Let us see how this interview progresses.

Pediatrician. Have you had any trouble sleeping?

Mr. Day. No, I haven't had any trouble sleeping at all.

Pediatrician. Do you have a good appetite? Have you been eating more or less than usual?

Mr. Day. About normal. I wouldn't say more. I don't eat very much anyway.

Pediatrician (to mother). Have you been eating a bit more?

Mrs. Day. Yes.

Pediatrician. Tell me more about your sleeping.

Mrs. Day. I don't get to sleep until 3:00 or 4:00 in the morning. I just toss and turn in the bed all night. And then either my daughter calls me or my son calls me and I get up with them. So the only time I can sleep is about 9:00 in the morning, when I fall asleep.

*The family's name has been changed.

Pediatrician. What can you tell me about your mood?

Mrs. Day. It's low, terribly low. My daughter noticed something was wrong. She looked at me and said, "Mommy, your stomach hurt?" But now she just looks at me. My husband told her we were bringing a new baby home, and she's been looking for this new baby. She won't say anything, but she'll look at me strange and she'll look at her father strange. You know, she was looking for a new little baby. She just looks at me now— she doesn't say any more, "Mommy, does your tummy hurt?" She'll just sit there and look at me.

Mrs. Day's sadness, change in eating habits, and sleep disturbance are not unusual for parents who are mourning the loss of a newborn infant.

The mourning reactions of parents are extremely difficult for children to interpret and understand unless the parents communicate their own feelings and give explanations. A helpful explanation might be, "Mommy is sad about the baby dying. That is why I am crying and look so unhappy. I don't feel like talking or doing the things I usually do right now." The ideas that arise from a sibling's death may be devastating. This girl may well be imagining that her mother's thoughts and reactions are entirely different from what they really are. She may feel guilty because of her angry thoughts about the baby. She may have wished that the baby would die and may believe that the mother's quietness is because of this. Obviously there is a problem of communication between this mother and her children. It sounds as if the children are also having a sleep disturbance. It would be appropriate and probably helpful for the mother to point out the similarity of the children's reactions of sadness to her own. Both the children are sufficiently old that it would be appropriate to help them put their feelings into words.

Pediatrician. What did you tell her about this baby?

Mrs. Day. Well, my husband didn't want to tell her anything. He only said the baby didn't come home, so I just told her the baby died. And she just sat there and looked at me kind of strange—she didn't know what I was talking about. She's almost 3 years old. But my son, he doesn't understand. He just runs around the house. He knows that I look different, that's all. He'll be 2 years old in five months.

Pediatrician. Do you find yourself crying sometimes?

Mrs. Day. Yes.

Pediatrician. What does this mean to the children?

Mrs. Day. At first when I came home, I was crying and my daughter didn't understand. She wouldn't come to me. She wanted to go upstairs to my mother, and she didn't want to be bothered with me, so my husband said, "You should have spoken to her before you went in the house and hugged her," but I just looked at her so strange because she reminded me of the new baby, and I just stared at her. And my husband said, "You shouldn't do that with a baby like that because she's not used to it." I don't know, I was completely numb, and my son was completely numb with me. I couldn't say anything to my two kids. I just looked at them. For two days they rejected me. All she wanted to do was to go upstairs.

As is often the case, the young children are going through severe reactions to the separation from their mother for the birth and postpartum period. This probably accounts for the daughter's unwillingness to approach her mother. The children have found that their mother is not only different in appearance because of the birth but radically changed in behavior and responsiveness. What comes to mind are the striking observations of Brazelton (1974) that even 2- to 4-month-old infants are drastically disturbed and depressed when their mothers sit in front of them mute and without facial response for just 2 or 3 minutes. One of the features of mourning behavior is that it is self-centered. In spite of this, with some encouragement, a mother can usually find the extra ounce of strength to embrace her children and give them some explanation. The husband's criticism does not help the situation, but by holding back his own mourning reaction, he has been able to think of the needs of the children. In retrospect, if we had talked to the mother and father together in the hospital, we would probably have provided the mother with an opportunity to release her feelings sufficiently for her to be able to recognize the needs of the children at home and could have provided a more satisfactory homecoming.

Mr. Day. The children were in a kind of trance. Their mother comes home and has lost a child. She's so cruel all at once that she doesn't see anything around her, like she's closed in a tube or something, rejecting everything else on the outside, so that when she came in the house the first thing she did was reject the children, which she shouldn't have done. She should have extended more love and affection and kindness to the children, which is hard to do in some situations.

Because he has repressed his own mourning reactions, the father does not realize how stunned, shocked, and self-centered a mourner becomes. He vividly describes the mother's inability to see and respond to things around her.

Mrs. Day. There was one particular incident that I remember that was very, very strange when we first came home . . .
Pediatrician. Yes?
Mrs. Day. Well, for one thing, I was very upset when the milk started coming in my breasts all of a sudden. They gave me a shot that prevents the milk from coming back in my breast, but all of a sudden when I got home the milk began to form, and that made it worse, because I had milk and no baby. So I called Dr. M., my obstetrician, and he said to stop drinking so many liquids. I cut down on liquids, but the milk still came

to my breasts. There was nothing I could do about it. I still have it now, so that's hard on me, too, because I'm sore on one side where they gave me the shot, but there's nothing I can do. That makes me wonder, too, you know.

She is probably indicating that she has a number of fantasies about the meaning of this mysterious production of milk in spite of her state of "shock."

Pediatrician. You were all prepared for the baby and there was no baby?
Mrs. Day. Yes. That brings it back to me. I think about her a whole lot. I told my husband that I didn't even *name* her. The nurses were calling her Pinkie. And my mother's upset too because she never did see the baby. She wanted to see the baby, but she didn't want to see her like that. She got all excited Friday and called my father at work and told him about it. She wanted to know if I would have a funeral, and one of my relatives called and wanted to know what I was going to do. I told him there was nothing I could do about it. So he called up his mother and told her and his Aunt Rosie. His cousin wrote him a letter, a sympathy card. She put on it that her daughter had a baby and it was the same way and that he came out of it and now is 15 months old and acts like he is 6 months. He doesn't do anything; he doesn't move around, just flops around. I didn't want my baby to be like this—just flop around. Now I sit around and just wonder about it. All the baby's things I have, from my other baby. I never threw them away, and she never used them up; there are no holes in them or anything like that. We still have all that stuff at home, and you look at it, and the more you look at it the more you think about it. I'm going to give all that stuff away so that I can't look at it anymore.

There is a natural tendency for parents to delay naming their premature and sick baby. This has resulted in a situation in which the mother is concerned that her own mother is upset because she did not name her granddaughter.

The cousin who writes about the 15-month-old who acts like a 6-month-old is characteristic of many relatives and friends who believe it will relieve the pain if they indicate that it is fortunate that the baby died because he or she would probably have been damaged. This matter is considered later on by the interviewer. This episode indicates the importance of good communication so that a physician can counteract this by explaining that the baby would have been perfectly normal if she had not died of respiratory symptoms. The baby clothes, just like the production of breast milk, remind the mother about her baby and cause her great emotional pain. It is important to appreciate that the pain of mourning cannot and should not be suppressed or eliminated. We would not interfere with the mother's plans to put away the baby's clothes, but we might indicate that there would be many other reminders of the baby and that there is nothing one can do to eliminate the pain associated with mourning.

Mrs. Day. I was taking those birth control pills. Would that have anything to do . . . because my girl friend said that her sister had a baby and that its heart was sticking outside of his skin.

Pediatrician. To my knowledge the birth control pills have no connection. When the birth control pills came in, there was no increase in this disease at all. Anomalies are not related to birth control pills either. Do you remember how you felt when you first saw the baby, some of the feelings and thoughts you had?

Mr. Day. I felt fine; I felt wonderful. Even though she was premature, I had heard that there was a good possibility for premature children to live, so I felt fine, I felt wonderful. I imagine that there were worse cases.

Pediatrician. Smaller babies?

Mr. Day. Smaller babies than mine that had succeeded and lived, and are probably fine right now, so this gave me encouragement for her future, that everything was going to be fine from day to day. I was optimistic about it.

It is surprising to find the father expressing such optimism about the baby. As the interview progresses, we obtain a clearer explanation of the parents' responses.

Pediatrician. How did you feel day after day when you saw the baby?

Mr. Day. Gradually, as the baby was getting worse, I began to feel different, but I still held high hopes. The doctor told me that there had been a great change in the baby in a matter of 3 or 4 hours, that the baby was getting worse. Then, knowing the baby was actually getting worse, I was thinking about time, and hoping as the clock ticked that she would improve. I never gave up hope. Right to the end.

The father had the advantage of seeing the baby during this period. In spite of the baby's poor clinical condition, the opportunity to see that the baby was breathing and that her heart was beating gave him a much more optimistic impression than the mother, who probably did not know about this bad turn of events but, because of the separation, was imagining that the baby was in poor condition.

Mrs. Day. That's right. Thursday night, I took a sleeping pill. I don't usually take sleeping pills but I asked for one, and I tossed and turned all that Friday morning until 5:00 A.M. I figured that something was wrong. I couldn't eat breakfast. I knew my baby was dead, but I didn't want to say anything, but I had a feeling that she was—my whole insides felt like they were falling out. I couldn't eat and I was sick, so the nurse said, "What's the matter?" I said, "I don't feel right." So she says, "Why don't you call and see how the baby's doing?" I did, and the doctor told me there was nothing else they could do for her. Well, then I knew she was dead. But they wouldn't tell me—but I just had a feeling she was dead. Then they called and told me she was dead.

At this point some comment about the mother's feelings would be appropriate. We might make a comment such as, "What terrible news! You know it is perfectly natural to feel like crying as we go back over these sad events." In retrospect we can see that the jump to the next item was a bit rapid. It might have been wise to wait longer to obtain her reaction to the news about the baby's death, and perhaps the reaction to this information being given by telephone.

Pediatrician. Could you tell me about the first time you saw the baby? Do you remember how you felt then? Were you optimistic?

Mrs. Day. Yes, when I looked at her . . . but she was so tiny. She was breathing hard; I knew she wasn't going to make it.

Pediatrician. You were not as optimistic as your husband.

Mrs. Day. I told him I wasn't. But he said, "Have hopes." He said she was going to be all right, but I knew she wasn't. I said she was going to die, but he said, "She's going to be all right, have hopes." She moved for me. She kicked for me, but she didn't have any life in her hands—she would only move her little fingers. I touched her little legs and she kicked a little bit and I touched her little hands and she didn't move much but she moved her feet, and that's about it. I would have liked to see her when she died, though, I mean, to say goodbye to her, you know; she was still mine, but in a way she wasn't mine.

The mother's impression that the baby moved for her was a helpful measure in increasing her attachment to the baby. If the baby had lived, this might have been the beginning of a reciprocal interaction that would gradually have developed into a series of communications between mother and baby that would progressively strengthen the attachment bonds.

This mother then expresses a desire to say goodbye to her baby, a request that many other parents have made. As a result, we have been offering parents an opportunity to be with their babies as they die or after they die. It is desirable to provide as much privacy as possible. Many parents will choose to return home or to their rooms in the maternity unit, and they will ask to be notified when the baby has finally died. It is difficult to predict precisely when a baby will die, so that even though it seems as if a baby will survive for only a few minutes, when parents choose to stay, it is wise to prepare them (and the nursery staff) that it might be a matter of several hours before the baby's heart stops.

Pediatrician. You felt badly that you didn't see her . . .

Mrs. Day. Yes, afterwards. I would still have liked to see her. She was still my baby. But my husband said no, and I listened to him. I didn't see her (very softly).

Based on Mrs. Day's comments and those of other parents, we started several years ago to offer parents an opportunity to see their dead baby and to touch and hold him or her. If the physician had talked to the two parents together, it is probable that the parents would have come to the decision that the mother could touch her baby. We believe that when a baby dies, a caretaker can make a major contribution to the long-term well-being of the parents and their family by doing his or her best to help them be aware that the baby really was born, did live, and is now dead. Confirmation of the baby's death will usually help to initiate and facilitate their mourning response.

Pediatrician. How have you felt since? Have you ever felt irritable in the last few weeks? Do you find yourself getting upset more easily?

Mrs. Day (laughing). It doesn't take much for me to get upset. Sometimes when my husband says something, I get mad at him, you know—but it doesn't last long.

Pediatrician. Is this different than usual? Do you jump on him often?

Mrs. Day. I snap at him, see (laughing), and he'll say, "You're so evil." My mother says, "You'd better cut that out." But we don't get into many arguments. He'll say, "You know it's for the best. Don't think about it. Think about something else." He's been taking me out to make my mind go somewhere else, but as soon as I get back home and get into bed, I lie there and just think—I don't know (sighs), I don't think I'll ever get over this (louder), and I don't think I'll ever have another baby. I couldn't take it.

The mother's irritability and anger are part of the mourning reaction. The father's tendency to label her reactions as cruel or evil is understandable because he does not appreciate the intensity of her mourning. His attempts to keep his wife from thinking about the baby are not very successful, but we would usually try to help a husband appreciate that his efforts to take his wife out and divert her mind were going against her natural inclinations and were suppressing her mourning response. In Culberg's (1972) study in Sweden, efforts to delay or suppress the mourning reaction resulted in a prolongation of the mourning response and a longer period of time before mothers were able to get back to normal.

Pediatrician. Do you think about the baby more when you have time to yourself?

Mrs. Day. Well, I go upstairs to keep from thinking about it. I go upstairs with my mother, and we'll talk about something else different, see, and I kind of forget about it until I go back downstairs. My daughter keeps me busy.

These parents demonstrate the support that comes from an extended family. The outcome might have been much less satisfactory if Mrs. Day had not had her own mother nearby to listen understandingly to her tell about her sadness or whatever else she wanted to discuss.

Pediatrician. Your daughter helps a lot?
Mrs. Day (laughs). She talks a lot, so she helps.
Pediatrician. She keeps you busy.
Mrs. Day. My son does too. Back and forth. "Get out of this, get out of that."
Mr. Day. I think that's the only approach to get over a thing like this. Keep busy as much as possible.

This father describes an approach that is characteristic of many men in the United States, British Commonwealth, and Sweden. As a boy grows up, he is trained to act "like a man" and not to cry or show feelings such as sadness. Following the model of his own father, he develops a pattern of keeping busy to keep his mind on other matters when a death or serious illness occurs. Many fathers take on additional employment and assume extra community responsibilities so that they are constantly occupied, often traveling great distances each day to meet these obligations and avoid facing their feelings. This often has the effect of interfering with their communication with their wives.

Based on our initial series of interviews with parents after the death of a newborn, at the first two interviews we have made a point of discussing with the parents the problems of a male in the United States. We encourage the wives to help their spouses express their feelings and tell their husband that it is perfectly all right to cry and to talk about how sad or mad or disappointed or guilty they feel. We are not aware of any studies which show that this results in fathers' mourning more appropriately, but our experience leads us to believe that most are helped by this type of discussion.

Pediatrician. That's one approach.
Mr. Day. That's the one I know of. And like she mentioned before , I thought it would be nice if I took her out to dinner and to socialize and to make various little suggestions to her as to her liking . . . where she would like to go out.

Again the common reaction is seen of the father that he has to fight against his mourning reaction not only by keeping himself busy but also by keeping his spouse busy. It is our practice to anticipate this possibility at our first contact with the parents by saying that it is desirable to arrange to lighten up on commitments and responsibilities.

Pediatrician. So you've gone out to dinner?
Mr. Day. To dinner and to a dinner dance and drive-in clubs—to enjoy ourselves together and to keep her mind off past experiences.
Pediatrician. Do either of you ever feel that there was something you didn't do or should have done that might have helped the baby?

Mrs. Day. No. I think we had the best doctors for her. Dr. P. told me, "We're going to give you the best doctor in the hospital." I don't feel that I could do any better than the doctors did. I mean, the doctors tried their best to save her, so it wasn't the doctors' fault or anything. The doctors were wonderful, especially Dr. W. He worked with her and wasn't going to give up, but he couldn't do it alone. See, if she had to go, she just had to go, and it's nobody's fault—it's just that she wasn't meant for us, that's all.

Some mothers who have lost a premature infant find that they can blame the death on an act or omission of the physician or the hospital. However, we have been impressed that a majority of the mothers do not put the blame on the physicians or on the system, even when there may be a reasonable excuse for doing so. We suspect that most mothers feel extremely guilty for having produced an abnormal baby—that is, a tiny fragile baby before it was ready to come into the world.

Mr. Day. Will you repeat that question again, please?

Pediatrician. Have you ever had any feelings or thoughts that there was something that you had done, or that we had done or hadn't done that would have made a difference for the baby?

Mr. Day. I understand now. What could we have done? Medically speaking, we couldn't have done anything, because we're not doctors. At the time that the baby was in such distress, we had suggested to the nurse that was taking care of her—since they had to spend round-the-clock hours with her—we had suggested, both of us, that if possible, we would like to do the things that they were doing, *if possible*.

This comment was surprising to the interviewer. Since that interview with Mr. and Mrs. Day, several parents have expressed an interest in becoming involved in the care of their babies in the last minutes or hours of their lives. When we consider that the average parents have spent twenty years plus seven to eight months preparing for a baby, we realize that they believe they have done an incomplete job in producing such a small baby. Because their baby has been taken away from them for care by the experts, it is understandable that many parents may have a strong desire to have a part in their baby's care—and in the process to have a chance to touch and really get to know their baby, who will probably live for only a few more hours. When faced with a baby whose outcome is clearly going to be fatal, Dr. Raymond Duff at Yale–New Haven Hospital, Connecticut, asks parents if they would like to have all of the tubes and apparatus removed so that they can hold their baby while he or she dies.

Pediatrician. I remember that you had mentioned this to me.

Mr. Day. Yes, to keep the burden off the nurses and the other doctors that were performing their duties. . . . I would have liked to lighten their load.

I think it would have been wonderful. . . . I would probably be there now. I could really appreciate life; life is worth living. I could really appreciate it. I could really talk to people and really make them understand.

Pediatrician. You feel that you didn't get your own hands into it?

Mr. Day. There's not much that I can say. . . . All I can tell you is my personal feelings.

Pediatrician. You felt left out of it. You have a good pair of hands and we could have taught you quickly how to do it—then you would have felt that you yourself had a part.

Mr. Day. That's it.

Mrs. Day. Then he would have got upset.

Mr. Day. No.

Mrs. Day. Yes, you would have (quietly, then laughs). Yes, you would have got upset.

Pediatrician. Do you feel that you are getting back in the swing of things? Or do you feel there is still something different about life from day to day in the way you feel?

Mrs. Day. Well, I miss my baby, I know that, and as I say, I'm not going to get over it. I have a certain feeling for her, you know. I carried her for seven months, and I came to the hospital to have her, but then I had to leave without her. You know, when you see other people leaving the hospital with their babies, well, it makes you wonder why your baby isn't there, and why you aren't taking your baby home, and the lady who was leaving at the same time I was leaving had her baby all wrapped up in a bundle in her arms—and our baby was down in the basement. I didn't want to turn around to say anything to her, but I had to, so I said, "I hope you have success with your baby," and she said she was sorry I lost mine. But it hurt me *bad*.

Several mothers who have lost their own infants have told us about an almost overpowering urge to grab another newborn baby and run away with him or her. These mothers tell us how they have seen a baby of about the same size as their own in front of a supermarket or some other public building and have found themselves touching or almost ready to seize the baby and run off.

Mr. Day. There's a kind of mysterious missing link, in an individual, when suddenly he loses a part. This is something that's very, very hard to explain. I'm trying to do my best to explain. My feeling is that there is something missing from day-to-day living.

Pediatrician. Something isn't right.

Mr. Day. Something isn't right. Now I can enjoy myself. I can go out. I sleep well. I eat well. I have other children that I enjoy. I have a wonderful wife, a wonderful home, but there's still that missing piece. This is the way I feel; I think it will always be there. I don't think that you can eliminate it.

Many parents have described a feeling of great emptiness, reporting how their arms or body ache because of the emptiness left by the loss of their infant.

Pediatrician. I wanted to go into two or three points. Your feelings are normal for someone who's just lost a baby. Your difficulty in sleeping, in taking up the care of your children, and in getting back into the swing of things is really very normal.

Mrs. Day (quietly). Last night I couldn't sleep, and every time I think about her, I always say I didn't get to name her. And my husband says, "Why didn't you? Forget about naming her, she's gone now." But I will say, "I didn't name her." And my husband looks at me and he says, "Well honey, you didn't name her, so don't think about it so much. Think about the other two kids and raising them." But that's always in my mind.

Pediatrician. What does that mean to you? Why do you say that bothers you so much?

Mrs. Day. I wanted another little girl so bad. My husband wanted a boy. So every time he came home, when I was pregnant, he says, "Has my son been acting up?" Well, she didn't start kicking until about the fifth month. In the sixth month she really got active, but before that she wasn't active at all, she wasn't doing anything, but finally she started kicking and moving. And my husband says, "That's a boy," and I said, "You're wrong, it's a girl." So after we had her I got my wish—it was a girl. So when she was in the nursery, it worried me, because I said my husband's thinking about names. Thursday he gave me some funny name, and I said I didn't want that name. So we were talking about names, and all of a sudden, she died, and I didn't give her a name. The nurses were calling her Pinkie, so I said, "Well, Pinkie would be a pretty name." Then the other day my mother went to the flower show, and somebody called her little girl April, and I thought April would have been a pretty name for the baby because that's an odd name, and my mother said, "You should have named her April before she died." So every time it comes to me, I remember that I didn't name her.

Pediatrician. Do you worry about your other two children more than before the baby died?

Mrs. Day. Yes. Is she going to get into anything, is she going to take anything, is she going to wander off, or is somebody going to pick her up?

Pediatrician. What do you mean?

Mrs. Day. Well, that she'd go outside into the street, and you know, how young fellows sometimes pick babies up. I just sit down and sometimes the craziest things come to me all of a sudden.

Pediatrician. But you have more of these worries now than before the baby died?

Mrs. Day. Yes. My husband is worried too.

Mr. Day (laughs). I've always worried about them. Of course, I'm health conscious. I want to know how they're feeling all the time. When I'm away, I call to see how they're doing, whether they're eating or not eating—this is the sort of thing I'm worried about, I worry about their health.

At this point the autopsy findings were presented and discussed. The baby's lungs showed many hyaline membranes, and there was an intraventricular hemorrhage. The interviewer emphasized that the baby was physically perfect in all other respects.

Mrs. Day. Do you know why she came early?

Pediatrician. This is a very important question. Along with our obstetricians we are trying to figure out how to predict which mothers are going to deliver prematures. But at the present I can tell you that we don't know. We have no answers but many questions.

Mr. Day. I was telling my wife about premature babies; I was telling her that when something happens to a baby, I don't know, I am assuming that this is Mother Nature's way of letting you know that something's wrong— a premature child.

It is a common practice to attempt to comfort the mother whose newborn infant has died by explaining that there was really something wrong with her baby, that she never would have been normal and healthy. This type of statement just reinforces the belief of mothers that they have really been very inadequate and have produced very unsatisfactory babies.

Pediatrician. You mean that something might be wrong with the baby?

Mr. Day. Yes.

Pediatrician. In the first month or two a large number of babies are lost. When these babies are examined, many have abnormalities. But this isn't true if they are born after the sixth month.

Mrs. Day (to husband, who is mumbling). Are you nervous, or something?

Mr. Day. Yes, I am.

There is a question whether this nonverbal behavior indicates that the interviewer has challenged one of the beliefs that supported Mr. Day's confidence that the outcome had been reasonably satisfactory. There is always the risk that a physician will say too much and remove one of the props supporting a parent during this difficult period.

Mrs. Day (to pediatrician). If I had carried her for nine months, would this still have happened, I wonder?

Pediatrician. Probably not. At 1400 grams—her weight—about 50% of the babies have this disease. By the time a baby is full term, it's less than 1%. If you had another baby, there's no increased incidence of having another baby with this problem.

Mr. Day. You mean, if you have another one. Having one does not increase your chances of having another. It's not like Rh disease or certain congenital anomalies. This particular disease is called . . . what?

Pediatrician. Hyaline membrane disease. The other name is respiratory distress syndrome. It has two names.

Mr. Day. In other words, she had two things.

It is fortunate that the interview went on sufficiently long that the father could ask more questions and indicate the areas about which he was confused. So often with the pressure of time health professionals neglect to ask the parents to tell them what they have understood.

Pediatrician. No, the same thing.
Mr. Day. One brings on the other.
Pediatrician. No, no. It's the same disease with two names. Actually there's a third name—the Kennedy baby's disease, because President Kennedy's baby had the same thing. They named the Kennedy baby's disease the respiratory distress syndrome of infancy and also hyaline membrane disease because you see hyaline membranes under the microscope. So these are the three names that people give it.

As we look back on our interview, we can see that we made comments we wish we could retract. There was no value to be gained by adding a third name while the father was already struggling with two.

Mr. Day. All three names are the same.
Pediatrician. The same thing. A third of the babies who die from this have brain hemorrhages, so finding the brain hemorrhage here was not that unexpected, although we didn't anticipate it because the baby was so good up until the last.
Mrs. Day. My husband was telling me that the baby would have brain damage.
Mr. Day. Because I checked in the medical book. I read up on it.

More and more parents are finding that they can search out their own answers in medical books. Some of the father's impressions about the poor quality of the baby may have been based on the reading he is reporting. Once again we can see that it is helpful to allow parents enough time to explain what they have done and what they understand.

Mrs. Day. Does it make me forget things? Lately I've been very absentminded. I forget where I put things, and then I go look for it and can't find it.
Pediatrician. Is that right?
Mrs. Day. My husband says I'm cracking up (laughs). That's a cute expression.
Mr. Day. I never used that.
Mrs. Day (laughs). Yes, you did. When I lay something down, I never can find it. I'm talking to my mother and I forget what I'm saying sometimes.
Pediatrician. You were asking about what may have made the baby premature? Do you ever have any thoughts that you might have done something that might have made the baby premature?

Asking the same questions during an interview by using different words will often focus the discussion closer to the concerns that are actually bothering the parents.

Mrs. Day. My mother always tells me about . . . I was fooling with my husband, you know, we always wrestle, and I always pull on him and I used to pick up things—strain—I don't know about straining myself. I think I'm the hard-head type, when you say don't do things.

Mr. Day. Lots of mothers do the same things.

Mrs. Day. I carry my son—you know, he's quite heavy. I was carrying him on my hip to take him up to the barbershop to get a haircut, and the baby kicked me all the way back home.

Mr. Day. I don't think this has anything to do with what he's talking about . . . this brain damage and . . .

Mrs. Day (interrupts). No, no, but he's talking about the baby coming early. . . . This is my mother's old-fashioned talk, and she says that if you play, you must pay. My husband and I play a lot, and I run up and down the steps a lot. I run up and down the street a lot.

Mr. Day (voice rising). People have been pregnant and been in the Olympics and swimming, and running. I don't think this has anything to do with it.

Mr. Day tries and tries to eliminate his wife's guilt and sadness when it would be desirable for her to continue to express her concerns.

(Mr. and Mrs. Day talk together.)

Mrs. Day. Their babies weren't down at the bottom of their stomachs. My baby was.

Pediatrician. This is one of the things that is under question. One group says that exercise is better. Other people say that rest is better, and I can tell you that neither group knows the right answer.

Mrs. Day. That's right, that's right (laughs loudly).

Pediatrician. So the doctors are just like you and your wife. Do you have any other questions that we can help you with right now?

Mr. Day (softly). No, no other questions. Jean, is there anything you would like to say? What about the physical and mental condition of the mother at the time of carrying the child with this respiratory disease?

In retrospect we wish we had asked Mr. Day further about what he had in mind. It may well have been that he was relating certain aspects of the physical or the mental state of the mother to the baby's problem.

Although this interview was long and became repetitious, new information continues to emerge. It was difficult to understand the father's early optimism, but it can be appreciated much more easily when we realize that he was a premature infant himself.

Pediatrician. Were you really?

Mr. Day. Yes, 2¼ pounds.

Mrs. Day (laughs). Thanks a lot.

Mr. Day. Yes, I was proud to say that.

Pediatrician (surprised). 2¼ pounds?

Mr. Day. Yes, 2¼ pounds. I weighed 2¼ pounds. I didn't have the medical advisors' service that they have today, either.

Pediatrician. Isn't that interesting. 2¼ pounds! I would like to have you come back to see me in about two months, mainly to see how you're doing.

Mrs. Day. It's been very helpful when the doctor is interested like this. It keeps your mind clear. As I was coming up here now, I looked in where the babies are—I can't think of the name right now—and there were little babies in there, and I was thinking, once my baby was in there. That's why I hate to go past that room.

Pediatrician. It was hard for you to come up here?

Mrs. Day. No, it's not hard for me to come up here, but it's hard for me when I go past. . . . See, I can look in and see the babies in there and I think, well, my baby was once in there (sighs heavily).

Mr. Day. Well, as I said before, if these discussions can help you in the future with other patients, to improve the individual, I'll be glad to help as much as possible . . . as much as we can.

We have been repeatedly impressed by the cooperativeness of parents and particularly by their appreciation for an opportunity to improve care for other patients and the education for physicians. This may give the parents a greater meaning for the life of their baby.

Mrs. Day. It helps me to talk about it. . . . My husband says, "Don't talk about it so much." It kind of eased my nerves a little bit.

Pediatrician. We have the impression that if you talk about something that worries you, it's better. There have been some studies about grieving after death and they indicate that if you tend to hold everything back, it tends to make the resolution more difficult years later.

Mr. Day (interrupting). What about the individual that *never* talks about it?

Pediatrician. We don't know.

Mr. Day. This would be a finding also. You would have to study into this. This is something now that I have . . . (long pause) . . . I think, as I said before . . . it's part of life. These things are bound to happen. And we have to learn to cope with them. And I just go on living day to day, and I have other things and other duties to perform. If I break down now, somebody will have to pick these people up . . . somebody's going to have to pull them together and help them if I break down. So I just keep going and try to keep busy (louder) and keep from thinking and keep from worrying about these things. So I just don't talk about it. With some people it's just the opposite. I can see how talking may help you, but it keeps you from doing a lot of other things.

Pediatrician. What you say is very true, but maybe in life there has to be a period where you recover . . . we don't know. In general, we have known that it takes a lot of emotional and physical work to bottle things up. Sometimes things just have to get out.

Mr. Day. It takes a long time.

Pediatrician. Oh, yes.

Mr. Day. Maybe I'm doing this under a tremendous strain, but I'm the only one to determine this.

Pediatrician. Yes.

Mr. Day. By closing this door upon something that has happened, as if it didn't happen, maybe it's wrong. Maybe it's wrong for me four or five, ten, fifteen, twenty years from now . . .

Mr. Day (loudly). I'm doing what I think is right because I have other responsibilities.

Mrs. Day. Put that ruler down; you're making me nervous (laughs).

Mr. Day (continues loudly). Because I have other responsibilities.

Mrs. Day (laughs again). You make me nervous . . . you know, this is what I was thinking about. When . . . I suffered with her so long . . . and then to lose her . . . from 7:00 that Monday morning until 6:35 that Tuesday to have her. It's a wonder I don't lose my mind . . .

Mr. Day. What do they call it when they . . .

Pediatrician. A cesarean section.

Mrs. Day. Yes, that's what he was going to do when she hadn't moved.

This was a long interview. If the physician's time is limited, it is likely that the information will come out at a subsequent interview if the physician is ready to sit and listen.

COMMENT: In this chapter the authors study the impact of an infant's death on his family, physicians, and nurses, and they attempt to help them master this stress. They approach this hard task not only with scientific objectivity and skill but bring it to that measure of compassion and humility which constitutes the most essential aspect of our work with the bereaved. It is difficult to achieve and maintain in ourselves, even harder to teach to others, yet without it even the most accurate procedure and words will not prove helpful.

The authors base their practical guidelines on three premises: (1) the bereaved person is helped to accept the death of a loved one by perceiving its concrete reality; (2) having acknowledged the external reality of the loss, the bereaved person needs to adapt himself or herself to it internally through the process of mourning; and (3) if the bereaved person fails to accomplish the mourning task, he or she will be unable to resume healthy progressive functioning. We fully agree with these premises and, in regard to the first, also support the authors' suggestions—opportunity to be with the dying, to see the body, to participate in its disposal by way of the customary rites, and to understand the cause of the death.

Our understanding of the mourning process differs, however, from that of the authors, and we would therefore stress somewhat different aspects in helping the bereaved individual. Mourning, a silent intrapsychic process, consists on the one hand of detaching ones emotional ties from the image of the deceased loved one and on the other hand of changing one's own image, to an extent, so as to become like the deceased, that is, identifying with some aspects of his personality. Depending on such factors as the nature of the relationship with the lost person, the bereaved individual's proportion of detachment and identification varies, so does the duration of the mourning process. The painful affects of sadness, loneliness, and anger usually accompany the process of detachment, but their expression does not guarantee the normal progression of mourning or does it necessarily facilitate it, since each person mourns in his own way and mourns each loss differently.

In mourning an infant a parent faces a particularly difficult task because (1) he can only utilize the painful long process of detachment, since identification would not prove adaptive (how can a parent become part child again?) and (2) he deals not only with the loss of a loved one but also with a loss of a part of himself (parental attachment consists of a mixture of object love and self-love). When a premature infant dies, these difficulties are heightened. The child has not yet become a person to be loved in his own right, and his death represents primarily a loss of self and of self-esteem to the parent. The inner adaptation to such a loss differs from mourning the death of one who has been known and loved as a unique individual. The father in the preceding interview understood this well when he said, "There's a kind of mysterious missing link, in an individual, when suddenly he loses a part. . . . I have a wonderful wife, a wonderful home, but there's still that missing piece." The mother, too, expressed it through her feeling depleted, fearing further losses, and needing to fill the void. The authors note that many parents have described a feeling of great emptiness. In dealing with such a loss it is particularly important for the parent to be active to reassure himself of his "wholeness" and ability to function as a competent parent. This need probably entered into the father's somewhat defensive busyness ("I am responsible for them") and underlies both parents' wish to cooperate with the physician in helping other bereaved parents.

These considerations suggest some shifts in approach. It seems important to stress to the parents that they have to accomplish an extremely painful, difficult job inside themselves which is even harder than mourning because they have lost, in their infant, a part of themselves as well as a relationship which was yet to come. Although it may be helpful to mention possible manifestations of distress, it needs to be emphasized that each individual copes with it differently. When individuals understand and respect each other's ways of grieving, they will be able to find the necessary and mutually helpful opportunities for sharing painful thoughts and feelings. The parents' need for activity and restoration of self-esteem is best channeled into the task of supporting each other and especially into assisting their children in mastering the stress. Hard though it may be to help youngsters to understand the tragedy and to meet their needs, ultimately a parent's self-esteem is augmented most by being an effective parent. He could never forgive himself if, in his concern over one lost child, he were to lose the continuity of his relationship with the other children. Even very young children prove to be caring companions in grief, if given the chance. In working it through with his child, the parent often gains mastery himself. It would seem wise in the second interview, if there are children at home, actively to direct the mourning parents to this task for the children's sake but also their own. Clinically, one of the best indications of the parents' healthy progress in mourning is their ability to discuss and feel the loss with their children.

The authors have thoughtfully pointed out that physicians too, can partly cope with their helplessness in the face of an infant's death by being active in helping the parents. Hopefully, such activity includes much listening to, and learning from, the parents to increase the health professional's knowledge and effectiveness.   E. FURMAN

RECOMMENDATIONS FOR CARE

1. *Parental contact with infant.* If a mother loses an infant any time after she has felt fetal movement, she will usually go through a long period of intense mourning. To help with the mourning process, we encourage mothers to see and handle their infant after he has died. Some of our mothers have cleaned and diapered the baby after his death. Others have gone to the mortuary, looked at the baby closely in private surroundings, and picked him up. In the situation where the mother is still confined in another hospital, parents have requested a picture of the infant after he has died. Each of these arrangements is upsetting to some of the nurses and physicians, but it has been our experience that each helps to make the death real. At first one might think that it is only good to remember the baby as a normal, active infant, but it is our present belief that it is important for some parents to see the infant after he has died so that they have a clear, visual proof that the baby really died, and they should be offered this opportunity. Many mothers have told us about having lost a baby in the past and wishing for years that they could have seen, touched, handled, or even seen a picture of him before he was taken away. Many had none of these opportunities.

2. *Funeral arrangements.* We have found it valuable, if the parents choose, to have a funeral. This facilitates the grieving process. Our own suggestion is a simple funeral with only the immediately family present. We do have arrangements for our hospital to dispose of the infant with cremation and burial in the hospital's plot, without charge, if the family so desires. When parents decide to have their baby cremated, we encourage them to go ahead with a small private service in their own place of worship.

3. *Second interview.* After the death of an infant we meet with both the parents together, and sometimes with their own parents, usually within

the first 3 days but at least within the first week (first interview immediately after the death, p. 216). This meeting generally lasts for about an hour. We spend several minutes discussing mourning, grieving, and the importance of accepting one's feelings instead of pulling oneself out of the depression or trying to get back to normal activities. We especially advise husbands to be honest with their wives, to tell them if they have had a sad or a rough day. They will often be afraid of expressing their emotions for fear that they will hurt their wives and cause them to cry. This openness permits the wife to express the difficult feelings she has had, and the couple can communicate and work out their grief together.

It is valuable to have the couple's parents present at this early discussion so that they can appreciate the needs of their children and can provide a major support and listening post for them. If a grandparent is not available, we encourage the mother to share her thoughts with another close friend. It is necessary to explain to the parents that many of their friends will not know how to react to the death of their neonate. They will often say something to the effect that if the baby was damaged, he is better dead. And in the United States they may believe that since the mother and father never took the baby home, there will be little grief and mourning. In other words, there will have been little attachment and therefore little feeling of loss.

Since most young people have had little or no experience with neonatal death, the parents appear to benefit from hearing how other people react to the loss of an infant. We explain that normal healthy people generally feel angry after they have lost someone close to them—angry at themselves, at the doctors, and at the nurses. Guilt is also experienced for things that were or were not done. We explain that the most valuable thing they can do is to let their feelings out and not rush to pull themselves back to any of their usual daily tasks, such as work, cleaning the house, visiting friends, going out to dinner, parties, and shows, or watching television unless they really feel like it.

It is important that this long discussion take place at least a day after the death of the infant. The parents are usually too overwhelmed on the day of the death to think about their own future and their own needs. Generally they only hear that the infant has died. In our discussions we encourage them to telephone and talk with us, to continue the relationship. We make an appointment for the parents to come back in three months.

4. *Avoiding tranquilizers.* We strongly encourage that parents take no tranquilizers. This tends to dull the mourning reaction in such a way that it may never fully develop, and the parents are left without having fully worked through the experience. On a few occasions we recommend a sedative to be taken solely at bedtime.

5. *Planning for another baby.* During the initial discussions we strongly encourage the parents to refrain from having a replacement infant until they have completed their mourning reaction. We explain that it is difficult to take on a new baby at the same time one is giving up the baby who has died. These two processes are moving in opposite directions and are extremely difficult to accomplish simultaneously. Therefore we ask the parents to wait six months to a year before planning for another baby. We encourage them to plan for a new baby in its own right, not to replace the baby who has just died. This has been noted by Engel (1964).

6. *Group discussions.* Recently we have found that many mothers who have just lost babies find it helpful to read the diaries of other mothers who have experienced the same loss. We are presently starting to organize a discussion group for a small number of mothers whose infants have died. Many of these mothers have mentioned that only a mother who has lost a baby can really appreciate the pain involved. A similar group has been helpful for mothers in several large cities whose babies have died from the sudden infant death syndrome (SIDS). Up to the present time it has been difficult for parents who have lost a newborn to find any other parents who have had a similar experience. Perhaps the hospital neonatal intensive care nursery should be the organizing point for these parents, just as the coroner has been for the SIDS mothers in our community.

7. *Third interview.* At this time we discuss any questions the parents may have. On the surface it appears that the parents are coming back to ask questions or to learn something more about the autopsy data, if there has been an autopsy. However, the major reason that they should come back is for us to determine whether the mourning process is progressing normally or whether there is evidence of pathological grief as defined by Lindemann (1944). This may show itself by no grief at all or by continuing, unremitting grief. (A more complete definition can be seen on p. 211.) During this session we chat with the parents to see how they are doing and ask some of the following questions:

Have you gone out at all?

How are your other children doing?

Have you been able to talk about the death with each other and with the children?

How is your eating?

How are you sleeping?

Are you watching television yet?

Have you had friends over?

In other words, we are trying to learn about their daily patterns of living, focusing on whether grieving at this time is still going on, is slightly lessened, is felt in dips of sad periods each day with some crying, or whether there is a change in daily habit patterns, such as sleeping, eating, interest in television, movies, visiting, hobbies, and eating out. It is often helpful to ask each parent to comment about changes in the behavior of his or her spouse and ask how the spouse's mourning process is progressing. In our experience grief usually continues for a period of seven to nine months. Generally by this interview it has lessened, since the parents have had the opportunity to release their strong feelings about the infant and hence are able to resume their normal way of life. Often we have noticed that the marriage appears to be stronger after this period of mourning; the parents appear to be better prepared to face the ups and downs of life.

We make the appointment for the three-month visit, and if the parents do not keep it, we call them, since we believe the visit is important. About one half of the parents find the thought of returning to the unit very difficult, although they usually seem relieved once they do come.

8. *Pathological grief.* Each year a small number of patients, even with these special interventions, experience pathological grief. As soon as we are aware of this, we believe that it is extremely important that they be referred to a psychiatrist.

9. *Other children.* If there is another child in the family, it is important to explain to the child what is happening. The surviving children sometimes feel overwhelmed and somehow guilty or responsible for the infant's death. It is important to help these children discuss their feelings. It is also wise to remind the parents to explain that they themselves are crying because of the sadness of the loss of the baby, not because they are angry at the other children, and how good it is to have them nearby.

It is not unusual for some of the siblings to need special guidance. When this is the case, it has been most useful to have the parents discuss the problems with a child guidance worker.

10. *Value of listening.* The specific suggestions just presented are misleading because there is so much emphasis on what the physician says. During visits with the parents much of the time is spent listening, often with long periods of silence or crying. On a busy day this sitting and listening is particularly difficult for a physician, but it is time well spent.

11. *Training house officers.* Interns and residents have an extremely difficult time discussing these issues with parents in their early months and years of training. They usually believe that their job is the treatment of the infant and have severe guilt feelings, wondering if they failed to do something that could have saved his life. This feeling is perpetuated by the procedures in the hospital such as the perinatal mortality committee meetings each week. Therefore, at the suggestion of Barbero

(1973), we have made a strong effort to join house officers the first four or five times they talk with parents who have lost an infant. They observe how we handle the interviews, and then we observe their next three or four encounters. After the interview we discuss it for about half an hour. We ask them what they might have done differently, how we might have talked differently to the parents, what the strong points were, and what the difficult points were in this encounter. In a sense it can be compared with the procedure in showing them how to insert a catheter. We show them once or twice, then we watch them, and finally they do it on their own. We believe that this is an essential part of the training in perinatal care for any physician planning to specialize in pediatrics.

12. *Staff meetings.* When the nurses, physicians, and other staff members of the unit are working well, they often experience mourning reactions after the death of one of the infants for whom they have cared. We have found it extremely important for the nurses and physicians to have a time to talk about their feelings. Our own unit works best when we have group meetings every other week and openly discuss our own feelings about the problem. Strong reactions relating to the death of some of the infants are often voiced. In one case a nurse asked, "You don't tell us why the baby died, Dr. _____. We wonder if we caused the death by our bagging. Did we produce the intraventricular hemorrhage? Would you please explain why each of the infants died? It would help us." We have had some house officers who experienced considerable difficulty with the newborn service because they expect themselves to be almost perfect in preventing the death of every infant under their care. In any active neonatal intensive care unit there are a number of deaths each week. This is difficult for certain house officers and nurses, and they need special personal help in coping with this high mortality rate. Surprisingly, it has usually been those house officers who demand perfection in themselves and expect to give an extremely high quality of care who have been most distraught in the nursery. Some have developed diarrhea, weight loss, and other worrisome symptoms. In a true sense the nursery is like an extended family, with the director and head nurse playing an important role in maintaining high morale.

The future

Although we have only begun to understand the complex process of the attachment of parents to their newborn infant, those responsible for the care of mothers and infants should reevaluate hospital procedures that interfere with early, sustained mother-infant contact. The introduction of practices that promote a mother's and father's interaction with their infant and help them to appreciate his wide range of sensory and motor responses should be considered.

We foresee that in the future the professionals will turn over one of their traditional roles in caring for the infant and mother to other members of the family. Twenty-five years ago the visiting policies in children's hospitals allowed parents to see their sick child for an hour once or twice a week. When changes in this policy were originally suggested, many nurses and physicians believed that children's wards would become unmanageable, the children would be too distressed, and their health would suffer. It is now agreed that this change to unrestricted visiting and living-in of parents has been extremely important in the overall health of the child as well as his family, but the change did not evolve easily. For example, children do cry more when parents are nearby during a procedure, but they are much more like children than like the depressed robots we used to see. Pediatricians who have observed the change, however, have seen that the sensitivity and ingenuity of parents often result in much better care for a child than could be provided by professionals alone.

> COMMENT: We must not forget that this attention to the strengths of normal people and their healthy newborns will emphasize the sadness and separation which will be heightened when we must separate a sick infant from his parents. Hence we should build in safeguards, not only for the parents but more for hospital personnel, who will find it difficult to be responsible for suffering parents in such a new optimistic environment. It actually will be easier for parents to find the supports they need in such a new brave world, since the resources will be less drained, but the physicians and nurses may also be less experienced in dealing with their own anguish.

T. B. BRAZELTON

As health providers integrate new procedures of caring for the family in the hospital into the present complicated network of hospital care, it is essential that the major advances and contributions of modern obstetrics and neonatology are not lost. Efforts to make childbirth and post-partum care more family oriented should not disrupt the progress of these two rapidly advancing disciplines. Unless a major attempt is made to blend the essential components of these three approaches to perinatal care, some parents will leave the hospital completely. Although some will achieve a more humanistic childbirth experience, it is inevitable that others will suffer tragic consequences. Therefore we strongly urge that child-birth in the future take place in the hospital but that the hospital offer a wide range of services to meet the special medical and personal needs of each parent and family. Thus there will be facilities for the present traditional childbirth as well as rooms within the maternity unit with an entirely different environment. In these, parents might invite three or four close friends or relatives, and the mother may labor and give birth in the same room with her midwife in the position she finds most com-fortable with no drugs or anesthetic, but the facilities of the hospital, such as fresh blood and a resuscitator for the infant, will be available for the rare emergency. This should include surgical facilities if there is need for a cesarean section in the event of acute fetal distress. Normal births, however, can proceed without the precautions and monitoring appropriate for a high-risk delivery. Vaughan (1975) has commented, "It may really be a disaster that the medical model—or, still worse, the surgical model—has been adopted for the birth of a baby, which is actually a *social* event. I think it is about time that we re-created the birth of an infant as a social event, taking it out of the medical arena and giving it back to parents and families."

These advances in the range of services offered to families will not come easily. The changes that have occurred in both neonatology and obstetrics are the result of years of detailed studies aimed at increasing the survival rate and the quality of the survivors. Health providers now enter an era in which it will be necessary to review closely each of their cherished procedures and techniques.

References

Ahrens, R.: Beitrag zur Entwicklung des Physiognomie und Mimikerkehnens, Z. Exp. Angew. Psychol. **2**:412-454, 1964.

Ainsworth, M. D. S., and Bell, S. N.: Attachment, exploration and separation: illustrated by the behavior of one-year-olds in a strange situation, Child Dev. **41**:49-67, 1970.

Ainsworth, M. D. S., Bell, S. M., and Slayton, D. J.: In Richards, M. P. M., editor: The integration of a child into a social world, New York, 1974, Cambridge University Press.

Altmann, M.: In Rheingold, H. R., editor: Maternal behavior in mammals, New York, 1963, John Wiley & Sons, Inc.

Ambuel, J., and Harris, B.: Failure to thrive: a study of failure to grow in height or weight, Ohio Med. J. **59**: 997-1001, 1963.

Anthony, E. J., and Benedek, T.: Parenthood, its psychology and psychopathology, Boston, 1970, Little, Brown & Co.

Avery, J.: Personal communication, 1973.

Barbero, G.: Personal communication, 1973.

Barnard, K.: A program of stimulation for infants born prematurely, Seattle, 1975, University of Washington Press.

Barnett, C. R., Grobstein, R., and Seashore, M.: Personal communication, 1972.

Barnett, C. R., Leiderman, P. H., Grobstein, R., and Klaus, M. H.: Neonatal separation: the maternal side of interactional deprivation, Pediatrics **45**:197-205, 1970.

Bell, J. E.: The family in the hospital, Bethesda, Md., 1960, National Institute of Mental Health.

Benedek, T.: Studies in psychosomatic medicine: the psycho-sexual function in women, New York, 1952, Ronald Press Co.

Benfield, D. G., Leib, S. A., and Reutor, J.: Grief response of parents following referral of the critically ill newborn, N. Engl. J. Med. **294**:975-978, 1976.

Berg, R. B., and Salisbury, A.: Discharging infants of low birth weight: reconsiderations of current practice, Am. J. Dis. Child. **122**:414-417, 1971.

Berkson, G.: In Lewis, M., and Rosenblum, L. A., editors: The effect of the infant on its caregiver, New York, 1974, John Wiley & Sons, Inc.

Bernal, J. F., and Richards, M. P.: In Barnett, A., editor: Ethology and development, vol. II, London, 1972, Little Club Clinics in Developmental Medicine.

Bettelheim, B.: How do you help a child who has a physical handicap? Ladies Home J. **89**:34-35, 1972.

Bibring, G.: Some considerations of the psychological processes in pregnancy, Psychoanal. Study Child **14**:113-121, 1959.

Bibring, G. L., Dwyer, T. F., Huntington, D. S., and Valenstein, A. F.: A study of the psychological processes in pregnancy and of the earliest mother-child relationship. I. Some propositions and comments, Psychoanal. Study Child. **16**:9-27, 1961.

Blau, A., Slaff, B., Easton, R., Welkowitz, J., Springain, J., and Cohen, J.: The psychogenic etiology of premature births, a preliminary report, Psychosom. Med. **25**:201-211, 1963.

Blake, A., Stewart, A., and Turcan, D.: In Parent-infant interaction, Ciba Foundation Symposium 33, Amsterdam, 1975, Elsevier Publishing Co.

Boston Women's Health Book Collective: Our bodies, ourselves, New York, 1971, Simon & Schuster, Inc.

Bowlby, J.: Nature of a child's tie to his mother, Int. J. Psychoanal. **39**:350-373, 1958.

Bowlby, J.: Attachment and loss, vol. 1, New York, 1969, Basic Books, Inc., Publishers.

Brandt, E. M., and Mitchell, G.: In Rosenblum, L. A., editor: Primate behavior: developments in field and laboratory research, vol. II, New York, 1971, Academic Press, Inc.

Brazelton, T. B.: Psychophysiologic reaction in the neonate. II. Effects of maternal medication on the neonate and his behavior, J. Pediatr. **58**:513-518, 1961.

Brazelton, T. B.: The early mother-infant adjustment, Pediatrics **32**:931-938, 1963.

Brazelton, T. B.: Implications of infant development among the Mayan Indians of Mexico, Hum. Dev. **15**:90-111, 1972.

Brazelton, T. B.: Effect of maternal expectations on early infant behavior, Early Child Dev. Care **2**:259-273, 1973.

Brazelton, T. B., School, M. L., and Robey, J. S.: Visual responses in the newborn, Pediatrics **37**:284-290, 1966.

Brazelton, T. B., Koslowski, B., and Main, M.: In Lewis, M., and Rosenblum, L. A., editors: The effect of the infant on its caregiver, New York, 1974, John Wiley & Sons, Inc.

Brazelton, T. B., Tronick, E., Adamson, L., Als, H., and Wise, S.: In Parent-infant interaction, Ciba Foundation Symposium 33, Amsterdam, 1975, Elsevier Publishing Co.

Bronfenbrenner, U.: Early deprivation in mammals: a cross-species analysis. In Newton, G., and Levine, S., editors: Early experience and behavior, Springfield, Ill., 1968, Charles C Thomas, Publisher.

Broussard, E., and Hartner, M.: Maternal perception of the neonate as related to development, Child Psychol. Hum. Dev. **1**(1):16-25, 1970.

Budin, P.: The nursling, London, 1907, Caxton Publishing Co.

Caplan, G.: Patterns of parental response to the crisis of premature birth, Psychiatry **23**:365-374, 1960.

Caplan, G.: Principles of preventive psychiatry, New York, 1964, Grune & Stratton, Inc.

Caplan, G., Mason, E., and Kaplan, D. M.: Four studies of crisis in parents of prematures, Community Ment. Health J. **1**:149-161, 1965.

Carr, E. F., Oppé, J. E.: The birth of an abnormal child: telling the parents, Lancet, **2**:1075-1077, 1971.

Cassel, Z. K., and Sander, L. W.: Neonatal recognition processes and attachment: the masking experiment. Presented at the Society for Research in Child Development, Denver, 1975.

Cohen, R. L.: Some maladaptive syndromes of pregnancy and the puerperium, Obstet. Gynecol. **27**:562-570, 1966.

Collias, N. E.: The analysis of socialization in sheep and goats, Ecology **37**:228-239, 1956.

Condon, W. S., and Sander, L. W.: Neonate movement is synchronized with adult speech: interactional participation and language acquisition, Science **183**:99-101, 1974.

Crook, J. H., editor: Social behaviour in birds and mammals, New York, 1970, Academic Press, Inc.

Crosse, V. M.: The premature baby, ed. 4, Boston, 1957, Little, Brown & Co.

Cullberg, J.: In Psychosomatic medicine in obstetrics and gynaecology, 3rd International Congress, Basel, 1972, S. Karger.

Daniels, L. L., and Berg, G. M.: The crisis of birth and adaptive patterns of amputee children, Clin. Proc. Child. Hosp. D.C. **24:**108-117, 1968.

D'Arcy, E.: Congenital defects: mothers' reactions to first information, Br. Med. J. **3:**796-798, 1968.

Darwin, C.: The descent of man and selection in relation to sex, New York, 1871, D. Appleton & Co.

De Chateau, P.: Personal communication, 1974.

De Chateau, Peter: Neonatal care routines; influences on maternal and infant behavior and on breast feeding (thesis), Umea, Sweden, 1976, Umea University medical dissertations, N.S. no. 20.

Desmond, M. M., Rudolph, A. J., and Phitaksphraiwan, P.: The transitional care nursery: a mechanism of a preventive medicine, Pediatr. Clin. North Am. **13:**651-668, 1966.

Deutsch, H.: The psychology of women: a psychoanalytic interpretation, vol. II, Motherhood, New York, 1945, Grune & Stratton, Inc.

Dillard, R. G., and Korones, S. B.: Lower discharge weight and shortened nursery stay for low birth-weight infants, N. Engl. J. Med. **288:**131-133, 1973.

Dolhinow, P., editor: Primate patterns, New York, 1972, Holt, Rinehart & Winston, Inc.

Drotar, D., Baskiewicz, A., Irvin, N., Kennell, J. H., and Klaus, M. H.: The adaptation of parents to the birth of an infant with a congenital malformation: a hypothetical model, Pediatrics **56:**710-717, 1975.

Elmer, E., and Gregg, G. S.: Developmental characteristics of abused children, Pediatrics **40:**596-602, 1967.

Engel, F.: Grief and grieving, Am. J. Nurs. **64:**93-98, 1964.

Evans, S., Reinhart, J., and Succop, P.: A study of 45 children and their families, J. Am. Acad. Child Psychiatry **11:**440-454, 1972.

Ewer, R. F.: Ethology of mammals, New York, 1968, Plenum Press, Inc.

Faber, H. K., and McIntosh, R.: History of the American Pediatric Society, New York, 1966, McGraw-Hill Book Co.

Fanaroff, A., and Baskiewicz, A.: Unpublished data, 1975.

Fanaroff, A. A., Kennell, J. H., and Klaus, M. H.: Follow-up of low birthweight infants—the predictive value of maternal visiting patterns, Pediatrics **49:**288-290, 1972.

Forfar, J. O., and MacCabe, A. F.: Masking and gowning in nurseries for the newborn infant: effect on staphylococcal carriage and infection, Br. Med. J. **1:**76-79, 1958.

Fraiberg, S.: In Lewis, M., and Rosenblum, L. A., editors: The effect of the infant on its caregiver, New York, 1974, John Wiley & Sons, Inc.

Frommer, E. A., and O'Shea, G.: Antenatal identification of women liable to have problems in managing their infants, Br. J. Psychiatry **123:**149-156, 1973.

Giles, P. F. H.: Reactions of women to perinatal death, Aust. N.Z. J. Obstet. Gynaecol. **10:**207-210, 1970.

Gleich, M.: The premature infant. III, Arch. Pediatr. **59:**172-173, 1942.

Goffman, E.: Stigma: notes on the management of spoiled identity, London, 1968, Penguin Books, Ltd.

Goldberg, S.: Infant care and growth in urban Zambia, Hum. Dev. **15:**77-89, 1972.

Goldblum, R., Ahlstedt, S., Carlsson, B., and Hanson, L.: Antibody production by human colostrum cells, Pediatr. Res. **9:**330, 1975.

Goodall, J.: In the shadow of man, Boston, 1971, Houghton-Mifflin Co.

Goren, C., Sarty, M., and Wu, P.: Visual following and pattern discrimination of face like stimuli by newborn infants Pediatrics **56:**544-549, 1975.

Greenberg, M., and Morris, N.: Engrossment: the newborn's impact upon the father, Am. J. Orthopsychiatry **44:**520-531, 1974.

Greenberg, M., Rosenberg, I., and Lind, J.: First mothers rooming-in with their newborns: its impact on the mother, Am. J. Orthopsychiatry **43:**783-788, 1973.

Grota, L. J.: Factors influencing the acceptance of caesarean delivered off-spring by foster mothers, Physiol. Behav. 3:265-269, 1968.

Hales, D., Trause, M. A., and Kennell, J. H.: How early is early contact? Defining the limits of the sensitive period, Pediatr. Res. 10:448, 1976.

Harlow, H. F., Harlow, M. K., and Hansen, E. W.: In Rheingold, H. R., editor: Maternal behavior in mammals, New York, 1963, John Wiley & Sons, Inc.

Harper, R., Concepcion, S., and Sokol, S.: Is parental contact with infants in the neonatal intensive care unit really a good idea? Pediatr. Res. 9:259, 1975.

Hasselmeyer, E.: Handling and premature infant behavior: an experimental study of the relationship between handling and selected physiological, pathological, and behavioral indices related to body functioning among a group of prematurely born infants who weighed between 1,501 and 2,000 grams at birth and were between the ages of seven and twenty-eight days of life, Dissertation Abstr. 24:7, 1964.

Helfer, R., and Kempe, C., editors: The battered child, Chicago, 1968, University of Chicago Press.

Hersher, L., Richmond, J., and Moore, A.: In Rheingold, H. R., editor: Maternal behavior in mammals, New York, 1963a, John Wiley & Sons, Inc.

Hersher, L., Richmond, J., and Moore, A.: Modifiability of the critical period for the development of maternal behavior in sheep and goats, Behaviour (an International Journal of Comparative Ethology) 20:311-320, 1963b.

Hinde, R. A., and Spencer-Booth, Y.: The study of mother-infant interaction in captive group-living rhesus monkeys, Proc. R. Soc. [Biol.] 169:177-201, 1968.

Hwang, P., Guyda, H., and Friesen, H.: A radioimmunoassay for human prolactin, Proc. Natl. Acad. Sci. U.S.A. 68:1902-1906, 1971.

Iyengar, L., and Selvaraj, R. J.: Intestinal absorption of immunoglobulins

by newborn infants, Arch. Dis. Child. 42:411-414, 1972.

Jackson, E., Olmstead, R., Foord, A., Thomas, H., and Hyder, K.: Hospital rooming-in unit for 4 newborn infants and their mothers: descriptive account of background, development, and procedures with few preliminary observations, Pediatrics 1:28-43, 1948.

James, V. L., Jr., and Wheeler, W. E.: The care-by-parent unit, Pediatrics 43:488-494, 1969.

Johns, N.: Family reactions to the birth of a child with a congenital abnormality, Med. J. Aust. 1:277-282, 1971.

Kahn, E., Wayburne, S., and Fouche, M.: The Baragwanath premature baby unit—an analysis of the case records of 1,000 consecutive admissions, S. Afr. Med. J. 28:453-456, 1954.

Kaila, E.: Die Reaktionen des Sauglings auf des menschliche Gesicht, Z. Psychol. 135:156-163, 1935.

Kaplan, D. N., and Mason, E. A.: Maternal reactions to premature birth viewed as an acute emotional disorder, Am. J. Orthopsychiatry 30:539-552, 1960.

Kattwinkel, J., Hearman, H., Fanaroff, A. A., Katona, P., and Klaus, M. H.: Apnea of prematurity, J. Pediatr. 86:588-592, 1975.

Katz, V.: Auditory stimulation and developmental behavior of the premature infant, Nurs. Res. 20:196-201, 1971.

Kaufman, C.: In Anthony, E., and Benedek, T., editors: Parenthood: its psychology and psychopathology, Boston, 1970, Little, Brown & Co.

Kennell, J. H., Chesler, D., Wolfe, H., and Klaus, M. H.: Nesting in the human mother after mother-infant separation, Pediatr. Res. 7:269, 1973.

Kennell, J. H., Klaus, M. H., and Wolfe, H.: Nesting behavior in the human mother after prolonged mother-infant separation. In Swyer, P., and Stetson, J., editors: Current concepts of neonatal intensive care, St. Louis, 1975, Warren H. Green, Inc.

Kennell, J. H., and Rolnick, A.: Discussing problems in newborn babies with their parents, Pediatrics **26**:832-838, 1960.

Kennell, J. H., Slyter, H., and Klaus, M. H.: The mourning response of parents to the death of a newborn infant, N. Engl. J. Med. **283**:344-349, 1970.

Kennell, J. H., Jerauld, R., Wolfe, H., Chesler, D., Kreger, N. C., McAlpine, W., Steffa, M., and Klaus, M. H.: Maternal behavior one year after early and extended post-partum contact, Dev. Med. Child Neurol. **16**:172-179, 1974.

Kennell, J. H., Trause, M. A., and Klaus, M. H.: In Parent-infant interaction, Ciba Foundation Symposium 33, Amsterdam, 1975, Elsevier Publishing Co.

Klaus, M. H., and Kennell, J. H.: Mothers separated from their newborn infants, Pediatr. Clin. N. Am. **17**:1015-1037, 1970.

Klaus, M. H., Kennell, J. H., Plumb, N., and Zuehlke, S.: Human maternal behavior at first contact with her young, Pediatrics **46**:187-192, 1970.

Klaus, M. H., Jerauld, R., Kreger, N., McAlpine, W., Steffa, M., and Kennell, J. H.: Maternal attachment: importance of the first post-partum days, New Engl. J. Med. **286**:460-463, 1972.

Klaus, M. H., Trause, M. A., and Kennel, J. H.: In Parent-infant interaction, Ciba Foundation Symposium 33, Amsterdam, 1975, Elsevier Publishing Co.

Klein, M., and Stern, L.: Low birth weight and the battered child syndrome, Am. J. Dis. Child. **122**:15-18, 1971.

Klopfer, P.: Mother love: what turns it on? Am. Sci. **49**:404-407, 1971.

Konner, M. J.: Aspects of the developmental ethology of a foraging people. In Jones, N. B., editor, Ethological studies of child behavior, London, 1972, Cambridge University Press.

Korner, A., Kraemer, H., Haffner, M., and Cosper, L.: Effects of waterbed flotation on premature infants: a pilot study, Pediatrics **56**:361-367, 1975.

Kramer, L., and Pierpont, M.: Rocking waterbeds and auditory stimuli to enhance growth of preterm infants, J. Pediatr. **88**:297-299, 1976.

Lang, R.: Birth book, Ben Lomond, Calif., 1972, Genesis Press.

Lang, R.: Personal communication, 1974.

Lanier, B. O., Goldman, A. S., and Harris, N. S.: Plasma cell antigen bearing lymphocytes in primary immunodeficiencies, Pediatr. Res. **9**:331, 1975.

Leiderman, P. H., Leifer, A. D., Seashore, M. J., Barnett, C. R., and Grobstein, R.: Mother-infant interaction: effects of early deprivation, prior experience and sex of infant, Early Dev. (Research Publication of the Association for Research in Nervous and Mental Disease) **51**:154-175, 1973.

Leifer, A. D., Leiderman, P. H., Barnett, C. R., and Williams, J. A.: Effects of mother-infant separation on maternal attachment behavior, Child Dev. **43**:1203-1218, 1972.

Levy, D.: Observations of attitudes and behavior in the child health center, Chicago, 1951, Year Book Medical Publishers, Inc.

Liebling, A.: Profiles: patron of the preemies, New Yorker Mag. June 3, pp. 20-24, 1939.

Lind, J.: Personal communication, 1973.

Lind, J., Vuorenkoski, V., and Wasz-Hackert, O.: In Morris, N., editor: Psychosomatic medicine in obstetrics and gynaecology, Basel, 1973, S. Karger.

Lindemann, E.: Symptomatology and management of acute grief, Am. J. Psychiatry **101**:141-148, 1944.

Lott, D., and Rosenblatt, J.: In Foss, B. M., editor: Determinants of infant behavior. IV. London, 1969, Methuen & Co., Ltd.

Lozoff, B., and Misra, R.: Medical control over labour, Lancet **1**:1242-1243, 1975.

MacFarlane, J. A.: In Parent-infant interaction, Ciba Foundation Symposium 33, Amsterdam, 1975, Elsevier Publishing Co.

Mason, E. A.: A method of predicting crisis outcome for mothers of premature babies, Public Health Rep. **78:** 1031-1035, 1963.

Mata, L.: Personal communication, 1974.

McBryde, A.: Compulsory rooming-in in the ward and private newborn service at Duke Hospital, J.A.M.A. **145:**625-628, 1951.

Meier, G. W.: Maternal behavior of feral- and laboratory-reared monkeys following the surgical delivery of their infants, Nature (Lond.) **206:**492-493, 1965.

Meltzoff, N., and Moore, M.: Neonate imitation: a test of existence and mechanism. Presented at the Society for Research in Child Development, Denver, 1975.

Miller, F. J. W.: Home nursing of premature babies in Newcastle-on-Tyne, Lancet **2:**703-705, 1948.

Miller, L. G.: Toward a greater understanding of the parents of the mentally retarded child, J. Pediatr. **73:** 699-705, 1968.

Mills, N.: Personal communication, 1974.

Miranda, S., Hack, M., Fanaroff, A. A., and Klaus, M. H.: Neonatal visual pattern fixation: a possible predictor of future mental performance, Pediatr. Res. **8:**463, 1974.

Moss, H. A.: Methodological issues in studying mother-infant interaction, Am. J. Orthopsychiat. **35:**482-486, 1965.

Newton, N., and Newton, M.: Mothers' reactions to their newborn babies, J.A.M.A. **181:**206-211, 1962.

Oliver, J. E., Cox, J., Taylor, A., and Baldwin, J.: Severely ill-treated young children in North-East Wiltshire, Oxford, 1974, Oxford University Unit of Clinical Epidemiology.

Olshansky, S.: Chronic sorrow: a response to having a mentally defective child, Soc. Casework **43:**190-193, 1962.

Parke, R.: Father-infant interaction. In Klaus, M. H., Leger, T., and Trause. M. A., editors: Maternal attachment and mothering disorders: a round table, Sausalito, Calif., 1974, Johnson & Johnson Co.

Parkes, C. M.: Bereavement and mental illness. I. A clinical study of the grief of bereaved psychiatric patients, Br. J. Med. Psychol. **38:**1-12, 1965*a*.

Parkes, C. M.: Bereavement and mental illness. II. A classification of bereavement reactions, Br. J. Med. Psychol. **38:**13-26, 1965*b*.

Parkes, C. M.: Bereavement: studies of grief in adult life, New York, 1972, International Universities Press, Inc.

Parkes, C. M.: The nature of grief, Int. J. Psychiatry **3:**435-438, 1967.

Parmelee, A. H., Jr., Wenner, W. H., Akiyama, Y., Schultz, M., and Stern, E.: Sleep states in premature infants, Dev. Med. Child Neurol. **9:**70-77, 1967.

Phillips, C. R. N.: Neonatal heat loss in heated cribs vs. mothers' arms, J.O.G.N. Nurs. **3:**11-15, 1974.

Poirier, F. E., editor: Primate socialization, New York, 1972, Random House, Inc.

Powell, L. F.: The effect of extra stimulation and maternal involvement on the development of low-birth-weight infants and on maternal behavior, Child Rev. **45:**106-113, 1974.

Prugh, D.: Emotional problems of the premature infant's parents, Nurs. Outlook **1:**461-464, 1953.

Rawlings, G., Reynolds, E. O. R., Stewart, A., and Strang, L. B.: Changing prognosis for infants of very low birth weight, Lancet **1:**516-519, 1971.

Raphael, D.: The tender gift, Englewood Cliffs, N. J., 1973, Prentice-Hall, Inc.

Richards, M. P. M., and Bernal, J. B.: In Schaffer, H. R., editor: The origins of human social relations, London, 1971, Academic Press.

Ringler, N. M., Kennell, J. H., Jarvella, R., Navojosky, B. J., and Klaus, M. H.: Mother-to-child speech at 2 years—effects of early postnatal contact, J. Pediatr. **86:**141-144, 1975.

Ringler, N. M., Trause, M. A., and Klaus, M. H.: Mother's speech to her two-year-old, its effect on speech and language comprehension at 5 years, Pediatr. Res. **10:**307, 1976.

Robson, K. S.: The role of eye-to-eye

contact in maternal-infant attachment, J. Child Psychol. Psychiatry **8**:13-25, 1967.

Rose, J., Boggs, T., Jr., and Alderstein, A.: The evidence for a syndrome of "mothering disability" consequent to threats to the survival of neonates: a design for hypothesis testing including prevention in a prospective study, Am. J. Dis. Child. **100**:776-777, 1960.

Rosenblatt, J. S.: The development of maternal responsiveness in rats, Am. J. Orthopsychiatry **39**:36-56, 1969.

Rosenblatt, J. S.: In Aronson, L., Toback, E., Lehrman, D., and Rosenblatt, J. S., editors: Development and evolution of behavior: essays in memory of T. C. Schneirla, San Francisco, 1970, W. H. Freeman & Co., Publishers.

Rosenblatt, J. S.: Personal communication, 1971.

Rosenblatt, J. S.: In Parent-infant interaction, Ciba Foundation Symposium 33, Amsterdam, 1975, Elsevier, Publishing Co.

Rosenblatt, J. S., and Lehrman, D.: In Rheingold, H. R., editor: Maternal behavior in mammals, New York, 1963, John Wiley & Sons, Inc.

Rosenblatt, J. S., and Siegel, H. I.: Hysterectomy-induced maternal behavior during pregnancy in the rat, J. Comp. Physiol. Psychol. **89**:685-700, 1975.

Rosenblum, L. A., and Kaufman, J. C.: In Altmann, S., editor: Social communication among primates, Chicago, 1967, University of Chicago Press.

Roskies, E.: Abnormalities and normalities: the mothering of thalidomide children, New York, 1972, Cornell University Press.

Roth, L., and Rosenblatt, J.: Self-licking and mammary development during pregnancy in the rat, J. Endocrinol. **42**:363-378, 1968.

Rubin, R.: Maternal touch, Nurs. Outlook **11**:828-831, 1963.

Sackett, G. P., and Ruppenthal, G. C.: In Lewis, M., and Rosenblum, L. A., editors: The effect of the infant on its caregiver, New York, 1974, John Wiley & Sons, Inc.

Salk, L.: The role of the heartbeat in the relations between mother and infant, Sci. Am. **228**:24-29, May, 1973.

Sameroff, A.: In Avery, G. B., editor: Neonatology, Philadelphia, 1975, J. B. Lippincott Co.

Sander, L. W., Stechler, G., Burns, P., and Julia, H.: Early mother-infant interaction and 24-hour patterns of activity and sleep, J. Am. Acad. Child Psychiatry **9**:103-123, 1970.

Scarr-Salapatek, S., and Williams, M. L.: The effects of early stimulation on low birth-weight infants, Child Dev. **44**:94-101, 1973.

Schneirla, T., Rosenblatt, J., and Tobach, E.: In Rheingold, H. R., editor: Maternal behavior in mammals, New York, 1963, John Wiley & Sons, Inc.

Schreiber, J.: Personal communication, 1974.

Seashore, M. H., Leifer, A. D., Barnett, C. R., and Leiderman, P. H.: The effects of denial of early mother-infant interaction on maternal self-confidence, J. Pers. Soc. Psychol. **26**:369-378, 1973.

Segall, M.: Cardiac responsibility to auditory stimulation in premature infants, Nurs. Res. **21**:15-19, 1972.

Selman, E., McEwan, A., and Fisher, E.: Studies on natural sucking in cattle during the first eight hours post partum. I. Behavioral studies (dams), Animal Behav. **18**:276-283, 1970.

Shaheen, E., Alexander, D., Truskowsky, M., and Barbero, G.: Failure to thrive—a retrospective profile, Clin. Pediatr. **7**:255-261, 1968.

Shaikh, A. A.: Estrone and estradiol levels in the ovarian venous blood from rats during the estrous cycle and pregnancy, Biol. Reprod. **5**:297-307, 1971.

Shinefield, H. R., Ribble, J. C., Boris, M., and Eichenwald, H. F.: Bacterial interference: its effect on nursery-acquired infection with *Staphylococcus aureus,* Am. J. Dis. Child. **105**:646-654, 1963.

Siegel, H. I., and Rosenblatt, J. S.: Estrogen-induced maternal behavior in hysterectomized-ovariectomized virgin rats, Physiol. Behav. **14**:465-471, 1975.

Silverman, W.: Personal communication, 1967.

Silverman, W. A., and Sinclair, J. C.: Evaluation of precautions before entering a neonatal unit, Pediatrics **40**: 900-901, 1967.

Skinner, A., and Castle, R.: Seventy-eight battered children: a retrospective study, London, 1969, National Society for the Prevention of Cruelty to Children.

Solkoff, N., Yaffe, S., Weintraub, D., and Blase, B.: Effects of handling on subsequent development of premature infants, Dev. Psychol. **1**:765-768, 1969.

Solnit, A. J., and Stark, M. H.: Mourning and the birth of a defective child, Psychoanal. Study Child **16**:523-537, 1961.

Sousa, P. L. R., Barros, F. C., Gazalle, R. V., Begères, R. M., Pinheiro, G. N., Menezes, S. T., and Arruda, L. A.: Attachment and lactation, Fifteenth International Congress of Pediatrics, Buenos Aires, Oct. 3, 1974.

Spitz, R. A., and Cobliner, W. G.: The first year of life, New York, 1965, International Universities Press, Inc.

Spitz, R. A., and Wolff, K. M.: The smiling response: a contribution to the ontogenesis of social relations, Genet. Psychol. Monogr. **34**:57-125, 1946.

Stern, D.: In Lewis, M., and Rosenblum, L. A., editors: The effect of the infant on its caregiver, New York, 1974, John Wiley & Sons, Inc.

Stewart, A., and Reynolds, E. O. R.: Improved prognosis for infants of very low birthweight, Pediatrics **54**:724-735, 1974.

Tafari, N., and Ross, S. M.: On the need for organized perinatal care, Ethiop. Med. J. **11**:93-100, 1973.

Tafari, N., and Sterky, G.: Early discharge of low birth-weight infants in a developing country, Environ. Child Health **20**:73-76, 1974.

Terkel, J., and Rosenblatt, J. S.: Maternal behavior induced by maternal blood plasma injected into virgin rats, J. Comp. Physiol. Psychol. **65**:479-482, 1968.

Terkel, J., and Rosenblatt, J. S.: Humoral factors underlying maternal behavior at parturition: cross transfusion between freely moving rats, J. Comp. Physiol. Psychol. **80**:365-371, 1972.

Turnbull, A. C., Patten, P. T., Flint, A. P. F., Keirse, M. J. N. C., Jeremy, J. Y., and Anderson, A.: Significant fall in progesterone and rise in oestradiol levels in human peripheral plasma before onset of labour, Lancet **1**:101-103, 1974.

Van den Daele, L. D.: Infant reactivity to redundant proprioceptive and auditory stimulations: a twin study, J. Psychol. **78**:269-276, 1971.

Van den Daele, L. D.: Modification of infant state by treatment in a rockerbox, J. Psychol. **74**:161-165, 1970.

Vaughan, V.: Personal communication, 1975.

Voysey, M.: Impression management by parents with disabled children, J. Health Soc. Behav. **13**:80-89, 1972.

Walker, A.: Immunology of the gastrointestinal tract, J. Pediatr. **83**:517-530, 1973.

Warkany, J.: Congenital malformations: notes and comments, Chicago, 1971, Year Book Medical Publishers, Inc.

Williams, C. P., and Oliver, T. K., Jr.: Nursery routines and staphylococcal colonization of the newborn, Pediatrics **44**:640-646, 1969.

Winters, M.: The relationship of time of initial feeding to success of breast-feeding. Unpublished, Master's thesis, Seattle, 1973, University of Washington.

Wolff, P. H.: Observations on newborn infants, Psychosom. Med. **21**:110-118, 1959.

Wolff, P. H.: The causes, controls and organization of behavior in the neonate, New York, 1965, International Universities Press, Inc.

Yarrow, L. J.: Maternal deprivation: toward an empirical and conceptual reevaluation, Psychol. Bull. **58**:459-490, 1961.

Yarrow, L. J.: Separation from parents during early childhood. In Hoffman, L. W., and Hoffman, M. L.: Review of child development research, vol. 1, New York, 1964, Russell Sage foundation.

Zahn, M. A.: Incapacity, impotence and invisible impairment: their effects upon interpersonal relations, J. Health Soc. Behav. 14:115-123, 1973.

Zarrow, M. X., Gandelman, R., and Renenberg, V.: Prolactin: is it an essential hormone for maternal behavior in the mammal? Hormones Behav. 2: 343-354, 1971.

Zuk, G. H.: Religious factor and the role of guilt in parental acceptance of the retarded child, Am. J. Ment. Defic. 64:139-147, 1959-1960, 1969.

Author index

251

Subject index

254